STAYING VEGI

Lynne Alexander, now a Britis... America, where she attended New York and the University of ..., Berkeley. She was a professional harpsichordist and teacher for ten years until 1980, and is now a full-time writer. Her first novel, *Safe Houses*, was published to critical acclaim in 1985.

STAYING VEGETARIAN

*A guide to guesthouses
and hotels for vegetarians,
vegans and wholefooders*

Lynne Alexander

with Oliver Fulton

Fontana/Collins

To my fellow vegetarians and vegans

First published in 1987 by Fontana Paperbacks
8 Grafton Street, London W1X 3LA

Set in Linotron Times

Made and printed in Great Britain
by William Collins Sons & Co. Ltd, Glasgow

Contents

Introduction

This is a highly personal guide to over eighty different places to stay in Britain that claim to provide not only bed and vegetarian breakfast but also vegetarian evening meals. (The one exception is Barrow House in London, which is bed and breakfast only.) It contains reviews of large and small hotels, guesthouses and private homes.

The eighty-two places in this book were mostly chosen on the basis of their own claims – they advertised, often extensively, or were listed in books or magazines for vegetarians; a few others came from personal recommendation. Not all are exclusively vegetarian: many non-exclusive places make a big pitch to vegetarians, and we felt these too should be investigated. Many of them fulfilled their claims and much more; some were perfectly acceptable to anyone who doesn't mind the company of carnivores and the smell of their bacon; while a few (a small minority, I'm happy to say) were disappointing. (After all, anyone can claim to cater for vegetarians. My mother, for instance, always took the bones out of the soup before serving it to me.) It is not always easy to tell from an advertisement which places are conscientious and serious, and which are just unscrupulously extending their sales campaign to a new market. And then again, there's no law that says that thorough-going vegetarians are universally characterised by good taste, cleanliness and the excellence of their cooking. The only way to know is to visit them; and the only way that standards will be improved is to tell the truth about them. Inevitably, then, some of our reviews are negative – not to hurt or anger the proprietors, but in the cause of public service.

Like other independent guides, our inspection visits were undeclared and anonymous. We booked and visited each place just as if we were ordinary guests. We paid for ourselves, ate the same food and slept in the same beds as any other visitor; there is no other way to find out how an ordinary guest is treated. And then we wrote down what we found, as honestly as libel law and good taste permit. Lack of cleanliness and the use of non-vegetarian ingredients were the two issues on which we were prevented from being as explicit as we would have liked. Alas, if a place advertises that its food is in fact vegetarian, it is defamatory to suggest otherwise. If we had no definite proof, we could not voice our suspicions or uncertainties (e.g. that the cheese and biscuits, soup stocks, frying fat, etc, were not entirely animal-free), and there were a number of places where I for one felt uneasy. Where I was confident, however, I have tried to make it quite clear: read the entries carefully.

The result is, I hope, fair, but it is not objective; the essays are personal and spontaneous, not formalised reviews or inspections. There are no point-by-point rating systems, no stars or 'highly recommendeds'. I believe that trying to reduce such very non-standard places as you'll find in this book to a set of standard categories would squeeze all the life out of them. Instead, by giving our personal reactions in a style which tells you quite a bit about ourselves, we give you the chance to make up your own mind. Remember, no inspector with a clipboard can be proof against the effects of moods, weather, personality differences or individual tastes. Our prejudices are here in print for you to take or leave as you will. Don't use *Staying Vegetarian* as a bible; use it as a guide or set of guideposts from which you can choose the direction that suits you and your own particular needs and prejudices.

And who might you be, gentle or not-so-gentle reader? Well, the polls say there are more than 3 million of us vegetarians in Britain, and our green, leafy, mobile ranks are growing all the time, and striking terror into the hearts of the butchers. But you don't have to be vegetarian to stay at one of these places. You may be considering becoming vegetarian or vegan; interested in health, good food or both; on a special diet; or related to, or travelling with, any of the above; or you might simply like offbeat or smoke-free places, which happily many of these are. If any of these fit, there is somewhere in *Staying Vegetarian* for you.

I should like to apologise to the proprietors of those places that were not reviewed. We did our best, especially to cover all the exclusively vegetarian ones we knew of, but inevitably some slipped through the net. These, along with others recently opened, are listed in the **Other Places to Stay** sections. If we missed you entirely, we're doubly sorry. Do write and let us know about you. We also welcome feedback from our readers.

I should like to thank Sara Randall and Duncan Fulton, and Margaret and John Crompton for their substantial contributions; also David Barton and Mary Hamilton, Alison Fuller, David and Anne Green, and Margaret Jones; and Brenda Beaghan and Moira Peelo for their company. To Oliver Fulton, my partner, fellow-vegetarian of ten years' standing, co-author, travelling companion, bucker-upper, trip planner and map reader *par excellence*, my love and appreciation for sharing the pains as well as the pleasure. It couldn't have happened without him.

Lynne Alexander
January, 1987

IX
HIGHLANDS
AND ISLANDS

VIII
SOUTHERN
SCOTLAND
AND BORDERS

V
NORTH WEST
AND LAKE
DISTRICT

IV
YORKS
AND
NORTH
EAST

VII
NORTH WALES,
MID-WALES
AND BORDERS

III
THE GREAT
EMPTY MIDDLE

VI
SOUTH
WALES AND
BORDERS

II
THE SOUTH
EAST

I
WEST COUNTRY

How to use this book

General

Staying Vegetarian is divided into nine geographical areas. In each of these you will find:

Places Reviewed
Listings of Other Places to Stay and Places to Eat.

Places Reviewed is arranged in alphabetical order by name of guesthouse, hotel, etc. Each one is given a number which appears on the map preceding that area's section.

Other Places to Stay was compiled from lists available to us, personal enquiries or recommendations, and recent 'classified' advertisements, some of which have telephone numbers only. We've added comments on any information we possess but most of them have not been tried by us. Bear this in mind – and good luck!

Places to Eat. Since this is a book about where to *stay* and not where to eat, we have limited these lists (with a few exceptions) to the relatively small number of exclusively vegetarian (XV) restaurants. For a complete guide to restaurants catering for vegetarians (not limited to XV) we recommend *Where To Eat If You Don't Eat Meat: A Guide to Eating Out For Vegetarians*, by Annabel Whittet (Grafton Books), which includes brief reviews of each restaurant; or either *The Vegetarian Handbook* or the *Vegan Directory*, both of which include comprehensive listings.

Our basic lists are included to help people *Staying Vegetarian* who may be looking for somewhere to have lunch, who are staying in a B & B which doesn't provide evening meals, or who are hungry for greater variety (you may not want to eat at your guesthouse or hotel every night). Your hosts may well be able to recommend other places to eat in the area. Failing that, wine bars and bistros frequently have vegetarian dishes. Try also Italian,

Indian, Mexican and other ethnic places; potato bars and crêperies. Even some enlightened pubs have gone veggie.

Descriptions and abbreviations used in the text

Catering

Exclusively vegan or **XVgn**. This means all catering is vegan (no dairy products of any kind).

Exclusively vegetarian or **XV**. This means catering is entirely vegetarian; no meat or meat-derived products used anywhere. Occasionally some places serve exclusively vegetarian dinners but offer traditional breakfasts for those who want them – we've said when this was the case. Exclusively vegetarian places are usually happy to cater for vegans as well, but do check.

Vegetarian and traditional or **V-T**. This means there's a bias towards vegetarian food, but non-vegetarian food is also served. Be wary of margarine, cheese, biscuits and stocks.

Traditional and vegetarian or **T-V**. This means it's basically a traditional-type place but they do cater somewhat seriously for vegetarians. Be extra wary of margarine, cheese, biscuits and stocks.

V/Vgn prop. This means the proprietor claims to be vegetarian or vegan.

B&B. Bed and Breakfast.

EM. Evening meal.

NOTE: We have not used the category 'wholefood' on its own since it seems to mean all things to all guesthouses.

Smoking

No smoking or **NS**. This means you are not allowed to smoke anywhere in the house (smoke-free).

Smoking not in evidence. This means that we were not aware of any rules forbidding smoking, but that nobody smoked when we were there. Often it seemed like the kind of place where people just wouldn't smoke.

Smoking restrictions. Usually means no smoking in the dining room, at least, but other parts of the house may be as well. Check.

No known rules. This means that we weren't aware of any rules, and although people didn't smoke when we were there, we suspect they might have.

Smoking allowed. This means smokey. Beware.

Price Categories

These are basic rates for dinner, bed and breakfast, in 1986, for single room or half of a double, or whichever is the cheaper. Where prices depend on whether you go in low or high season or which room you have, we have indicated the range; e.g. Low to Medium, or High to Very High.

Very Low (VL): Under £12.50

Low (L): £12.50–£15.49

Medium (M): £15.50–£18.49

High (H): £18.50–£22.49

Very High (VH): £22.50–£29.99

Very Very High (VVH): £30 and over.

I
THE WEST COUNTRY

Cornwall, Devon, Dorset, Isles of Scilly, Somerset

For its size, the West Country is the part of Britain best supplied with amenities for the travelling vegetarian. We stayed, as it turns out, in fifteen guesthouses; and Other Places to Stay lists plenty more, even if they don't all meet our fairly restrictive criteria. Devon, in particular, is exceptionally well supplied with places to stay and eat, though Cornwall is a bit disappointing. But in the area as a whole you can find anything from hotels and big houses to little family homes in town or country, and many of them stay open year round. If only the rest of Britain were as lucky.

Places Reviewed

1. The Blenheim Hotel, Brimley Road, Bovey Tracey, S.Devon
2. Brookesby Hall Hotel, Hesketh Road, Torquay, S.Devon (XV)
3. Chough's Nest Hotel, North Walk, Lynton, N.Devon
4. Grimstone Manor, Yelverton, S.Devon (XV)
5. Halsdon House Vegetarian Hotel, Great Torrington, N.Devon (XV)
6. Hazelmere Guest House, 50 Shirburn Road, Torquay, S.Devon (XV)
7. Holway Mill, Sandford Orcas, Nr Sherborne, Dorset (XV)
8. The House at Bridge Corner, Bridge, Redruth, Cornwall (XV)
9. The Manor House Hotel, Woolfardisworthy, Bideford, N.Devon
10. Moorhayes Vegetarian Farm House Hotel, Talaton, E.Devon (XV)
11. Neubia House Hotel, Lydiate Lane, Lynton, N.Devon
12. Penhaven Country House Hotel, Parkham, Nr Bideford, N.Devon
13. Penmarric Lodge, Penare Terrace, Penzance, Cornwall
14. Ullacombe House, Haytor Road, Bovey Tracey, S.Devon (XV)
15. Woodcote Hotel, The Saltings, Lelant, St Ives, Cornwall (XV)

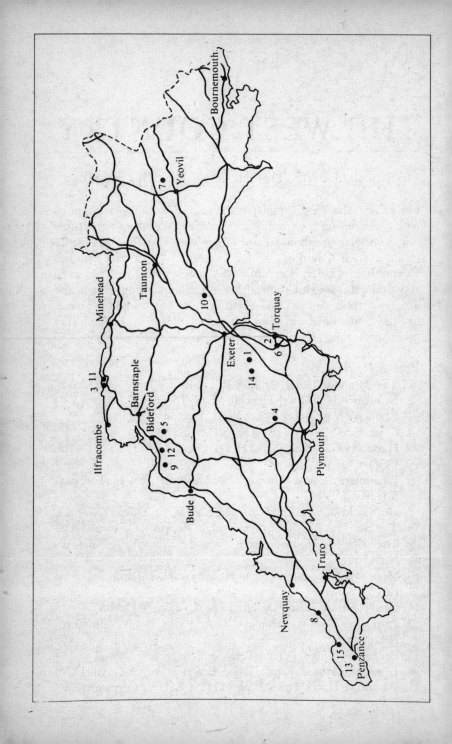

1. The Blenheim Hotel

'Dogs are specially catered for and are allowed on the condition that the owners accept responsibility for any damage, and must be kept on a lead when passing through the hotel.' (From the brochure)

Charm at the Blenheim came from my fellow-guests alone: a sweet old man and a feisty Irishwoman on holiday with her dog, though neither she nor her dog wore a lead when passing through the hotel.

As for the Blenheim, it's one of those large, creaking boarding houses, with a damp, musty smell about it, that has seen better days. It was cold (no central heating, a couple of fires here and there). My bedroom had an electrical gadget which looked like a vertical waffle iron on clawed feet and was about the same vintage as the other guests. There was also a plastic apricot-coloured shower cubicle (not an object of great beauty) which gave out a trickle of tepid stuff at the tune of £1.50 per go. The bed had grey pilled sheets, feathers flying out of pillows – I won't go on; suffice it to say I slept in my clothes, unmoving. A spider crawled across my face.

Decoration was, shall we say, Late Nursing Home period.

The food was not exactly young and foolish either. Dinner was an anonymous green soup and thin sliced brown bread; a lump of quiche accompanied by carrots, overcooked broccoli, boiled potatoes; plus (for me, specially) brown rice and plain (*al dente*) lentils. For dessert, tinned fruit or profiteroles. Instant coffee, tea or herb tea were available.

Breakfast was tinned grapefruit sections, juice or prunes, plus a choice of dry cereals. The Irish lady managed to wangle porridge ('Psst,' she whispered to the waitress, 'could you be a sweetheart and tell Mrs Turpin I'd like some porridge, and if it's to my liking, I'll have it every morning, oh and with cream don't you forget

3

now . . .'). The rest of us were not given the chance to say 'me too'. Cooked (carnivorous) breakfasts included kippers, haddock, bacon, sausage, etc, and thin commercial toast. Tea from the bag (herb teas available too) or coffee; choice of honey *or* marmalade (I can believe it).

I didn't get to meet Mrs Turpin, who was immured in the kitchen. As for Mr Turpin, he kindly explained to me that allergies to dust were primarily a liver imbalance.

The Blenheim is to be congratulated for its special catering to the needs of dogs.

CATERING Traditional; vegetarians and other diets catered for. Licensed.

SMOKING Smoking restrictions.

PRICE CATEGORY Medium.

FURTHER INFORMATION Mr and Mrs John Turpin,
The Blenheim Hotel,
Bovey Tracey,
South Devon TQ13 9DH
Phone (0626) 832422

2. Brookesby Hall Hotel

Brookesby Hall was my last stop on a whirlwind tour of Devon veggie places. It was early April. A cold, evil wind blew me into Torquay but the evening proceeded to settle in mild (well, mild-er) and rosy-ish on the 'English Riviera'. Brookesby Hall is in the quiet 'exclusive' Lincombe Conservation area, facing south, set high up in its own ¾ acre gardens and looking out over the roof of the Imperial Hotel to Torbay and across to Brixham and Berry Head. It is a very large Victorian villa; as the brochure says, 'modernised yet retaining many original features'. It is an elegant house but rather enormous and draughty (in early April anyway) in spite of the central heating, and a bit forbidding with its impressive mahogany staircases, enormous windows (with opaque glass etched with little sailboats) and teardrop chandeliers. The hallway has been newly decorated and is very light and airy with lots of spanking white trim and pale wallpaper. The single bedrooms are small and a bit cell-like, while the double ones, with sea views, are huge and light, though with some pretty horrible old carpets and furniture. Some have private showers. The worst room, in my opinion, is the front lounge, unredeemed in its Edwardian gloom, with wall-to-wall sofas and murky fishtank. The upstairs bathroom gets a prize for sheer colour madness: red carpet, black wood trim, green, grey and yellow flowered wallpaper, yellow-orange tiles, turquoise curtains, and pink towels and bath mat (matching). The back lounge (facing the sea) is a lovely room, though, in spite of a fuzzy green eight-piece suite, brown satin wallpaper, swirly-whirly carpet, and so on. But sea and sky, and Mr Baker's unceasing upkeep, save Brookesby Hall from geriatric grimness.

The dining room, again facing the sea, is large and light, old-fashioned and formal with its starched white napkins and tablecloths ('Brookesby Hall Hotel' embroidered in curly writing) and heavy silverware. I had one of the window tables, which was lovely. Dinner began inauspiciously with a not brilliant vegetable soup. But the main course was a delicious cashew and almond loaf accompanied by baked potato, braised celery and carrots, and green beans. Dessert was called 'Apricot Yogurt Delight': magnificently creamy and apricoty (but no cream, I checked), topped with hazelnuts. Coffee, alas, was instant. The whole was accompanied by what sounded like Jeanette MacDonald and Nelson Eddy doing Opera Pops, selections from spaghetti operas, plus assorted 'classical' waltzes and marches. Catering for the older taste in music, I'd say. (I liked it.)

It was at Brookesby Hall that I did the unforgettable – locked myself out of my room at 5 a.m. Or rather, the door locked itself (and I had no key with me), and there I was, exposed in my elegant nightwear – T-shirt, baggy drawers and no bathrobe. (I had only meant to nip out, after all, for a quick visit to the loo; and back before anyone could admire my *assemblage*.) (Enter Aunt

Pearl wagging a finger, 'Always wear a pretty nightgown; you never know when you'll get locked out of your hotel room.' She's the one who said to her son, after President Kennedy was assassinated, 'Lawrence, didn't I tell you never to ride in a convertible?') Anyway, there I am, unbecomingly attired and freezing to death. So I dive into the nearest open room (the honeymoon suite, I think) and, whipping the bedspread off and wrapping it around me like a shroud (so as not to disturb the sheets: magnificent fine old cotton), I insert myself into the bed (no bride and groom, thank God). Alas, sleep does not come: the sheets do not thaw and the gulls are doing their Isadora Duncan spring madness dance, beating their wings against the bridal pagoda and ululating. It is time to rise and go now and resume my Jacob Marley imitation, though silently, silently, through the halls of the Hall. I find myself curled up in one of the green fuzzy lounge chairs facing the terrace and the sea and snooze awhile. Soon I wake up, bathed in weak spring sunshine, privileged witness to an early morning homosexual encounter between two huge chow dogs, Winston and Black Beauty. It is an awesome sight.

By 9 a.m. (having been rescued by Mr Baker, and chided for not waking him during the night) I took my seat in the dining room, bathed, dressed and more or less restored to normal. Breakfast (even if I hadn't been floating around like the ghost of Queen Victoria for the past four hours) was (yes, I'll say it) fit for a queen – the first really 4-star breakfast I encountered on this Devon trip: real tea, real porridge, homemade wholewheat bread (delicious), homemade yoghurt and stewed fruit, free-range eggs if wanted, and all to the accompaniment of Chopin's piano music.

It was a lovely warm morning with Torquay and the sea looking appropriately Mediterranean-ish. I took Mr Baker's advice and walked along the Marine Drive and some way along the coastal path. It was wonderful, warm and sparkling, and very empty of people. I began to think it would be a fine place to spend a week's holiday, especially if the weather were good. There's a woodland walk which begins on the doorstep and leads down to the coastal path, with sea views along the way, and it's not far from Dartmoor and towns like Totnes (good vegetarian café), Dartmouth and Kingswear, also with good coastal paths.

In sum, the food is excellent, the spot is scenic and walkable, there's a sun garden overlooking the sea, and Mr Baker (I didn't meet Hilda) is a lovely man. As long as you hang your key around your neck before going to bed, or unlock your door, you should have splendidly peaceful nights as well as restful days.

CATERING Exclusively vegetarian; vegan and other diets catered for.

SMOKING Smoking restrictions.

PRICE CATEGORY Low to Medium.

FURTHER INFORMATION Edward and Hilda Baker,
Brookesby Hall Hotel,
Hesketh Road, Meadfoot Beach,
Torquay, Devon TQ1 2LN
Phone (0803) 22194

3. Chough's Nest Hotel

The Chough's Nest is a 100-year old stone house, originally built for a Dutch millionaire, perched on the cliffs overlooking Lynmouth Bay: the last hotel at the end of Lynton's North Walk, which leads on to one of the most spectacular coastal paths in Britain. In addition to its panoramic views (from most rooms), the house is one of the best maintained I have stayed in: clean, cosy, warm, glowing with D.I.Y health and white paint, and hermetically sealed against the weather, which they get lots of. A very snug nest indeed.

The decor is very traditional British. The lounge has red and gold brocade curtains with scalloped rails, ditto velour three-piece suites on top of a scenic carpet, and a 'feature' fireplace adorned with knicknacks, gold painted acorns, pampas grass, copper and brass doodads, and the whole topped with crossed swords. Thank

God for the white walls and the sea which give it a light and airy feel, in spite of.

The dining room is all white but for one wall papered in flocked pineapples which don't quite go with the Persian-style Wilton. But never mind. You sit at rustic tables with gas lamps, looking out at the sea and sky, which is really lovely, even romantic. (Honeymooners are especially welcomed in the brochure.) The night I was there dinner was something special, and I don't just mean the food. It was Lorna Doone night – a weekly occurrence during which Sylvia and Bob Harrop, their children and other helpers dress up in seventeenth-century costume and serve food with names like Mother Meldrum's Brew and Badgworthy Broth, and vaguely 'period' music (very vaguely) plays on the cassette machine. I found it all pretty cornball but managed to ignore it and enjoy the food and the view.

Dinner on Lorna Doone nights is more elaborate, but I suspect it's always plentiful and good. Sylvia is the vegetarian and I think pretty conscientious and knowledgeable about her ingredients. She checked out if I was vegan before serving me dairy products, so I felt very relaxed. It was an enormous and delicious meal, in spite of the cutesy-poo names for the dishes (bear with me). First came John Ridd's salad appetiser: a fresh fruit salad with raspberries and blackberries, and big chunks of warm granary bread. The main course (nameless, blessed relief; presumably Lorna Doone characters don't eat vegetarian) was courgettes stuffed with an unusual combination of apples, nuts, broccoli and tomatoes, with a mushroom-lemon sauce; accompanied by two kinds of potatoes, creamed cauliflower in cream sauce and Brussels sprouts; plus a salad (with bottled dressing, I fear, though it came in a separate dish). For dessert there was Little Annie's favourite fruit salad or peach and blackberry pie with cream. I asked for the pie, with yoghurt instead, and it came homemade and delicious. Then Jeremy Stickle's Cheeseboard (no room, sorry), and finally Judge Jeffery's Coffee Pot, served with Cousin Ruth's homemade whisky truffles (yum yum). Actually there was so much to eat, I was quite ill the next day. For me, there could have been a lot less, but people who'd been on huge hikes were probably glad of the generous portions. Anyway, be prepared for quality *and* quantity.

To be honest, I hadn't expected much from the food, as their brochure advertises such goodies as 'crinkle-cut carrots' which immediately gives me goose bumps. But in fact the vegetables were fresh and real and the combination of tastes, mixing fruits and vegetables, really imaginative.

After dinner most of us retired to the lounge which was toasty warm in spite of the gale howling outside. Each family group occupied a corner and played its games while I sat reading in solitary splendour, curled up in one of the velour chairs (the one with the best view). I sat there for hours, leafing through old magazines and books (the library is not brilliant), enjoying the sunset and feeling vaguely part of the family atmosphere without having to take part. It's what the Dutch would call *gezellig*: cosy, snug. At 10 o'clock we were offered hot drinks, including herb tea.

Most if not all the bedrooms have sea views, but mine was extra-special, being the last attic bedroom. A bit on the chilly side and with its share of flocked pineapples and swirly-whirly carpet, but basically it was a simple white room with astragalled windows looking out over the sea and the curving Countisbury headland. I saw just about eye to eye with what I took to be a nesting chough at the top of a huge Scots pine.

Next morning the wind had died down and the sun shone onto a sparkly sea. Breakfast was orange juice followed by a choice of fresh grapefruit or cereals (including sugar-free muesli), warm granary bread or brown toast (not very special). Eggs with tomatoes and mushrooms were on offer for vegetarians (as well as the usual meaty fare for others). I asked for yoghurt and got more of the homemade kind. After breakfast I announced to one of the other guests that I had a chough nesting in the tree opposite my window. He smiled indulgently and said, 'My dear, I doubt that very much. The chough is very rare indeed; what you have seen is a common rook.' Oh dear.

The Chough's (or Common Rook's) Nest is a very good clean, comfortable, *superior* small hotel which caters very well for vegetarians, but is particularly special because of its setting. You can walk right out of the front door along the coastal path to the Valley of the Rocks. Exmoor and a hundred other walks are to be had a bit further afield. In fine weather there's a terrace to sit out on; then it must be glorious. It's a curious place really; the Lorna Doone stuff is too twee for words. (They are very serious about it. Bob is president of the local Lorna Doone Society and has even made a TV video, with the whole family in costume romping about on the moor.) It's all a bit too too for my taste, but saved, I think, by its wild and wonderful position; otherwise it might be utterly claustrophobic. It'a certainly very popular with families, as well as honeymooners. If you, and/or your children, can stomach the Lorna Doonery (you can always avoid Thursdays) – oh and another night there's a slide show of local beauty spots – then do go, it's a wonderful spot, good vegetarian food, nice people. I would go back myself for a longer stay. But don't go in high season; Lynton must be hell. Besides, they're sure to be booked up. And if you get my attic room (No.7) give my regards to the nesting chough.

CATERING Traditional and vegetarian; vegan and other diets catered for. Licensed.

SMOKING Smoking restrictions.

PRICE CATEGORY High.

FURTHER INFORMATION Sylvia and Bob Harrop,
Chough's Nest Hotel,
Lynton, N.Devon
Phone (05985) 3315

4. Grimstone Manor

Grimstone Manor belies its name. Architecturally it may be a bit of a jumble, but it is far from grim; more a glorious, odd and endearing concoction. On the right is the original seventeenth-century farmhouse, now painted a pinky-grey, with a new conservatory thrown out in front; on the left an eighteenth-century octagonal wing faced with chipped and peeling ochre paint; in the middle a porch with tall Italianate columns; a modern gallery above with sliding glass doors; an outside circular wrought-iron stairway, and one siding of slate shingles. Plonk the whole on the western slopes of Dartmoor about fifteen miles north of Plymouth, surround with acres of garden, grassland and splendid outsize trees and shrubs (Monterey pines, copper beeches, giant rhodo-dendrons), and you have some idea of Grimstone Manor as it looked when we visited it in summer 1986.

The old wing contains the original stairway in a hall of simple and classical proportions; the later Italianate hall and stairway are more extravagant, with an ornate curlicued double staircase, long windows with shutters, and a great blazing chandelier. A tiny garden set in the floor, framed in stone and spotlighted adds a meditative touch. The main meditation/group/work/play room – it would be mundane to call it a lounge – is huge and panelled, with a bay (added) at one end and the brand new swimming pool and jacuzzi through a door to the side. There are two fireplaces, the back one of simple stone as befits the kitchen it originally was, the front one of ornate marble. A wood floor was being laid the entire length of the room, to make it suitable for dancing, and a dividing curtain hung, so that two groups can work or play simultaneously. The bedrooms are also geared for groups: very simply furnished with rows of beds or even, up in the attic rooms, simply rows of mattresses lined up on the floor. They are all lovely, large, light rooms, looking out onto fields or trees. Some have private bathrooms. Besides the 'dorms' there is one double room for guests (which I didn't see as it was occupied by another couple) and a few single 'cells' which usually house course tutors. For the intrepid guest or course tutor who wants to get away from the madding group, there is a summer house, complete with futon on sleeping platform, and no facilities, as they say. The dining room, also geared for large parties (they have accommodated up to fifty recently) is light and spare, with a cork floor and stone fireplace, wood-burning stove and stacks of wood. Down the middle runs a vast refectory table and to the side, in a raised Victorian extension, are two squarish oak tables, for smaller parties and guests. My favourite part of the house is the new conservatory. Designed in and shipped all the way from East Anglia, it has tall, graceful, curved vaulting, a slate staircase repeating the roof's curve, Victorian grated walkway and exotic shrubs. It was a real treat to have tea there, sitting at a pine bench looking over the huge stretch of grass and handsome trees to the fields and villages beyond. A vase of exotic broom, a brass candlestick and our tea on a thick slate shelf made a perfect still life. Tea itself was real herb tea (not a bag); a fresh peach for me and a crunchy health bar for Oliver.

After tea we visited the new pool, picking our way through rubble (it was very much under construction then). The pool itself was finished and swimmable-in, though deathly (or delightfully, depending on your taste) cold for English outdoors. Eventually it will be enclosed and heated to 80°, which, with the addition of the jacuzzi, promises perfection. It combines luxury (all blue tiled, electrically operated cover) with ecological soundness: no chemicals and heated by solar panels. I don't know how the jacuzzi is to be heated and treated, but I'd favour it over the Trust House variety any day. Not quite an outdoor natural hotspring (like the one at Esalen in California) but not bad for England. And very welcome, I should think, after a day of contemplating belly buttons and ego trips; or just walking Dartmoor in the rain. The pool will be a must for those taking part in the sweatlodges conducted by the Indian medicine man, Harley Swiftdeer Reagan, Ph.D., D.D.

After our respective waterings (Oliver took the plunge, I retreated to a hot indoor bath), there was dinner. First drinks: a strawberry wine cup which was refreshing and delicious. One of us ordered a bottle of white wine from their small but thoughtfully selected wine list. For dinner there was courgette and potato soup with wholemeal croutons, a lentil and cider loaf with spicy tomato sauce, broccoli and sweet corn. Dessert was an oat and apple slice with clotted cream, followed by a distinguished cheeseboard with green grapes. Freshly ground decaf coffee, or tea, followed. I had a rather different menu, due to a suspected potato allergy: melon with mint for starters, and an instantly rustled-up (and very delicious) bean and tomato stew, raspberries for dessert (first of the season) with soya dessert. I was embarrassed about causing such a last minute to-do, but was put at my ease by Jean Whieldon (who is also allergic to potatoes) and was made to feel less troublesome and freakish than I have done at other places.

After dinner we walked out the door and up the hill, and found ourselves on Dartmoor in the summer mist among wild horses and their foals. It seemed very much part of the Grimstone magic. Back to a pot of chamomile tea (help yourself in the dining room) and bed. I feel it's unfair to criticise the bedrooms; they are not meant, like ordinary 'guest' bedrooms, to ooze charm and warmth. But you should know what you're getting yourself in for (unless you're lucky enough to land the one double room): a rather barnlike room with lots of beds (our bedroom had a double and enough singles for the seven dwarfs too; we could choose), possibly chilly outside summer, and with not such great mattresses and bedding. A pity, I think, they don't have more rooms for single and couple guests, but that's the way it is.

Breakfast was very special. I had jumbo oat muesli (specially made up with no wheat flakes, full of nuts and dates) and guaranteed to bring instant enlightenment. Also a salad of fresh fruits, melon topped with strawberries, soya milk and barleycup to drink. The others had muesli or other cereals followed by hot croissants, yoghurt and various homemade spreads (marmalade with lemon), followed (if you could) by a cooked breakfast of free-range, marigold-coloured eggs on toast with mushrooms and tomatoes.

In between times, Tony and Jean made time to chat with us. They are both warm, friendly, interesting and interested people. I didn't discover much about Jean's background (except that she is Canadian and spent nine months in Berkeley), but Tony told some of his amazing career history. Originally a teacher, he afterwards ran a small bus company, then became a farmer, then a farmer/psychoanalyst!) – then co-proprietor of Grimstone Manor. 'Groups' are their main thing, and range from the usual personal growth type stuff (e.g. Gestalt weekends, New Skills Workshop, Self and Body Workshop, Humanistic Psychology programme, Creative Dance Workshop, etc) to the more esoteric and way out stuff (Gestalt and the Sacred, Enlightenment Intensive, Ritual Theatre and the Dancing Path; and do not forget Harley Swiftdeer

Reagan (Ph.D., D.D.) – how could you? – who leads a workshop called 'Teachings of the Luminous Egg Cocoon'). Not my cup of tea (I remember being quite ill on Navajo tea) but impressive all the same. They have had eminent people, including Carl Rogers and Laura Perls. Most, say Tony and Jean, are 'very dynamic people'; almost all are from the States. The interesting thing is that while they have trouble filling the more traditional training/ therapy courses, the nuttier-sounding ones (sorry) fill up immediately. Somewhere out there a surprising number of people are graduates of Luminous Egg Cocooning, the sweatlodge experience, and Enlightenment Intensives; and what better way to do it than at Grimstone Manor?

I could go on and on describing this curious and intriguing place. At the time of writing it was very much in transition; or should I say (in the language of enlightenment and growth) like a splendid chrysalis in the stage of becoming. But by the time you read this, it will have undergone its final architectural transformation and be much more all of a piece. The later additions will all go, including the Italianate columns, the spiral staircase, the sliding glass doors. The whole thing will be painted a uniform pinky-grey. And though it will lose some of its endearing eccentricity, it will probably be more elegant. All the bathrooms will be finished and of course the pool/jacuzzi complex. It will be splendid. Still, I'm glad I went when I did; I feel a privileged witness to the 'becoming' stage. Not that the becoming will cease: Tony's next labour will be the gardens, which he means to turn into one of the finest in the south-west – and I have no doubt he'll do it.

I will certainly try to go back, probably as a guest, though I will consider going as part of a group. If you are into such things, I recommend it enthusiastically; but even if you're not, I recommend it for the food, drink, waterworks, general ambience and proximity to Dartmoor, and friendly, relaxed, assured care of Jean and Tony Whieldon and his daughters. As they say in their notes, they are not a hotel. If you go, you go as a guest in their home, and a splendid home it is. But be warned: there are limited dates available for guests between group bookings.

CATERING Exclusively vegetarian; vegans and other diets catered for. Licensed.

SMOKING No smoking.

PRICE CATEGORY Medium.

FURTHER INFORMATION Tony and Jean Whieldon,
Grimstone Manor,
Yelverton, Devon PL20 7QY
Phone (0822) 854358

5. Halsdon House Vegetarian Hotel

Halsdon House is a large town house (part of a terrace though it doesn't look or feel like it) on a side street of the small town of Great Torrington in North Devon. It's two minutes from Dartington Glass, a new swimming pool, the local theatre, good walks and views. The house is probably late nineteenth century, with high ceilings and big rooms. Sue Marsh told me how they'd found it – so derelict they didn't dare have a survey done; but cheap and needing love. So they bought it, loved it (it took six months to get it into shape), and opened in October 1985.

It's simply done: black and white lino entrance, white walls throughout with dark red gloss trim, plain carpets, mostly functional furniture with a sprinkling of grandma's attic-type stuff. There are also some Victorian touches in the heavy carved oak sideboards and chests, etched glass lamps, swiss cheese plants and pampas grass. When I was there it still had a bit bare and newish feeling, but they were working on it. By the time you go, there should be a large wall-hanging (commissioned from a neighbour) in the stairwell.

The lounge decoration is curious – part Art Deco and part Oriental – rattan *kitsch* around the bar. But never mind, it's very warm and comfy. The bar offers a good selection of wines – including organic wines from France – and beers, and the library beside it offers a varied selection of books: education, psychology, nature, poetry and fiction. (I rediscovered Browning.)

The bedrooms are large, clean and comfortable, with cotton sheets and duvets on the beds; though, again, perhaps a little too tidy and stark because of the bare walls. There's a huge bath on the landing (not en suite but convenient to all rooms with plenty of hot water) – Sue's pride and joy. As she said. 'It doesn't matter how cold or wet you get outdoors so long as you have a big hot bath to come back to.' I couldn't agree more. There are also seventeen central heating radiators in the house, so it's nice and warm.

The dining room, with five tables, is smallish and overlooked by a yellow brick building across the street; and not improved by window bottoms (in the lounge too) of bubbly opaque glass. There's a floor-to-ceiling stone fireplace on one side and a huge carved oak sideboard on the other; the colour scheme, in keeping with the rest of the house, is pink and burgundy.

The food was simple but delicious. For dinner I had a pasta shell savoury (with *fresh* tomato sauce) followed by millet croquettes (melted in the mouth), new potatoes, tomatoes, broccoli and carrots de luxe (tiny new carrots, wonderful), followed by fresh fruit salad and cream (I asked for yoghurt and was offered a choice of plain or Greek-style, yum yum). I had a glass of Muscadet which was very dry and good. Coffee, alas, was instant. Otherwise it couldn't be better; or could it? Well, maybe. The fact is, Sue also runs a restaurant for non-residents (normally open only weekend nights, but special mid-week bookings can be made) with a later sitting and a menu which changes monthly. She also does special dinners, like the Indian feast whose menu set me drooling. The current restaurant menu included mushroom soup (homemade, of course) or marinated white beans with homebaked wholewheat rolls, followed by a pine kernel bake and, finally, a choice of carob-chip ice cream (also homemade) or Stilton cheese balls and celery sticks or creamy cashew yoghurt. Although I thoroughly enjoyed my hotel dinner, next time I'd definitely arrange to be there over a weekend and book in for a restaurant dinner. It sounds fantastic, and well worth the difference in price (£2.50).

Breakfast was fruit juice, tea or coffee, choice of cereals (dry, including muesli), soaked prunes and apricots, eggs and mushrooms on offer, wholewheat toast (commercial). Good but not special. Yoghurt might have been possible if asked for.

Halsdon House is no country idyll. It's very much a town house and in a tiny town at that. I think the lack of views is a bit sad in such a beautiful place and in summer it could be a bit claustrophobic with no garden. But a two minute walk gets you to Castle Hill and a set of trails snaking down and along the River Torridge with a splendid view of the valley and fields beyond. Sue says Great Torrington is a great town to live in – very friendly people, laid back atmosphere (including the traffic warden). You could see it: rows of shops dotted around the market square looking relatively unspoiled and mostly untwee (though 'The Mole and The Haggis', a bookshop, were said to be 'nesting'). Of course if you come by car, you can go to the coast path or up onto Exmoor, Dartmoor or anywhere.

If there are any shortcomings, they are more than made up for by the relaxed atmosphere created by the proprietors, Sue and Norman Marsh, who are incredibly warm and friendly people. After dinner, Sue and I sat around over a glass of white wine, folding some of her new brochures, and chatted for hours, with Harley the dog (also very friendly) getting in on the act whenever he could. After a while Norman joined us and they talked very openly about what it was like giving up the London rat race and risking all on their hotel venture. They seem very happy with it and so far business is ticking over even in winter.

They deserve lots of encouragement. They are 100 per cent vegetarian, so you can relax completely with the food, as well as enjoy it; and Sue is more than happy to cater for vegans and other special diets (Norman is on a gluten-free diet). Another plus: Halsdon House is a hotel not just a guest house, which means they don't chuck you out first thing in the morning. So if the weather is bad or you're not up for a big walk, you can just laze around for a while with a cup of coffee and a book.

A simple, unfussy place run by lovely people and serving fabulous food. Warmly recommended.

CATERING Exclusively vegetarian; vegans and other diets catered for. Licensed. Vegetarian pet food provided.

SMOKING Smoking restrictions.

PRICE CATEGORY High.

FURTHER INFORMATION Norman and Sue Marsh,
Halsdon House Vegetarian Hotel,
Great Torrington, N.Devon EX38 8DX
Phone (0805) 22948

6. Hazelmere Guest House

For the committed vegetarian Torquay is a place of pretty extreme contrasts. On the one hand there is Brookesby Hall, long-established and run by experienced hoteliers, a house of stature in the best Riviera-villa area. On the other there is Hazelmere Guest House, newly opened and run by young people whose enthusiasm makes up for their inexperience – a little semi-detached guest-house in a respectable but distinctly downmarket area well away from boarding house territory. Karen and David Norman bought Hazelmere (alias No.50) as a one-family house, and turned it – with considerable effort and a shoe-horn or two – into a place that can cope with ten plus guests, at a pinch. (Their tales of the purpose-built boarding houses that they looked at and rejected are enough to freeze your blood.) It does undeniably feel like a seaside boarding house none the less, from the beds for five (one double, one single, two bunks) in the very modest-sized room into which I was shown to the rather kitschy ornaments in the scarcely daylit dining room in the basement. But it is lovingly cared for: the paint and wallpaper are bright and new and everything is spotless. Even the tiny bits of garden at front and back are full of plant- and wildlife: each has a pond, the front with fish, the back with frogs and toads. The household consists of Karen, who became a vegetarian via a commitment to anti-vivisection, and who seems to have boundless youthful energy both for the practicalities of this full-time business and for conversation with her guests; David, who works as a careers adviser and spends his leisure hours on the business and on the constant task of maintenance and refurbishment; and Rex, a large black dog who was rescued from a brutal owner by an animal rights colleague, and then passed on as unsociable to Karen and David, who promptly socialised him into the gentle and affectionate creature that he now is.

Hazelmere's location is not, to be honest, much in its favour. The brochure says that you are within 15–20 minutes' walk of Babbacombe and its beach and even closer to the town centre. I didn't go to Babbacombe, but, as for the town, I'd say 15 minutes might just be possible on the way down; but you'd need to be a very fast walker to get back in that time. There is no view, which is sad from so high up above a place like Torbay; and you are quite close to a busy and noisy main-ish street. But you are, I suppose, strategically located for getting out of town – near the coach station, and near main roads if you have a car.

The food was not what you'd call gourmet: I had a sliced orange for starters, topped with chopped crystallised cherries; then a nutloaf with mushroom gravy, carrots and cabbage. Karen has recently acquired a food processor, and to judge by the nutloaf, which had all sorts of good things in it but had been overmixed to a uniform slightly mushy texture, she is still a bit too enamoured of it: even the neatly-sliced carrots were an excellent visual imitation of frozen ones – deceptively so, since the Normans buy everything fresh and, wherever possible, organic. Pudding was a banana baked in its skin – very soft and delicious if difficult to eat and rather black and evil looking – sprinkled with chopped almonds and with cream if wanted. The food is not quite vegan, but very nearly, and definitely will be for all if anyone staying requests it. Breakfast was a choice of cereals, including muesli which came with fresh fruit and prunes, then a choice of mushrooms or tomatoes or beans or eggs on toast, plus more toast with a wide range of jams or marmalade. Granose margarine as standard; big choice of drinks including herb teas, instant decaf, barleycup, etc, as well as regular tea and coffee.

For most of the year Hazelmere simply offers accommodation.

But there are special events: an elaborate sounding Christmas party of several days; an Easter Bonnet competition (sic); and David, who is a positively distinguished bird-watcher (he is co-author of a recent but already classic book on birds and where to see them in Devon and Cornwall), has arranged special bird-watching and walking weekends with transport provided, and will do so again if specifically asked, though he doesn't intend to advertise them. Karen and David are particularly anxious, without discouraging visitors of Torquay's average age, to appeal to young and active people. They are certainly enthusiastic (and very reasonably priced) and should do well with people who want to come and use them as a base for an active holiday and aren't too fussy about their immediate surroundings. I would like to think of them moving to a more spacious and perhaps more countrified house in a year or two. O.F.

CATERING Exclusively vegetarian/vegan; other diets catered for.

SMOKING Smoking restrictions.

PRICE CATEGORY Very Low.

FURTHER INFORMATION Karen and David Norman,
Hazelmere Guest House,
50 Shirburn Road,
Torquay, Devon TQ1 3JL
Phone (0803) 313139

7. Holway Mill

As we drove east into Dorset on our way home from a rather disappointing Cornish trip, the sun came out, the lanes got narrower, the hedgerows higher, the cars got fewer and fewer, the birds hopped about, and generally the world seemed a more promising place. Especially after staying at seven mediocre places – but in any case it will stand comparison with the very best in this book – Holway Mill fulfilled our highest expectations.

You will find it tucked away in the north-west corner of Dorset, 2½ miles north of Sherborne, and a quarter of a mile outside the picture postcard village of Sandford Orcas. It's very much in a world of its own, surrounded by fields, downs and narrow lanes (very) with twelve-foot hedges. It is utterly silent round about, almost eerily so, especially in warm, misty, summer weather.

The mill complex is of beautiful gold-hued stone. The main house was originally built as a small farmhouse in the early 1700s and went through major restoration in the late 1960s. The barn, also magnificently restored, is not used much except for storing Chris Woodard's family crests and for barn dances. There are two acres of lawned gardens, with nice, unmanicured flower beds, a 'solar heated' swimming pool (more about this later), and a small patio overlooking all.

The inside of the house is gorgeous: large, elegant, airy rooms, filled with lovely antiques, both dark oak and light pine; fabrics, cushions, plants, interesting modern prints, old flower prints, and ethnic hangings and more, add to the feel of a lovely tasteful home. It's not only beautifully furnished, it's also comfortable, even opulently so. Our bedroom was huge, christened 'the Nursery', as it houses a collection of old childrens' books and toys and a lovely oak cradle stuffed with cushions. The colours are restful: soft greens and pinks, plump duvet on top of traditional wool blankets (fine cotton sheets) and gigantic thick bath towels. Our room had a sink and a new corner shower; about the only piece of ugly modernity in the house. (Not too ugly to use and enjoy, however.) One of the other rooms ('the Mastersuite') has its own private bath, and the other two bedrooms have close access to the landing bathroom.

The lounge is very pretty: again soft pinks and greens with heavy stripped oak beams and unusual carved pelmets; flowery three-piece suite around a lovely old pine fireplace (log fires in the winter). There's also a front entrance room/library, with books on nature and vegetarianism, and samples of animal-free products to buy, including Faith product soaps and Holway Mill's own home-made jams and preserves; also books. There's no heavy sell, but it's all there for the interested.

We had tea on arrival in the lounge. I tried nettle tea (they have something like forty-two varieties of herb tea), and there were delicious homemade biscuits to go with it. Afterwards we strolled into the village to visit the Manor House. Back to Holway Mill, hot from our walk, we made for the waters. The labradors went with us to the pool, though only one of them was brave (or foolish) enough to take the plunge. I hesitated myself, as it was rather too natural looking (green in fact), and deathly cold. Once up and down was enough to freeze the carcase; the dog did a few doggy paddles; and Oliver pretended it was the Lancaster Trust House pool (usually about 90°). All very well to advertise 'solar heated swimming pool' – so it is perhaps by definition – but noticeably without benefit of solar heating panels.

Never mind. The icy plunge set us up for dinner (nothing like a little virtue to whet the appetite). The dining room, too, was an inspiration: all white, with wide French doors leading out to the gardens. Very simple and beautiful, with one enormous pine refectory table (seats twelve) plus two smaller round tables, an oak dresser and old tools, jugs and dried flowers hanging from the huge beams above us. The food combined taste, health-consciousness, freshness and an eye for colour and presentation. Dinner was entirely vegan, planned around my diet, and none the worse for that (the vegetarians present didn't look like they were suffering). To start, a lentil and pineapple pâté with fresh whole-wheat rolls. The main course was baked courgettes stuffed with bulghur accompanied by three salads: flageolet beans, mandarin orange and sliced winter radish, and grated carrot, cabbage, nuts and raisins. Dessert was fresh peaches with blackcurrant sauce (and cream for the lacto-vegetarians). Followed by real coffee, decaf, barleycup or one of the variety of herb teas. I had hawthorn, with After Eights, in the lounge. Most of their fruit and vegetables are organic and very fresh, from a local market gardener. Also, they are a licensed restaurant, open to the public for dinner at weekends. Their wine list was quite extensive and interesting, including a number of (fairly expensive) local English wines.

After dinner, we went for a walk in the moonlight along a quiet lane (it seemed to be the local lovers' lane) and when we came back, stood around chatting with Caroline and Chris, and admiring the two labradors as they careened around the house after their ball. The Woodards are very friendly, able to strike exactly the right balance of relaxed openness and businesslike distance.

Breakfast was another treat. I enjoyed just looking at the table with its spread of things, even if I couldn't consume everything: six huge jars of cereals, including two kinds of muesli; stewed rhubarb, yoghurt, black bread from Harrods, plain milk and soya milk, an assortment of homemade jams – blackcurrant or apricot and almond, and organic honey. Then there was a huge bowl of fresh fruit. Wholewheat toast followed and cooked breakfast, with free-range eggs, was on offer.

We had, reluctantly, to leave after only one night's stay, but vowed to return, maybe in autumn or winter, when the log fires are burning. I want to be there for one of Caroline's special ethnic food feast weekends (Russian, Greek, African, Spanish, Near Eastern, Caribbean, French, Italian). For those interested in local history and archaeology, Chris does day tours of the area, to Glastonbury and local Arthurian sites to the north, and to Hardy and Wessex countryside to the south. Apparently he also does lecture slide shows. If you're into pottery, you can arrange to use the pottery kiln. You can hire cycles, play croquet, badminton or just read and eat. A wonderful, wonderful place, though I'm afraid to praise it too highly or it will get so booked up I'll never be able to go.

CATERING Exclusively vegetarian; vegan and other diets catered for. Licensed.

SMOKING No smoking.

PRICE CATEGORY Medium.

FURTHER INFORMATION Caroline and Christopher Woodard,
Holway Mill,
Sandford Orcas,
Nr Sherborne, Dorset ET9 4RZ
Phone (096 322) 380

8. The House at Bridge Corner

I actually walked to the House at Bridge Corner, with a pack (well, a small rucksack) on my back. The cliffs between Portreath and Godrevy Head (home of Virginia Woolf's lighthouse) at the end of St Ives Bay, are lovely walking – sufficiently dramatic and occasionally awesome, but with access to some nice beaches in between; and, best of all, astonishingly level. There is really only one down-to-sea-level-and-back climb in the whole stretch. So even the ugliness and scruffiness of Portreath itself hadn't discouraged me much; and the last mile out of it and inland up to Bridge followed a leafy old miners' track which made a nice contrast. I arrived cheerful and hungry, and was not disappointed.

The house is a friendly, small, Edwardian double-fronted villa, with a big kitchen extension at the back. It is curiously low-set (the Jemmetts say the road has been raised a lot since it was built) and seems to crouch in its little front garden, with a certain amount of traffic whizzing past on its way to Portreath from Camborne (from anywhere, in fact). But the back faces the little bridge of Bridge, and my bedroom, which was on that side, was filled with the sound of the little river gurgling below. It was mostly quite simply decorated; quiet colours – blue walls, grey carpet; a plain but comfortable bed with a small but very well stocked bookcase with good fiction beside it, and a couple of rather large and lumpy Edwardian pieces of furniture, one of which (a chest of drawers) had one of the most hideous things on it that I've ever slept with: a huge glass wash basin and matching jug, in electric blue and pink, with black palms and camels painted on it in silhouette. It turns out that the Jemmetts collect such things – the guests' room downstairs is full of early-to-mid-twentieth-century artefacts, ranging from the comically endearing and even occasionally attractive, to the downright appallingly camp. Before coming down, though, I had a comfortable hot shower in the family bathroom, which is clean if quite full of children's bits and pieces.

Downstairs there are, or will be, three quite elegant rooms, each with fairly staggering original fireplaces with lots of marble as well as cast iron. When I was there two rooms were not yet decorated, so I had my supper in the temporary sitting-cum-dining room, eating at a little round table in the bay window looking out to the garden, before subsiding into a huge leather armchair to browse in more of the library, looked on by, amongst many other objects, a naked marble couple who were introduced to me as Marcus and Lavinia. I don't mean to put you off – there were lots of plants, flowers, and signs of thoughtful if pleasantly idiosyncratic taste, and no doubt the sense of clutter will diminish when it's all spread over three rooms instead of one. I felt thoroughly comfortable and at home.

But it was the food that was really spectacular. Supper (and breakfast, too) was one of those deceptively simple meals, that both looked and tasted superb – every course was a treat for the eyes as well as the other senses. It began with a grated beetroot salad, with pumpkin seeds, raisins, etc, nestling in three lettuce leaves and garnished with slices of the very first radish from Amy's (the Jemmetts' younger daughter) garden. Then came courgettes stuffed with bulghur and red peppers and slow-baked, with a wonderful walnut and garlic sauce, minty new potatoes, and braised carrots with rosemary. And finally, a strawberry mousse, semi-frozen, made with extra-fresh strawberries and garnished with mint leaves; and peppermint tea to round it all off. Chris Jemmett gets most of her fruit and vegetables from an organic smallholder, which is a good start; but she really knows how to assemble them into something remarkable.

Breakfast was, if anything, even better to look at. I found it waiting on the table, all assembled in little dishes chosen from the household's collection when I came down. There was a bowl of muesli pre-soaked in orange juice, with a circle of peeled grape halves decorating the edge of the dish. There was Granola – 99 per cent nuts, seeds and fruit; there were toasted wheat flakes, toasted buckwheat; a green apple and a knife on a plate; there were prunes; orange juice; there was a little round homemade loaf, one person's size, on a tiny breadboard, and homemade toast on offer as well; and there were four 1930s jars containing peanut butter, jam, marmalade and honey, the last with a ceramic bee crawling up it. It's difficult to convey what a lovely composition it made in the morning sun; but it was the kind of meal that you remember long afterwards for the combination of sensory pleasures.

The House at Bridge Corner seems to me the very best kind of family B & B. Chris and Nick Jemmett, though somewhat shy, were very friendly and kind – I was even offered a lift to set me off on a good walk in the morning; their daughters, who wait on you at mealtimes, are enchanting; and the monster Alsatian, though she may bark if you prowl in the garden, is equally friendly face to face. It is certainly a family home; but you have enough space to prevent you feeling you've kicked the owners out of their day-to-day living area. If you get tired of the house there's a very friendly pub just down the street. It's a bit trafficky, and the village doesn't amount to much, but at least it's not Portreath, which is a visual disaster. As a place to use as a base, fill in the gaps in your knowledge of modern English literature, and to eat in real style, it can't be beat. I'm looking forward to my next Cornish coastal walk. O.F.

CATERING Exclusively vegetarian.

SMOKING Not in evidence.

PRICE CATEGORY Low.

FURTHER INFORMATION Chris and Nick Jemmett,
The House at Bridge Corner,
Bridge,
Redruth, Cornwall
Phone (0209) 842377

9. The Manor House Hotel

'Vegetarians! Good Food is Essential!' said the advertisement at the back of the *Guardian*. Too true – though it's a slightly odd way of putting it. Agreeing enthusiastically, I rushed off to the Manor House, Woolfardisworthy (pronounced and often spelled, as hereafter, Woolsery).

The house looks large, one of the tallest two-storey houses I've seen: a big Georgian south-facing front tacked onto a Tudor back end, which has been extended into a vaguely fake-Tudory dining room, seating, at a guess, sixty plus. My bedroom was a grand room at the front, said to have a fine view of Dartmoor, if Dartmoor would cooperate (it wouldn't). It was large and barn-like: no armchairs, only one upright chair despite the two single beds; and though well heated it smelled vaguely damp from the distinctly unmodern en suite bathroom, which came equipped with thin and skimpy towels, an old rag for wiping the bath and an ineffectively-flushing loo. Beds OK, if old, but only one non-rubber pillow between the two; tired old wallpaper and paint. Most of the rest of the house felt similarly tired. The non-smoking (one good mark!) lounge was the only room that had been fully redone by the Watkins. But, a bit ominously for the rest, it was comfortable, certainly, but not showing a lot of taste or style. The bar/sitting room where I spent the evening had an enormous fireplace in which a gloomy fire went out; the dimmest lights I've ever failed to read by; tired leather furniture which looked like red plastic (or vice versa? I couldn't see): general effect by Hammer. I hasten to say it's next on the Watkins' list. *Anything* will be an improvement.

There's a huge vegetarian menu (you choose at the bar) – a brown leather folder for carnivores, green leather (!) for veggies. Choice of *seven* starters and *seven* main courses . . . the finger of suspicion points to the freezer. Starters are elaborate and fussy. Corn on the cob, yes: but with *cinnamon* butter? Melon, with

27

walnuts, cherries *and* grenadine. Salad of orange segments and endive – with sorbet? Also asparagus mousse with yoghurt and chive sauce, which I regret not trying I think. Out of a sense of duty to my readers, I avoided sensible things like soup or garlic mushrooms, and chose a chestnut-stuffed pepper with mushroom sauce, followed by a main course of 'spinach and goat's cheese roll', imagining a slim slice of elegant roulade.

The dining room was, if possible, even dimmer than the sitting room, so the description that follows is without benefit of careful visual inspection. (Also I was distracted by the music: supermarket muzak for the first course was suddenly replaced by Lohengrin in time for the culinary *pièce de resistance*, but it faded back to muzak for the pudding.) The stuffed pepper wasn't bad: if the food comes from a freezer at least it's properly reheated, not microwaved. A bit rich, but chestnuts are; and quite nicely seasoned. The main course was something else. 'I hope you're hungry,' said Vicky Watkins menacingly, lowering an enormous pasty (about size 8EE) in front of me, along with another plate with seven vegetables on it. (Is this sevenishness a fetish, I wonder?) The pasty was better than it looked: when I ordered, she'd warned me it wouldn't be goat cheese but Stilton, 'I think'. *I* think not; but the pastry was light, though white, and there was lots of spinach and not too much cheese, though I couldn't find the promised accompaniment of 'rice, caraway, lemon and garlic' either inside or outside. The veges were awful: overboiled potatoes and carrots; onions and potato croquettes baked in a lot of oil and, if you please, *more* spinach and *another* half pepper with the same chestnut stuffing. No one could possibly have eaten the lot. The puddings you can imagine: mine came with aerosol-piped cream and more cream from a jug. Wine list not bad, but my Beaujolais, after a lot of song and dance about (a) its splendour and (b) its not-being-quite-warm-enough-yet, came almost hand hot. A pity, as it would have been quite nice, I think. Breakfast – well, what would you expect? White toast, packet cereals; yoghurt on offer, but asking for natural caused a small panic.

I didn't feel comfortable; but if *you* like rich hotel meals, out of the freezer and overstuffed to justify high prices, *and* you're a very trusting or non-compulsive vegetarian, you might get on OK. The

Manor House may soon be a bit less seedy, though I don't honestly think it will ever be elegant. The Watkins' rows of curly-headed children, who may bring you your breakfast, are gorgeous (if with wicked looks in their eyes). But don't go for the village – the church was locked, the Farmer's Arms was being rethatched, and the rest is endless housing developments with teenagers tuning their motorbikes. O.F.

P.S. There is a new swimming pool.

CATERING Traditional and vegetarian. Licensed bar.

SMOKING Smoking restrictions.

PRICE CATEGORY Very High.

FURTHER INFORMATION David and Vicky Watkins,
The Manor House Hotel,
Woolfardisworthy,
Bideford, N.Devon
Phone (02373) 380

10. Moorhayes Vegetarian Farm House Hotel

Moorhayes was the first place I visited. Though it had only recently opened, I thought then that it was wonderful, though I had nothing to compare it with. But now, measuring it against the other places in this book, I can still safely say it's special. One of the reasons, of course, is the fact that Jenny and Duncan Hulin are in the unique position of managing Moorhayes without having to finance it themselves. I don't know the details, nor do I wish to give away trade secrets, but the gist of it is that the owner of Moorhayes is able and willing to invest, improve and advertise to the hilt where many another veggie proprietor would fear to tread. For example, if you look in the back page of *The Guardian*, you'll see their frequently running advert – a hefty outlay right there. And there's a lot more.

They spent two years converting Moorhayes – a seventeenth-century Devon longhouse – tastefully and lovingly renovating, decorating and furnishing. The result is luxury without ostentation. Our large en suite bedroom (with a tiny shower/loo room) was very pretty in a pink chintzy style, with super comfortable double bed (soft cotton sheets and duvet), all mod cons (TV, kettle, extra heater) and some handsome pieces of antique furniture. The old and new harmonise nicely. The rest of the house is equally comfortable and pleasing to look at: fresh white painted walls, nubbly oatmeal carpeting, original slate dining-room floor, walk-in fireplace, more handsome polished antique furniture, wood-burning stove, secluded sun-bathing area, and so on. Lots of dried flower arrangements in December; fresh ones I presume in summer.

They are constantly upgrading and improving. When we were there, Duncan was talking about the possibility of a sauna. I urged him to consider an outdoor California-style hot tub, which he seemed interested in, but I doubt if even they have the kind of money to indulge in such follies (though it would be my idea of perfection to loll in a hot bubbly tub under freezing Devon stars after a long day out on Dartmoor). Who knows, by the time you go, maybe there'll be some kind of exotic waterworks. If not, the enormous old-fashioned bathtub, with gallons of hot water, should still do fine.

The food was so good we decided to stay an extra night. There was a wide choice of dishes and the menu was different each night. Particularly memorable were the carrot and orange soup, fresh baked rolls, *al dente* steamed vegetables, felafel patties, wholewheat pizza. For dessert, tangy tofu cheesecake. Real coffee, tea or herb teas. They also do (on alternate weekends when we were there, but check for current timetable) South Indian specialities, which must be fabulous (I shall go back). The restaurant is open to the public on weekends and is very popular. Even on a quiet winter weekend, it was fully booked both nights. Bring your own bottle, or they serve non-alcoholic wines. Breakfast was equally wonderful, with fresh and stewed fruits, homebaked wholewheat rolls, yoghurt and honey, free-range eggs, toast and various spreads. Herb teas, coffee and coffee substitutes.

The only criticism I had was that the dining room in December was cold and draughty. I kept wishing there'd been a fire in the enormous fireplace, but, alas, it was filled with dried flowers – very pretty but burning logs would have been warmer. There was a wood-burning stove in the living room, which made it very cosy indeed, though it tended to be monopolised by the Hulins' huge Dalmatian (the only carnivore around) who growled like Lon Chaney's Wolf Man every time we tried to join him. It's pure bluff (I think).

Don't be put off by the Spanish hacienda-type exterior – inside it's tasteful and in a completely English farmhouse style. If you value delicious food, magnificently clean, comfortable and stylish accommodation, do visit Moorhayes. It's 10 miles from Exeter; Dartmoor is not much more than half an hour's drive away, and the South Devon coast is very close. Lots of peaceful country lanes for cycling (they have a few bicycles available for guests' use) and you can walk in Ashclyst Forest. Also indoor games and an interesting library in the lounge, with books on nature, local interest, photography, antiques, health, etc; stacks of fat magazines too. Then there are the Hulins to chat to. When we were there, it was just the two of them doing everything, so their time was limited. By now, Jenny has the baby she was expecting, and I hear they have acquired help in the kitchen, which should help matters – just as long as the cooking doesn't lack her special touch. Whatever the changes, I'm sure it's still a perfect place for a vegetarian holiday.

CATERING Exclusively vegetarian and vegan; special diets catered for. Non-alcoholic wines.

SMOKING Smoking restrictions.

PRICE CATEGORY High to Very High.

FURTHER INFORMATION Duncan and Jennie Hulin,
Moorhayes Vegetarian Farm House Hotel,
Talaton. E.Devon
Phone (0404) 822895

11. Neubia House Hotel

The Neubia House Hotel, Lynton, is a simple, unpretentious place, with no side at all. True, it's a cut above the long row of boarding houses on the main street of the rather dull little town; but unlike the Chough's Nest it's not pretentious enough to sneak round out of Lynton's narrow valley and face the spectacular coast. In fact, it is probably one of the lowest situated houses in the town: tucked in – with its own private car park, thank goodness – between the front and back streets, looking out rather hesitantly (it doesn't seem to have a front) over the roofs of a garage and the Lynton Dairy ('cream freshly clotted daily', but don't panic, cream evidently clots in silence) and, if you crane your neck out of your window, with a bit of vertical Exmoor pasture and a line of trees on the skyline straight above you. All the rooms face south, with this same view; in fact, I had the odd sensation of staying in the thin half of a rectangular loaf sliced the wrong way.

If the general impression is a little claustrophobic, that's fair enough. After a day walking along the North Devon cliffs I felt desperately shut in, and went quickly out to grab the rest of the daylight before supper. However, early season Lynton doesn't have much to offer between shop-closing and pub-opening time (indeed I doubt if either shops or pubs would help very much) and I was reduced to taking the quaint but utterly unheated cliff railway to Lynmouth, where I froze and decided it was no better. So, dying for a hot bath, I took the train back up and retired to my room. The bath was indeed hot, though exiguous: Neubia House has en suited its none too large rooms by the simplest method of cutting a chunk out of each, and I'm glad I hadn't brought any cats to swing. But at least there was daylight in my bathroom instead of the usual cupboard. I doubt if that's true of every room, however, and in return I also had what sounded like the main cold water supply pipe for the whole house. My fellow-guests that night were early retiring and late rising, so the noise didn't much matter. But I couldn't hear my private TV even at the most anti-social volume while the water was running; if offered a choice you might be well advised to avoid Room 4.

The dining room, on the ground floor but feeling a lot like a basement, has a tiny bar, rather the scale of my bathroom, at one end. But drinks are cheap (and rather impressive in variety: a sharp ear will detect a trace of Aberdeenshire in Dorothy Murphy's accent, and she has a patriotically formidable selection of malt whiskies to prove it, along with a good selection of pre-drinks, beer and wine, all at very modest prices) and the company was friendly . . . just as well, as we sat in each others' laps. So we discussed our routes to Lynton and the unseasonable (sic) cold with true British animation, and chose from the menu before dispersing to our separate tables. There were four starters, all vegetarian, I think: I had avocado and tomato salad, which came as very simple slices with rather a lot of non-home-made inferior mayonnaise or superior salad cream – *I* wouldn't know the difference, he said snobbishly. The vegetarian main course – there is one every night – was mushrooms in paprika sauce; an excellent stroganoff with all the proper things, accompanied by scalloped potatoes and some beautifully *al dente* steamed vegetables – cauliflower and leek (this was April) simply decorated with slivers of celery and carrots. Altogether very delicious and plentiful. The puddings were less exceptional: rum and raisin cheesecake was rich but very natural and homemade tasting; but I chose it in preference to a rather elaborate looking apricot and almond flan with tinned looking apricots and (I think) white pastry. Then cheese, if you could – a wide choice – and coffee or tea. Piped music throughout: classical pops, not too loud. The general ambience wasn't attractive: a dimly lit basement room, and not much effort at cheering it up with decoration or good food presentation. But as a meal to eat with your glasses off, not half bad.

I retired to the lounge, which is two rooms knocked together one floor above, and made my eyes jump with the huge array of chairs and the colours of carpets, curtains, furniture, wallpaper, etc. The whole house is done up in a rather dire style with a range of super-swirly carpets I haven't seen the like of since house-hunting in Edinburgh in the early 1970s. So I went to my room and stared up at the TV perched on its curiously high shelf (and listened too when the water wasn't running) before falling into a peaceful sleep in the comfortable and very warm bed: the whole house is very well heated.

Breakfast was mostly rather conventional 'traditional', but with brown toast as standard at least, and special super-wholewheat bread available for vegetarians, along with sunflower or other spreads and honey, instead of butter and marmalade; also sugar-free muesli.

Altogether a pretty comfortable experience. *Not* visually pleasing, but not at all bad for most of the other senses. It was a great relief to find the Vegetarian and Vegan Society stickers firmly on the door after four days at the mercy of the commercial veggie-bandwagoneers of North Devon, and to find their claims lived up to inside. Dorothy Murphy is a very genuine vegetarian, and radiates conscientiousness and intelligence about vegetarians' and vegans' needs. If Neubia House weren't 400 yards from the Chough's Nest (which is certainly not to everyone's taste either), you'd be very pleased to find it.

Oh, and don't let me put you off Lynton: the town itself isn't much cop, but between Devon's best piece of coast, Exmoor on top and the valleys in between you don't have to go far to find some of the very best bits of the West Country. O.F.

CATERING Vegetarian and traditional; vegans catered for. Licensed bar.

SMOKING Allowed but not in evidence.

PRICE CATEGORY High.

FURTHER INFORMATION Brian and Dorothy Murphy,
Neubia House Hotel,
Lynton, N.Devon EX35 6AH
Phone (059 85) 2309

12. Penhaven Country House Hotel

'I knew nothing about hotel keeping except what I'd picked up in three months on the road with the Rolling Stones.' Alan Wade, *Daily Express*, February 1985 (framed with pride above the bar).

Saw *Guardian* advert boasting vegetarian proprietor, special catering for vegetarians, etc, etc. Sent away for brochure. Sounded posh, poetic ('. . . streams to meander with and the magic of a woodlands wild life to enjoy'); expensive but worth it for special treat. Phoned to book. Got de luxe room en suite (no ordinary double available). Received confirmation of deposit with request to fill in special booking form. Carefully wrote: *Ms* Lynne Alexander and Mr Oliver Fulton. Reply came back: 'Thank you, Mrs Fulton.' A bad start.

Rotten weather, worst week in April. Not their fault. Enter driveway, see white Gothicky-style house set in lovely parkland with daffodils blooming. All is forgiven. Push open lozenge-shaped door, hit in face by essence of cigarette smoke. Can't breathe. Floors carpeted in thick red stuff. Lady proprietor (Maxine Wade, I presume) greets us, leads us up to room. Cigarette smoke follows. Notice 3-D wallpaper, clown painting (sad) on landing. Say house is unusual (attempt at pleasantry). Get no reply. Room has lovely view. Bed has pink tufted headboard. Furniture made of plastic wood laminate. Mrs Wade instructs on use of remote control TV. En suite bathroom has no view; in fact no window. Bathroom door does not close properly, rattles when window opened. Cigarette smoke creeping up from below. Put suitcase against bathroom door.

Nice hot bath (yes, plenty of hot water though towels skimpy) and down to bar/lounge while Oliver has his. Plant self fairly conspicuously in front of fireplace: floor-to-ceiling stone monstrosity with firedogs, yule logs and niches pasted onto Victorian

35

cornices. I wonder if Mick Jagger taught prop. Alan Wade interior decoration too? He comes over to poke fire and nearly trips over me. Says sorry but he didn't see me. Does not offer me a drink (must be because I am invisible). Solitary male persons in lounge I doubt would be invisible, even midgets. Am reminded of the Castle View Hotel in Chepstow (another ExecHotel) where I was also not offered a drink. Stride up to bar and order sherry. Give room number and name: *Msszz* Alexander. So there. He looks the other way. I ask for the vegetarian menu. He produces one out of his sleeve and says all the right things about Fresh Vegetables. Something about a medieval garden, would like to convert all guests. Talks scathingly about salesmen who visit him, trying to sell frozen (ugh) veges, including frozen peas which they say are tastier than fresh (imagine!). Wag heads together. Am cheered up. He may be blind but he still has tastebuds. Order mushroom pâté and toast followed by cheese and onion croquettes with veges from garden (of course), followed by unspecified sweet from trolley. Oliver orders vegetable soup (ditto) followed by cauliflower beignets. Decide to share bottle of Muscadet, and a good thing too.

Waiter pulls out my chair, spreads napkin on my lap. Poor Oliver. Mr Wade bends over Oliver and asks, '*Were* you having any wine, sir?' Takes away glasses. Returns glasses all nice and chilled plus wine in real ice bucket. Shows label to Oliver. Oliver shows to me. 'Ah,' he says, 'a second opinion.' I hold out my glass to receive The Taste. Mr Wade looks uncomfortable. I say – completely over the top, offensive, aggressive and absurd, but pushed to it – 'I'll do the tasting, I know more about wines than he does.' Not true, but forgivable in the circumstances. Mr Wade sidles off.

Switch to waitress. Brings basket of rolls, brownish. '*Did* you want a roll, Madame?' Oh I get it, ladies first with the food. No I did not want a roll. Wait a minute, what is all this past tense waitpersonese? I hate it. No I don't want one, I say. I can smell Oliver's soup across the table – either packet stuff or beautifully designed to taste like it. My mushroom pâté tastes of nothing but salt and flavouring. Can this be happening? '*Were* you finished with your toast, Madame?' Yes I *am* finished. Main course brings luminous orange croquettes (mashed potatoes fried in orange-coloured breadcrumbs). Oliver gets three pieces of cauliflower with curried apple sauce. Says bravely how good it is, I mean was. I manage one bite of mine and am not polite about it. *Did* I want some potatoes with my potato croquette (Duchess, mashed or fried)? I take fried but the flavouring is overpowering; my mouth begins to pucker. The salsify (five pieces), unadorned/adulterated, is very good. Leeks in a peanutty sauce. Deep fried cabbage. Oliver says if God had meant the humble cabbage to be battered and fried he would have seen to it Himself. I am hungry. All this food and nothing edible. Cocktail music is washing over us. I think we could have had a better dinner at the Water Witch in Lancaster (baked beans on jacket potato) for a tenth of the price, and with better noise/sound effects; less fawning and cetainly better grammar from bar people. At least the pub has no phobias about present tense construction and is definitely less chauvinist.

Bus boy pretends shock. *Didn't* Madame like her dinner? Madame says she's had enough mashed potatoes for one night, thank you very much. Dessert trolley wheeled in. I order cheese and biscuits. Biscuits of a brand made with animal fat. Oliver orders cheesecake. Stuck together with masses of what tastes like gelatin. I eat whole bunch of garlicky cream cheese; delicious. Ask for more; get small dollop. No sweet. (Cheese *or* sweet; generous to a fault this place.)

'*Were* you wanting coffee, sir?' Into the lounge with us (yes me too, remember me?) where rock music is blasting. Tweedy couples, mostly elderly, do not seem to notice. Smoke thick. Coffee is real (surprise, surprise). Drink greedily. Even eat lump of fudge out of hypermania. Lift *Tatler* and go to bed.

Wake at 3 a.m. in sweat, head pounding, stomach gurgling, mouth like pot of glue. Oliver too. Howling wind and rain. Window rattles. I forgive it as it's old and real; the only real things about the place.

Morning dawns. Shower a trickle; have another bath. Bacon smells float up to us. Breakfast: tea bags. Grapefruit with darling little red cherries. Stone cold toast, mostly white. I ask for prunes and porridge. Prunes come (straight out of packet) *in* porridge. Oliver's eggs good (yes, free-range from noisy chickens outside)

37

on darling little triangles of crustless white toast (he ordered brown). No cream for porridge. I ask for croissant. It comes, pale and flaccid.

Sun comes out. Oliver's face brightens at suggestion of leaving. '*Were* you wishing your bill, sir?' 'No, I'll have it and kindly change the Mr and Mrs Fulton to Ms Alexander.' Obedient but stony silence. Croissant eating grin. I pay. It hurts.

We leave. Agree Penhaven Country Hotel is worst place out of forty-nine so far visited. Oliver says personally he'd rather spend a night in jail. What should the booby prize be? (suggestions please).

CATERING Traditional; vegetarians catered for. Licensed bar.

SMOKING Allowed.

PRICE CATEGORY High.

FURTHER INFORMATION Alan and Maxine Wade,
Penhaven Country House Hotel,
Parkham, Nr Bideford,
North Devon EX39 5PL
Phone (02375) 388

13. Penmarric Lodge

To tell the truth, I never looked forward to Penmarric Lodge. Penzance, admittedly, is an attractive if seedy town – like a cross between Mallaig and Hull – with an end-of-the-railway, start-of-the-voyage air to it, and a suitably squalid harbour with a niffy mixture of small boys and old men fishing, smashed boats and nautical junk, bearded swains leaning out of trawlers to chat up leggy girls off yachts, crab stalls, scruffy pubs, and so on. And of course, the Egyptian House on Chapel Street. So I was hoping for, and indeed got, an interesting evening stroll after my evening meal.

But Wendy Lorenson hadn't endeared herself to me over the phone. She grilled me at length – and at my long-distance expense – about exactly how and especially why I was coming, and though too polite to tell her to get lost, I found her interrogation distinctly over the top. I booked, agreeing 'because she might want to go to the beach' to arrive after 5.30, asked for and was rather grudgingly promised an evening meal 'though there's a very nice vegetarian restaurant down the street', and sent my deposit and a letter confirming one night's stay, arrival after 5.30, and evening meal. A few days later, a phone call: when was I arriving, and would I mind not coming till after 5.30 . . .?

The address (Penmare Terrace) and something about the brochure had suggested that Penmarric Lodge was likely to be less than the grandest of lodges, with its name owing more to boarding house convention than to strict accuracy. So my heart lifted momentarily when I saw a rather dotty, double-fronted Victorian detached house, with a strange wood-and-glass tower on the roof and a palm tree in flower in the garden, even if it was at the corner of two grey granite terraces in the dull upper part of the town. Pausing merely to note that The Lodge has a wrought iron gate labelled (more modestly?) Men Dhu, I rang the bell and, after an alarmingly long pause, was let in by Ms Lorenson's daughter (she herself was indeed still out at 5.45). Once inside, my heart fell again; but since – in a nutshell – I do not recommend Penmarric Lodge, I do not propose to burden you with a detailed description of its interior. It seems reasonably clean, the water is hot, the beds are mediocre (and the pillows something worse, see below), the furniture and decoration are boarding house-cluttered, and do not lift the spirit. But it is, to be blunt, the proprietor that is the problem. She arrived back after 6.00 and opened the conversation by asking how many nights I was staying (I had already told her twice); then, evidently wanting some tea for herself, thought to offer me a cup (it was now 6.30). I asked about my supper, and learned – surprise, surprise – that she was too tired to cook me a meal. 'Did I say I would?' Well yes, madam, you clearly did. Oh well, there was a good vegetarian restaurant *just* down the street and when we finished our tea she would give me directions. Fortunately, I established that it closed at 7.30, and managed to extract the directions – which involved four or five streets – before then, though not before being sat down and, to the background of some revolting 'soothing' music, which consisted of synthesised trash repeated ad nauseam, quizzed still further about my private affairs.

I made off, pleading – if excuse were needed – my evidently bizarre anxiety to get a meal before the café closed ('I expect they'd stay open if you telephoned,' said Ms Lorenson vaguely). And I was sufficiently irritated to make very sure not to come back till bedtime. As I say, I enjoyed my stroll no end; and come to that, Jenny's Wholefood Café (39 Causewayhead) is simple but excellent, and has better cheesecake, I swear, than New York's finest. Try it if you're in the area; there's no need to stay at Penmarric Lodge, after all.

There is (or was, these things change fast) an expressive Californian adjective, 'flaky'. It denotes a degree of laid-backness which has passed the bounds of social acceptability, even on the West Coast; and it came to my mind at Penmarric. I suppose I might have put up with either the nosiness or the flakiness, but the combination was too much. And the flakiness extends, I'm afraid, to breakfast (no pun intended). There could hardly have been a sharper contrast than with my previous day's breakfast at the House at Bridge Corner. There was (a) a bowl of shop-bought muesli with a few bits of sliced banana around it; (b) some toast made from very ordinary bread. Period. Oh, and she played the same damned tape over again at breakfast – twice. One final straw: my pillow was one of those lumpy foam rubber jobs, guaranteed to give even yogis a stiff neck. I'd expect better from almost any seaside boarding house, but since Wendy is, she says, a professional masseuse, I reckon it's inexcusable. All I can say is that Penmarric Lodge is just about top of my never again list. I know there's not a lot of choice in West Cornwall, but even so. If you've bought this book, you too deserve something better. O.F.

CATERING Vegetarian breakfast; evening meal unknown.

SMOKING No known rules.

PRICE CATEGORY Low.

FURTHER INFORMATION Wendy Lorenson,
Penmarric Lodge
Penare Terrace,
Penzance, Cornwall TR18 2DT
Phone (0736) 62068

14. Ullacombe House

Ullacombe House is full of contrasts. The map on the back of the brochure is simplicity itself; but it seems a long two miles from Bovey Tracey and you begin to panic (well, I did) when you finally see a sign to Ullacombe Cottages (which are *not* what you're looking for). Through the gateposts for Ullacombe House at last, you find yourself on a track through an intensely gloomy wood, with thick laurels below the dense sycamores just to complete the sombreness. On a wet and dripping day I might even have turned back, except that there's nowhere to turn. But suddenly the track emerges into the open, you drive a few hundred yards more, through another pair of gates, and there you are on the doorstep of an enchanting house with a truly breathtaking view. The house was built around 1840, but has if anything a late Georgian feel to it: big and plain but handsome, with large windows beautifully picked out in a faded Georgian blue against the chocolate and grey granite. At your feet as you stand on the doorstep – from under which self-sown blue squills were flowering when I arrived – is a lower terrace of beautifully kept grass (I noticed croquet equipment) with a bank full of primroses, a little clump of tall yucca plants to show it's Devon, and then a view down a sweeping combe that opens out to the whole Teign Valley. It's so splendid that I got all self-conscious about my grossly red car, and offered to move it out of sight.

Inside, the whole house is wonderfully light and airy. Even my little single room at the back had the westerly sun streaming in over the high moor behind, with a friendly view of bits of Ullacombe Farm (unconnected), some gracefully tumbled sheds and a steep field above. The guests' drawing room and the best double bedroom ('the honeymoon suite', said the Rileys, ruefully contemplating the no expense spared extravagance of places like Moorhayes) have windows on two sides; and two of the three double rooms have The View (the other merely having *a* view which would do just fine anywhere else). The decoration is a bit mixed: odd combinations of beauty (of many different kinds), utility and kitsch (ditto) among the ornaments, pictures, etc, old prints, oriental rugs, some hideous carpets and knick-knacks; furniture some antique, some junky; and the paint, carpets, etc, are old but clean and somehow compatible with each other and the place.

John and Kianoosh Riley are warm and welcoming, so much so that I can't tell you much about them. Unlike most of the hosts in this book, they are genuinely interested in their guests, enough to want to find out about *you* instead of telling you the story of *their* lives. John talked to me about education and about Dartington; Kianoosh about cooking; and both of them about the house and the business (though I'm not sure that's a word they'd use), all of which they had somehow quietly established were *my* interests. I suspect they'd rise to the challenge of any visitor you could find for them.

Supper was formidably splendid. Mr Riley serves it from a kind of hatch, in which it appears from the disembodied hands and accompanied by the equally disembodied comments of Mrs Riley. You eat at a magnificent long table in what must once have been the kitchen, now superseded. The first course was a wonderfully thick and hearty soup, containing among much else white beans, sprouted beans and barley. There was a huge plateful of freshly made croutons to go with it. We all felt quite full afterwards, but were reproached for not eating more. I'm only glad I didn't, since the hatch next opened to reveal four huge tureens of vegetables – cauliflower baked in cheese sauce, which many others would have got away with as a main course; a spectacularly rich and tasty stew of aubergines in tomato sauce (ditto); baked sliced potatoes and carrots, which melted in the mouth; and swede reposing in a great nest of peas (the only non-fresh thing among them). Each of these was enough for at least six, and we were only three . . . The tureens sat in the middle of the table, temptingly enough; and when our plates finally arrived, they came with a wonderful kind of nut rissole on them as well, an inadequate word for a rich and dark, exotically scented (cardamom among others), well, *burger*, but with a difference. Then there was a salad, deliciously crisp and light, with Chinese leaves and alfalfa sprouts and a wonderful mustardy dressing. Then there was pudding: a lemon soufflé which contrived to be both dark and sticky and light and feathery in different bits, with a huge bowl of clotted cream. Then, though even I gave in at this point, cheese (with vegetarian rennet). All washed down with delicious water from the house's spring, or apple juice (or bring your own wine). Except that I'd been stupid enough to eat lunch, and I hadn't walked 25 miles, it was sheer perfection: like the house, a wonderful combination of simplicity, solidity, subtlety and beauty. Breakfast, by the way, was up to the same standard: homemade muesli ad lib (and I don't mean home-mixed, but much of it dry-roasted the night before); fresh fruit, bread or toast, local honey and marmalade, eggs if required (I didn't . . . or couldn't). Tea, coffee or herb tea (also available any time; kettle in your room).

So far, so perfect: that is, unless the sight of that vast quantity of lovely food sets up irreconcilable conflicts in you. Problems? Well, only two, really, and one doesn't bother me at all. First, Ulla-combe House is not 'modernised' – no en suite bathrooms, not even a washbasin in your room – though there are two loos and two baths which is not bad for a maximum of nine guests. Me, I'm happy to saunter down the passage in my dressing gown, but the Rileys are a bit self-conscious about it and fear some people may be discouraged. Please don't be: the compensations are much too good; and anyway, cutting chunks out of those lovely rooms, or even putting basins in them, would quite spoil their simple character. On the other hand, the house is also rather cold. There's no central heating, only some rather *ad hoc* and not over-generous portable heaters downstairs; and nothing in my bedroom – in early April – for the air temperature, though there was, mercifully, a comforting electric underblanket on the bed. This does seem more serious to me; I suppose that radiators, like washbasins, spoil the look of Georgian rooms, but after a long day's wet tramping on Dartmoor I do think warmth for chilled bones is almost as important as good food. The Ullacombe philosophy, as the brochure makes clear, is that you are a guest in the Rileys' home, and it's clear too that they have strong views on how such a home ought to be, which don't include central heating. Perhaps if we all suggest it they'll relent; meanwhile, pack your woollies and choose your season.

What else? Testimonials in the visitors' book (including one from the President of the Swedish Vegan Society) show that Kianoosh Riley caters both well and conscientiously for vegans also, if asked, or for any other diet you may have. If you're not a fully-fledged vegetarian, don't be put off by the slightly menacing 'For Vegetarians and Vegans Only' – if you'll eat it, they'll have you. Ullacombe is two miles uphill from Bovey Tracey, and one field's width from the open moorland of Dartmoor, directly below Hay Tor. If you can get yourself there by public transport (plus taxi?) you could certainly do without a car for a week's walking; with a car, all South Devon is in easy reach – you're less than ten miles from the main A38 Exeter–Plymouth road. So, if you need 1980s good taste, all ultra mod. cons, and have the cash for it, you'd better go to Moorhayes. If you want something simpler and very personal in a house of exceptional and unspoiled character, take a thick sweater and either your walking boots or a very large belly, and go to Ullacombe. I'm going to get married again, for the pleasure of a few nights in *their* honeymoon suite. O.F.

CATERING Exclusively vegetarian; vegan and other diets catered for.

SMOKING Not in evidence.

PRICE CATEGORY Low.

FURTHER INFORMATION Mr and Mrs J.J. Riley,
Ullacombe House,
Haytor Road,
Bovey Tracey,
Newton Abbot, Devon TQ13 9LL
Phone (03646) 242

15. Woodcote Hotel

The Woodcote Hotel is a two-storey, rambling, mock Tudor house with black painted porch across the upper storey, mostly cottage windows but for the large plate-glass dining-room window overlooking the Hayle estuary. You enter through a sliding glass door. A pleasant front lawn with a sweeping, turning circle completes the picture of a promising small hotel. It's set in a popular part of Cornwall, in walking distance of the coastal path and Woodland Trust walks, and short driving distances to beaches, archaeological sites, riding stables, bird and animal sanctuaries. It's quiet but for the peep-peep of wading birds and the not unpleasant toot-toot of the little train chugging past on its picturesque way to St Ives. Added to all this, it was one of the first (*the* first? – established in the early 1920s) to cater exclusively for vegetarians. But although exclusively vegetarian, the Woodcote manages to convey the atmosphere of a traditional seaside hotel. The proprietors, John and Pamela Barratt, are jokey but impersonal. John's smile, which he flashed like the Godrevy Point lighthouse in a fog, was frankly a turn-off, as was their rather chauvinistic banter. The inside of the house is very disappointingly bungaloid – modernised out of any character it may have once had, with flush panel doors, sliding glass doors, fire doors, arches, floor to ceiling tiles in the bath, wrought-iron light fixtures. The decoration is as plastic as are the smiles – all the chairs and settees upholstered in the same dark brown and dayglo orange polyester stretch fabric, and the carpets are swirly-whirly, though in quietish colours.

It was not redeemed by its food. For dinner there was French onion soup or salad (the usual, with a few beansprouts added) for starters. The main course was one of Pam's pasties, filled with a few scraps of vegetable matter (mostly potato) and accompanied by soggy cauliflower, spinach, and fried new potatoes; no butter or margarine but a jug of 'gravy'. Dessert was orange whip or ice cream. I opted for the vegan alternative – two fresh peaches –

45

which was the best part of the meal. Rosehip tea followed

It really was a pretty poor performance. Even at many traditional hotels one can often get decent steamed vegetables, if nothing else. Breakfast was no improvement: a range of dried fruits, all over-sweetened, muesli or Weetabix, followed by the usual cooked breakfast, with commercial brown bread or toast and eggs. My soya milk was watery.

I had a twin bedroom with no view, decorated in pink and lilac with cutesy-poo drawings on the wall. The duvet cover didn't look particularly clean and there was no top sheet between it and me. (Duvets are fine but only if their covers are washed as regularly as top sheets.) Otherwise it was comfy enough, with a bedside reading light, basin and kettle with herb tea bags provided. Except for the duvet cover, the place was spanking clean. It's a very snug house, with lots of radiators to warm you even if the food doesn't. There's no bar but you can bring your own wine (no corkage charge). I daresay a front bedroom, with a view of the estuary, would have made me less grumpy.

What more can I say? I certainly expected more from the brochure; from its pretty pencil sketch on the front to the paragraph, headed 'Our Philosophy': 'The emphasis at Woodcote is on individual freedom plus good old fashioned personal service supported by an imaginative and varied vegetarian/vegan cuisine.'

Sorry. Actions speak louder and all that.

CATERING Exclusively vegetarian; vegan and other diets catered for.

SMOKING Smoking restrictions.

PRICE CATEGORY Medium.

FURTHER INFORMATION John and Pamela Barratt,
Woodcote Hotel,
Lelant,
St Ives, Cornwall
Phone (0736) 753147

Other Places to Stay

CORNWALL

Nr Launceston: Oak House (formerly the Old Rectory), Altarnun
Phone (056686) 206
T-V, prop. V. Former rectory, comfortable looking house. Price category M.

Par: Linda Hudson
Phone (072681) 5609
XV house: 'detached, with lovely big secluded garden, 5 minutes to beach'. B & B + EM. Price category VL.

Nr Penzance: Chun Farm, Morvah
Phone (0736) 788300
XV (vegetarians only catered for). 'New barn conversion with views of the sea. Organic produce as available.' Just started advertising.

Nr St Ives: St Judes, St Ives Road, Carbis Bay
Phone (0736) 795255
XV, 'modern accommodation, overlooking St Ives Bay'. On main road. Price category L.

Torpoint: Wringford Farm, Cawsand
Phone (0752) 822729
XV organic farmhouse B & B + EM. 'Quiet, friendly atmosphere . . . beautiful uncommercialised part of Cornwall.' Price category L.

Nr Truro: Polsue Cottage, Ruan High Lanes
Phone (0872) 501596
V-T ('Many of our visitors are vegetarian'); small cottage with good views, 6 acre smallholding with organic market garden. Roy and Bridget Bowcock are former teachers; welcome walkers, painters, birdwatchers, sailors and especially other 'scribblers'. Price category VL. (Sounds nice. I tried but couldn't get a one-night booking.)

Zennor, Nr St Ives: Boswednack Manor
Phone (0736) 794183
V-T, V props. Mostly special interest holidays (see Chapter X) but take guests between courses or if space available. (We tried but failed.) Beautiful setting.

DEVON

Bampton: Loades, Millhead Cottage
Phone (0398) 31739
XV, B & B + EM 'if required – but no vegans'. Large period cottage, Georgian village.

'Between the Moors'
Phone (0884) 860012
XV. B & B + EM opt. 'Old vicarage with spacious accommodation in lovely setting.'

Dartmoor:
Phone (0647) 40782
V-T, B & B + EM, 'Japanese specialities, children welcome.'

Lustleigh:
Phone (06477) 310
XV. B & B + EM opt. 'Spectacular Dartmoor village with lovely walks'; guests' sitting room. Price category VL.

Nr Newton Abbot: Farmborough House, Chudleigh
Phone (0626) 853258
XV, between Haldon Forest and Dartmoor. Painting, yoga, New Age books and tapes. Price category VL.

North Bovey: Gate House
Phone (0647) 40479
V-T guesthouse. '15th century thatched house, views, pool.'

Nr Ottery St Mary: Harmony House, Southerton
Phone (0395) 68577
XV. Holistic guesthouse: Peace Garden, Healing Sanctuary, New Age book and tape shop. Natural Living and Awareness Centre. Restaurant.

Nr Paignton: Bonne Nuit, Lower Westerland Lane, Marldon
Phone (0803) 552394
XV, small friendly seeming guest house, nr Dartmoor and Torquay. Nice quiet position but house rather pink and twee. Clean and comfortable. Proprietors Tony and Diane Pill left the London rat race to settle in the country. Price category L. (We had a quick look round but unfortunately couldn't stay.)

Sidmouth: Avalon Wholefood Guest House, Vicarage Rd
Phone (03955) 3443
T-V, emphasis on health but V and special diets catered for.

Sidmouth: Enstone Guest House, Lennox Avenue
Phone (03955) 4444
T-V, traditional looking but V proprietor says he likes catering for vegetarians.

Nr Torquay: Braddon Hall Hotel, Braddons Hill Rd E
Phone (0803) 23908
V-T, 'V meals a speciality'. Recently moved from Stratford where they had a guesthouse with XV EMs.

Nr Totnes: Highfield House, Kingsbridge Hill
Phone (0803) 863887
V-T, B & B + some EMs by arr. Listed Georgian house overlooking Totnes and Dartmoor.

DORSET

Bournemouth: Saint Antoine Guest House, 2 Guildhill Road, Southbourne
Phone (0202) 433043
V-T. Traditional looking seaside guesthouse with V emphasis.

Bournemouth: Westminster Private Vegetarian Hotel, 14 Clifton Road, Southbourne
Phone (0202) 423826
XV seaside guesthouse. Price category L.

Charmouth: Charleston House, The Street
Phone (0297) 60347
V-T, B & B only – 'lots of vegetarian places to eat nearby'.

Charmouth: Knapp House, The Street
Phone (0297) 60574
V-T, B & B + EM opt. '95 per cent vegetarian; vegetarians especially welcome.' Price category M.

Charmouth: Margaret Watson
Phone (0297) 60751
XV, B & B + EM 'occasionally'. 'Cottage with warm welcome, lovely views, one mile sea, quiet farmland setting, superb walking country.' Price category VL.

Charmouth:
Phone (0297) 60444
XV, NS, B & B + EM by arr. 'Sea views, homemade bread, quiet position, lovely walks.'

Nr Lulworth Cove:
Phone (0305) 853633
'Wholefood' B & B only, NS. 'Comfortable family house, large garden; beautiful walking country.'

Lyme Regis: Pitt White, Uplyme
Phone (02974) 2094
T-V guesthouse, 'semi-vegetarians'. 'Peaceful country house near the sea. Any special diets catered for.' Price category VL.

Lyme Regis: River House Vegetarian Guest House, Coombe Street
Phone (02974) 3149
XV, long established, on narrow street of old houses; one minute walk to the sea front. Excellent food. (We visited five years ago and enjoyed our stay.) Price category VL. Book early – gets full in high season; we couldn't get a booking this time round.

Osmington:
Phone (0305) 832387
XV B & B only. 'One mile sea, children welcome.'

Swanage: Sunnybank Private Hotel
Phone (0929) 422767

T-V. Traditional seaside boarding house but with vegetarian sympathies. Mr Larsen is 'a lifelong vegetarian' and Mrs Larsen 'a cordon bleu cook'. Price category VL.

West Dorset:
Phone (0297) 89422
XV, B & B only. 'Seaside cottage, lovely views.' Weekly rates, winter breaks.

ISLES OF SCILLY

St Mary's: The Boathouse
Phone (0720) 22688
T-V, 'vegetarians welcome' (but not mentioned in brochure), small guesthouse on Town Beach. 'Superb views, own garden produce.'

St Mary's: Bayview Guesthouse
Phone (0720) 22798
T-V, 'vegetarian/wholefood/traditional.'

SOMERSET

Chard: Holmbush, Thorncombe
Phone (02977) 597 or (0297) 34710
XVgn. 'Tranquil, cosy cottage home of alternative healers.' A.O.N.B., eight miles Lyme Regis. Price category VL.

Glastonbury: Chalice Hill House, Dod Lane
Phone (0458) 32459
XV, B & B + EM by arr. The Ramala Centre 'for pilgrimage, retreat or holiday. Hard tennis court and mystical Glastonbury.' Price category M.

Nr Glastonbury: Nut Tree Farm, Stoughton Cross, Wedmore
Phone (0934) 712404
V-T, guesthouse, all diets catered for. Sounds serious, nice people.

Pensford: Viaduct House
Phone (07618) 745
XV and Vgn, mostly organic B & B + EM. Price category L.

Places to Eat

CORNWALL

Falmouth: Greens (XV), 45 Killigrew St. Phone (0326) 319391.

Penzance: Jenny's Wholefood Café (XV), 39 Causewayhead. No phone listing.

Penzance: Olive Branch Vegetarian Restaurant (XV), Market Jew St. Phone (0736) 62438.

St Ives: Sunflower Wholefood Vegetarian Café (XV), 3 Chapel Lane. Phone (0736) 794700.

Truro: Attic Feast Wholefood Restaurant (XV), Old Bridge St. Phone (0872) 40008.

DEVON

Barnstaple: Heavens Above (XV), 4 Bear St. Phone (0271) 77960.

Dartington: Cranks (XV), Dartington Cider Press Centre, Shinners Bridge. Phone (0803) 862388.

Exeter: Grants Wholefood (XV), 15 North St. Phone (0392) 214213.

Exmouth: Round the Bend (XV), 53 The Strand. Phone (0395) 264398.

Plymouth: College of Further Education, Kings Road, Devonport. Phone (0752) 264750. *No, not an error. Friday night said to be a feast for vegetarians (and vegans). 'One of our most forward-looking catering colleges.'*

Talaton: Country Table Vegetarian Wholefood Restaurant (XV) at Moorhayes Vegetarian Hotel (*see main review*). Phone (0404) 822895.

Tiverton: Angel Food (XV), Angel Terrace. Phone (0884) 254778. *Also wholefood shop.*

Torrington: Halsdon House Restaurant (XV). Phone (0805) 22948. *Also guesthouse, see main listing.*

Totnes: Willow Restaurant (XV), 87 High St. Phone (0803) 862605.

Bournemouth: Henry's Wholefood Restaurant (XV), 6 Lansdowne Road. Phone (0202) 297887.

Bournemouth: The Salad Centre (XV), Post Office Road. Phone (0202) 21710.

Charmouth: Gnomes Vegetarian Café (XV), The Street. Phone (0297) 60532.

Christchurch: Salads of Christchurch (XV), 8 High St. Phone (0202) 476273.

Poole: Inn a Nutshell Café (XV), 27 Kingsland Crescent, Arndale Centre. Phone (0202) 673888.

Shaftesbury: Harvest (XV), 4 Bell St. Phone (0747) 4444.

Nr Sherborne: Holway Mill (XV), Sandford Orcas. Phone (096322) 380. *Weekends only. Also guesthouse; see review*.

Wareham: Annie's (XV), 14a North Street. Phone (09295) 6242. *Possibly also a guesthouse though we received no reply from our enquiries*.

SOMERSET

Glastonbury: Rainbow's End Café (XV), 17a High St. Phone (0458) 33896.

Wells: The Good Earth (XV), 4 Priory Rd. Phone (0749) 78600.

II

THE SOUTH EAST

Greater London, Hampshire, Kent, Surrey, East and West Sussex

Places Reviewed

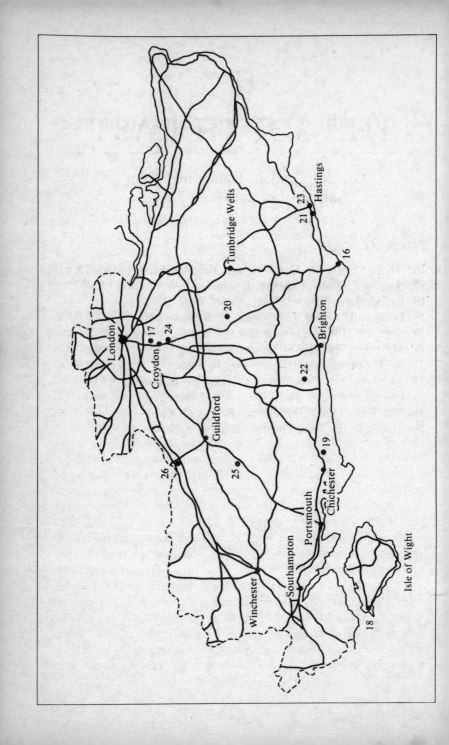

16. Abele Vegetarian Guest House

Abele is on a quiet, respectable street in Eastbourne, one short block from the Promenade, close enough to get a whiff of the sea but not a view of it. One of a row of red brick terraced houses with pretty astragalled windows, Abele is distinguished, if not improved, by a blue awning and plain plate-glass windows.

The house itself seems quite nice inside: cheerfully decorated bedrooms, dining room with piano and framed family portraits. But these homey touches seemed superficial; one night at Abele brought out its true boarding house nature: the lounge – small, dark and grim – most unwelcoming with its single window looking out onto an alley; the bathroom at the back of the house on the ground floor, so that you have to go through the lounge to get to it (tiptoeing through your TV-watching fellow guests in your robe and slippers as if you were just going out to sniff the flowers), and a considerable hike from the upstairs bedrooms. Flushes and gurgles from the potty next to my bedroom and Radio Two from the bedroom on the other side were hard to take. It's not all so dire. Once you make your trek down to the bathroom, it has cheerful apple green trim, lots of plants and plenty of hot water for a relaxing bath. And my bedroom – though the mattress was soggy and the wallpaper beginning to peel off – had clean cotton sheets and duvet. The hall is painted white which *is* unusual, and refreshing, for a boarding house.

The food is 100 per cent vegetarian. There are notices posted on their bulletin board to assure you that what you are eating is free of all animal products, in any shape or form – a great comfort to be thus reassured. The weekly dinner menu was also posted. For the week I was there it included pizza, lentil pasty, Scotch egg, and vegetable pie, all filling, substantial, if uninspired, dishes. Breakfast consisted of grapefruit or muesli and fruit, scrambled eggs with commercial wholewheat toast and ordinary tea. I asked for yoghurt (this was during my non-vegan, special diet phase) but they were out of it. There were various pots of commercial jams and honey.

My impression of the Longs (who look a bit like ageing hippies) was that they were not particularly friendly. It was the summer season, they were busy and harried, and, as I learned from Betty Long, they were planning to open a new restaurant soon in Eastbourne; so it's possible their attention was elsewhere. But I had the impression that, like their house, they'd taken on the characteristics of traditional boarding house proprietors – rather distant and businesslike. Perhaps it's an occupational hazard.

As it happened, I had to skip dinner because I was ill. While Vic Long did bring me an aspirin at about 6 o'clock (for which I was duly grateful), no one checked afterwards to see if I was all right, or offered to bring a cup of tea (visions of Writer Perishes in Seaside Resort). Perhaps that is asking too much, but you have only to read through these pages to discover numerous cockle-warming exceptions to the rule. I was charged for the dinner I hadn't eaten, which I didn't blame them for, but I did feel there was something lacking in the manner in which it was done. No regrets, no 'how are you?' Just a rather defensive and unfriendly attitude.

Perhaps my experience was atypical. I hope so. I thought the Longs seemed like nice people underneath, and their hearts are certainly in the right place. I would recommend trying their new restaurant for lunch. But for personal attention, gourmet vegetarian food, and smoke-free air, I would stay elsewhere (try Rita Welfare at Merryfield House).

CATERING Exclusively vegetarian; vegans catered for. Licensed.

SMOKING Smoking restrictions.

PRICE CATEGORY Low.

FURTHER INFORMATION Vic and Betty Long,
Abele Vegetarian Guest House,
5, Rylstone Road,
Eastbourne, E.Sussex
Phone (0323) 35781

17. Barrow House

So far as I know, central London boasts no vegetarian hotels, in fact not so much as a B & B. This is perhaps understandable and to some people no great inconvenience, since there are plenty of veggie restaurants and it's a rare B & B that can't boil you an egg – though vegans may find it harder. But anyone who wants to be safe from the smell of bacon and, equally important, wants all the other things that a vegetarian household promises – a warm reception, a clean house, healthy food and no cigarette smoke – would do well to board a train at Victoria Station for Streatham Common (15 minutes journey, trains every 15–20 minutes daytimes, half hourly at night). Three minutes' walk from this station takes you down Barrow Road, where the little terraced brick houses gradually expand to generous semis, and finally, at No. 45, to the handsome late Victorian Barrow House, a detached house with a small but endearing turret at one side.

Inside, Pauline and Michael McDonald will make you more than welcome, greeting late-night arrivals with a huge choice of herb teas and homemade goodies, and offering you their comfortable sitting room to watch their TV. If you simply want to sit and read or write, your own room will do fine: mine, lovingly furnished in high Victorian style (and including a circular bay below the turret) contained an armchair and a writing desk, both well-lit, as well as a splendid double bed (but with a dependable modern mattress) and not only pillows but a real live bolster. On the bedside table, characteristically thoughtful, was a latchkey and a train timetable.

The facilities, for a house which sleeps eight at most, include (in three separate rooms) three loos, a bath, a serious shower, a bidet, and a fireplace in the room with the bath. Altogether a splendid combination of Victorian elegance and late-twentieth century convenience. Other furnishings are equally lavish: you might want to bring your dark glasses if you expect a hangover, but I loved it.

Breakfast, too, is spectacular: unlimited quantities of fruit juice, coffee or various teas, lots of mueslis, healthy toast, homemade yoghurt, etc, etc. Boiled eggs if you wish. The McDonalds themselves are vegan, but cope cheerfully with lactos if required.

No possible complaints except that the house is possibly too warm in winter – terrific central heating, and double glazing. And blissfully quiet; you'd never know the railway is so close. The meals policy is strictly breakfast only, but Streatham, with a vegetarian and many ethnic restaurants, is a short walk.

Go, and enjoy. I've become a regular. O.F.

CATERING Exclusively vegetarian; proprietors vegan.

SMOKING No smoking.

PRICE CATEGORY Medium, even allowing for train fare from central London.

FURTHER INFORMATION Pauline and Michael McDonald,
Barrow House
45 Barrow Road,
London SW16 5PE
Phone 01-677 1925

18. Brandelhow

Ward Road is immediately adjacent to the Turf Walk and the sheltered beach of Totland Bay, on the far western coast of the Isle of Wight. The coast is a warren of footpaths and you can step out the front door and walk for miles along the cliffs or inland downs. White cliffs, heather in August, orchids in April; giant cypresses, birds, sea, sky, picturesque villages, and more, make it a fine place for a holiday. If you're very fit and so inclined, you can take your bicycle, but it must be pretty punishing. Totland Bay itself is a good place to be – off the beaten track but accessible by foot or road to Headon Hill, Alum Bay, Freshwater Bay, and so on.

The little cameo on the front of the rather old-fashioned brochure, depicting a distant farmhouse surrounded by trees with horses pulling a plough, has nothing obvious to do with Brandelhow itself, which is a red brick, double-fronted villa with a handkerchief sized front lawn, flanked on either side by larger and better-kept versions of itself. Having imagined something more romantic, I found the reality rather disappointing: the rusted sign saying 'Private Hotel', the peeling window frames, and a front door practically rotted away.

Inside things looked more comfortable and better cared for, though the decor is undeniably of the seaside boarding house variety. The dining room is papered in a pattern of giant ochre *fleur-de-lis*, with nautical pictures and a chandelier resembling an inverted wedding cake. The lounge in the back of the house is dark, filled with chairs, settees and telly; its only window looks out onto a tiny concrete yard with curly white patio furniture. It seems cruel to be a stone's throw from the sea and yet have no view of it. To make matters worse, there is nothing to read (not even guidebooks or maps) except for a pile of National Trust magazines. My single bedroom was rather a shoebox but with some redeeming features; namely, a view of splendid cypress trees and a suggestion of sea over the housetops, and most rare, a really comfortable bed with good cotton sheets, and a reading light over the bed. Evidently the other rooms – double and family-size – are much larger and that much more comfortable. The loos (two) and bathroom are clean and serviceable though not things of beauty, while the separate shower cubicle was rather unappetising. Some of the rooms do have private 'facilities', if that's one of your priorities.

The food is excellent; and now, thanks to more of us going, exclusively vegetarian. Drinks are non-alcoholic but there are pubs nearby. Vegans are extremely well, and cheerfully, catered for, but I must warn you that Pauline Stratton, who does the cooking, does not normally have people on special diets in the high season, though she rather grudgingly had me for one night. For starters I had an orange and grapefruit salad, nicely sweetened with honey and spices, while the others had celery and asparagus soup, which had potato in it. My main course was a special buckwheat and lentil bake with fresh tomato sauce; the others had a sesame–cashew roast with baked potatoes. Vegetables were cauliflower and carrots, nicely steamed. My dessert was fresh stewed apricots with soya ice cream and homemade oat flapjack; for the rest it was apple pie with blackcurrants, with cream or yoghurt. Choice of herb teas, tea or coffee followed.

Breakfast was equally delicious and individually designed. I had prunes, oats soaked in apple juice, a bowl of nuts and raisins, a jug of Plamil; plus oatcakes, rice cakes, honey and marmalade. For those wanting a cooked breakfast, there were vegeburgers, free-range eggs, tomatoes, mushrooms and thick slices of wholewheat toast.

The Strattons are both conscientious and caring people: Ken is a patient, sweet and gentle host and Pauline is an imaginative and talented cook and a friendly if forthright person. Though not the ultimate in gracious living, Brandelhow is comfortable and a good place to be based for a holiday on the Isle of Wight. It's on a quiet part of the island and convenient for beautiful walks and scenery. The food is healthy, delicious and now – their first year – strictly vegetarian, and vegans are very well looked after. People with special diets, in spite of my rather dusty reception, are welcome in the quieter seasons. They do not allow very young children or dogs (but older children are very welcome), so if you go you can be assured of a quiet, peaceful holiday.

CATERING Exclusively vegetarian; vegans by prior arrangement.

SMOKING Smoking restrictions.

PRICE CATEGORY Low.

FURTHER INFORMATION Pauline and Ken Stratton,
Brandelhow,
Ward Road,
Totland Bay,
Isle of Wight PO39 0BD
Phone (0983) 752238

19. Briarcroft

Briarcroft lies in the village of Oving, 3 miles east of Chichester. It's located down a quiet lane, opposite the village church and its splendid manor house. It's a smallish white box of a house, trimmed with yellow, with a steep tiled roof, and surrounded by a large lawned area in front and a substantial kitchen garden to the rear. The house is simple and homey, with small rooms, modest furniture, and the kind of decoration and ornaments typical of that kind of suburban house. The bedrooms are both small (one with double bed, the other with twins) and both look out onto the next door's hedge. Mine (the twin) had fishy curtains, a worn grey rug, and a monolithic white wardrobe. The beds were equally tortuous: one a hammock, the other a rack (both with nylon undersheets). (It seems quite ironic that a physiotherapist should harbour such beds in his own house.) The lounge is done in shades of brown, and dominated by an upright piano, a large TV, mementos of family life, an irrepressible electric clock, a few plants and a cornerful of rather tired dried grasses. It has a large window looking out to its neat front lawn and across the road to the grand trees of the manor house beyond. Bookshelves contain a rather motley collection, including many esoteric and spiritual titles: *Swedenborg*, *Sun Signs*, *Theosophy*, *The Zen Doctrine of No Mind*, and *Meditation on the Occult Life*.

The Dungeys are Quakers and vegetarians. Mrs Dungey grew up a vegetarian, as the daughter of Theosophist parents. After running a smallholding for many years, Mr Dungey decided to become a masseur and Mrs Dungey put her efforts into running a guesthouse and tending her garden, which is clearly her pride and joy and a near enough full-time job. She grows every imaginable vegetable and fruit, and all according to organic principles. She also bakes her own bread and makes her own yoghurt and preserves.

The food was simple but deliciously fresh, most of it straight out of the garden. Dinner was a composite vegetable stew of garden delights: carrots, onions, courgettes, broad beans, peas. The tomato sauce was too cornstarchy, but I suspect that was because of my no-wheat diet. The salad was very plain, undressed, but also from the garden: lettuce, cucumbers and tomatoes. Dessert was a blackcurrant pudding with Plamil – luscious. I was offered Ryvita and peanut butter too. Fresh mint tea made a refreshing end.

Breakfast was wonderful. No impersonal lineup of sweety-puffs, but an assortment of bowls filled with all kinds of alluring goodies for a make-your-own muesli: blackcurrants, oat flakes, fresh bananas and peaches, plus soya milk. That was followed by Ryvita and homemade marmalade, honey and Marmite. And again, garden mint tea. Of course, if you're unlimited by any dietary restrictions, you will be offered homemade bread and yoghurt, free-range eggs, mushrooms and tomatoes.

When you go to Briarcroft, you must expect not a guesthouse or hotel – with the independence or anonymity they imply – but a small family house which you will be very much a part of. At Briarcroft you share the lounge and bathroom, though not your meals, with your hosts. I had the lounge to myself until 9 o'clock, when the Dungeys came in to watch the news and after that we chatted for a while, which was pleasant. Before retiring, I was offered a kettle to take up with me, along with two herb tea bags.

The joint bathroom could be more of a problem for some. It feels very much like their bathroom – with their toothbrushes, flannels, footpowders and hair brushes ranged round. Moreover, there isn't a neverending supply of hot water, and there's no shower; also no central heating, though there are storage heaters. This lack of 'amenities' could be a distinct drawback for some, but I found Mrs Dungey's kindness, friendliness and conscientiousness made up for a lot; as did the fruits (and vegetables) of her inspired garden.

Briarcroft is not a luxurious house. It's a place where old things are treasured (there's what looks like a 1940s radio in the dining room) and where waste is not tolerated. You can see that from the slivers of soap and the minute pencil stumps saved up in a jar.

Their motto must surely be 'waste not want not'.

I hope I haven't given too negative an impression of Briarcroft. I enjoyed my brief stay very much. I think it would suit people who'd rather avoid the overdone swankish or gracious living places, and who aren't too finicky about 'facilities' and 'amenities'. You certainly won't waste money and you won't want for perfectly fresh, homemade and homegrown food – exclusively vegetarian and vegans most welcome. And if the beds are a punishment to the back, you can always arrange for a massage from Mr Dungey!

CATERING Exclusively vegetarian; vegan and other diets catered for.

SMOKING No smoking.

PRICE CATEGORY Low.

FURTHER INFORMATION Mrs Heather Dungey,
Briarcroft,
Oving, Nr Chichester,
W.Sussex
Phone (0243) 789394

20. Claridge House

Claridge House is a Quaker Centre ('for renewal, rest and study') maintained by the Friends Fellowship of Healing. It doubles as a conference centre and a country guesthouse, fitting guests in when space permits. There's a strong emphasis on spirituality and on peacefulness. I personally found the rest and refreshment angle more appealing, but whatever your reason for going, you'll find it a beautiful place and easy to get to if you live in London – it takes 50 minutes from Victoria Station. From there you walk a mile, take a taxi or the house car can pick you up.

Claridge House is a large red brick Victorian villa with a white façade. It's set in 1½ acres of lush landscaped grounds. When I was there in late May the cherries and early yellow azaleas were especially lovely, though the beeches and giant pines must always be good. The interior of the house is plain but very comfortable, the walls are painted white and the furniture is simple and tasteful, and in keeping with its Victorian tone of voice. The bedrooms are very comfortable and well equipped, though a bit cell-like and furnished in nursing-home style. Mine looked out on the garden, had old-fashioned cotton sheets and blankets, and a good reading light over the bed. Basin and kettle were also provided, though not herb tea bags, but Liz Walpole was happy to provide them when asked.

There are several splendid public rooms: a quiet room, a drawing room, and lounge or small conference room, the latter two having huge windows overlooking the gardens. The lounge has French doors leading out onto a terrace where tea (and other meals) are served in fine weather. The quiet room is where guests are invited to join the rest of the household in the Quaker tradition of meeting for 'quiet times' twice daily. It also houses a library, mostly religious or quasi-religious books (*God's Smuggler*, *Dying We Live*, *Suffering*, *The Secret of Staying in Love*, *Adventures in Prayer*, etc). On the whole, a fine house, though details like the bedroom furniture, the fire doors (no doubt statutory), and 'modernised' (flat panel-boarding) doors and stairways, spoil it. The other less than perfect features are the roar of planes overhead (it's on a main Gatwick flight path), and the whiz of cars past the front gates, especially at commuting hours (though the house is set back from the road).

The dining room – which unfortunately lacks a view of the gardens – has three refectory tables, two simple dressers and a wooden wall carving of The Last Supper. I found dinner in this room something of an ordeal, though that had nothing to do with my supper or indeed with The Last Supper, but everything to do with sharing a table with a rather remote ninety-three year old Quaker with a Father Time beard.

The food was very good. If it was extra-simple, that was the fault of my 'stone age' diet, which Liz Walpole coped with beautifully:

apple juice to start, followed by courgettes stuffed with a delicious ground sunflower seed stuffing, with side vegetables – grated carrot with caraway, and parsnips and onions. Dessert was fruit salad: simple and delicious. Breakfast was exactly what I asked for: stewed prunes, sunflower seeds, coconut, soya milk and herb tea. Yoghurt was available. Normally guests are offered muesli followed by toast (no cooked breakfasts). Because of the numbers of conference guests, breakfast is kept simple, to leave time to prepare lunch, which is a large meal, and then tea . . . Unlike most guesthouses, this is a full-board establishment.

A curious place Claridge House. It shares the problem of other such places (like Tekels Park and Runnings Park) in trying to combine a guesthouse with a conference/religious centre. I don't think the problem is insurmountable, though the success of your stay will depend to some extent on the group you find yourself sharing a table with, and your interest or sympathy with their aims. Liz and Mike are themselves very accepting people, and I certainly enjoyed chatting with Liz in the evening about diets and our respective forms of isolation. Guests are, more seriously, invited to discuss Healing and to share their problems; in fact, if you have a special reason for going to Claridge House, they ask you to forewarn them so they'll be 'better able to serve you'. But if you're not interested in this sort of thing, they certainly will not foist it on you; it's very much a take it or leave it approach. I am not in the least 'into' healing, nor a Quaker, yet I still felt very welcome.

Liz is a wonderful cook, Claridge House and its gardens are very inviting. If you need to get away from it all, if you are ill or recovering, if you are under stress, or if you simply want to get away to think or read or contemplate the garden or the Surrey countryside – there are some very pleasant walks in the area; Liz or Mike are happy to make suggestions – or go to Lingfield Races, I certainly recommend you consider Claridge House.

CATERING Exclusively vegetarian; vegan and other diets catered for.

SMOKING Smoking not in evidence.

PRICE CATEGORY Medium.

FURTHER INFORMATION Liz and Mike Walpole,
Claridge House,
Dormansland,
Lingfield, Surrey RH7 6QH
Phone (0342) 832150

21. Merryfield House

Merryfield House (3 St Matthew's Gardens) is a large, red brick
terraced house, probably turn of the century, up a steep hill in St
Leonards, on the East Sussex coast. It's a ten minute walk to the
train station, and a 15–20 minute walk to the sea front; not to
mention all the wonderful places a bit further afield, from Henry
James's house in Rye to Beachy Head near Eastbourne. Inside it's
very spacious; elegant and homey at the same time, with some
appropriate furniture from Chris's past antique business. Downstairs there's a dining/sitting room for guests (with a telly), another
guests' sitting room upstairs (also with telly), and bedrooms are on
the floor above. Mine was incredibly comfortable and clean, with
lovely cotton sheets and duvets and fresh-smelling, plump pillows
and thick towels; also another small telly for watching in bed. It
made such a cosy nest up there, I found myself watching a very bad
Agatha Christie. Next to my bedroom was a brand new shower
room and loo.

Dinner was magnificent. For starters there was melon with
grapes and good wholewheat bread. The main dish was a chick pea
stew accompanied by a sweetish rice pilau. Then there were two
fantastic salads: one silver beet (grown from seed brought back
from Australia) with croutons and mushrooms; the other was
tomatoes with toasted almonds and coriander. Dessert was hunza
apricots soaked in herb tea and stuffed with hazelnuts, with
banana and apple slices – *and* (had it not burned) a topping of
carob sauce. It really was a very special meal – an unusual and

imaginative combination of spices and flavours – each course beautifully cooked and presented. I couldn't get enough of the salads, which are Rita's speciality, but it was all extremely good. She's a fantastic cook. There were also lively chats between courses, about everything from vegetarianism to the rotten English weather.

Breakfast was juice, muesli (or other cereals) and wholewheat toast with various jams and peanut butter spreads; free-range eggs with mushrooms, etc, if wanted. Coffee, tea, herb teas or barleycup.

Merryfield House would have been an excellent place to stay without any additional hospitality, but the extra care and attention both Rita and Chris laid on made it very special indeed. They recommended places of interest I should see and then, since they were going, offered me a lift to Rye so that I could see Henry James's house (closed that day, natch). Then, in the afternoon, Chris offered to take me to Batemans – Rudyard Kipling's home – simply because he liked it so much himself, he wanted me to see it too. I wasn't able to take him up on his offer, but I'm very grateful for his and Rita's unusual generosity and warmth.

A wonderful, homey, smoke-free place with friendly, thoughtful people and extra-special vegetarian gourmet cooking. As their brochure says: 'We are not a "guesthouse" but an informal household for paying guests.'

CATERING Exclusively vegetarian; vegan and other diets catered for.

SMOKING No smoking.

PRICE CATEGORY Low.

FURTHER INFORMATION Rita Welfare,
Merryfield House,
3 St Matthew's Gardens,
St Leonards-on-Sea,
E.Sussex TN38 0TS
Phone (0424) 42453

22. Nash Country Hotel

I was sure it would be one of those super-posh country places; the kind with dining room muzak, flocked wallpaper, teary-eyed clown paintings and smoke-filled rooms – but cocking a ladle to the recent fad for 'wholefoods' with a freezerful of cheesy brown crepes. Well I'm happy to report it wasn't like that. The only flocking at the Nash Country Hotel is done by the waterfowl – geese and ducks (Muscovy I think) who range freely about the 8 acres of lawns, paddock and pond areas surrounding the hotel. The setting is lovely and peaceful, sheltered by splendid old trees – larch, cypress, beech, chestnut, apple – beyond which you look out to the South Downs topped by the magical trees of Chanctonbury Ring. The Nash site is very old – fourteenth century at least – with the original part of the house forming the present kitchen and scullery. But the main part was built by two Victorian Quaker ladies in 1840 (whose spirits were recently seen hovering round the grand piano). Joyce Elsden, the current proprietor, has made further improvements, adding a modern wing and renovating various farm buildings to make separate cottages for self-catering families.

The inside of the house is refreshingly simple and unspoiled; tastefully decorated and furnished in traditional style, though most of the panelled doors have been boarded over. The walls are mostly white, off-white or pale pastels with white trim, the carpets plain coloured. The lounge is a long handsome room, entirely done in soft apricot and deep turquoise, which may sound peculiar but is actually a rich and harmonious combination. Fresh flowers, a grand piano, prints, photographs, a Renoir reproduction, a wall of books (mostly twentieth century writers), a good reading lamp, and a TV in the opposite corner from the piano, add to the sense of country house comfort and unfussy elegance. Even when the other guests were watching the TV, it was possible for me to sit at the other end and read without being disturbed.

The upstairs is also simple and spacious, with a large open landing which doubles as a second lounge (no TV), with lots more books. The bedrooms are large, light and airy. Mine had a lovely view over the vineyards up to the Ring. It had rather functional furniture with touches of B & B baddies (fringed lampshade, flowered polyester curtains) but the carpet was plain and the walls cool green with white trim, so the overall effect was nice. There was a small black and white TV and a kettle (but no herb tea), cotton sheets and fresh blankets. The bathroom (opposite my room) was splendidly bare, clean and simple, with plain carpet and large bath in the middle of the room. Some rooms are en suite.

The atmosphere is friendly and informal. I arrived on one of the hottest days in August, after a 3 mile walk from Steyning (it's 5 miles from Shoreham and 11 miles from Brighton); longing for a swim but without a bathing suit. 'Never mind,' said the manageress, 'just go in your bra and pants, no one will mind.' And so I did, improvising with a large red bandana. The pool is about the size of a fishbowl and distinctly frigorific, but with the swifts flying round overhead in a blue sky, it was just what was needed; though I doubt that there would be many days when the flesh would willingly take the plunge. Solar heated is, I believe, the current euphemism.

The rather pokey dining room has a lovely view over the lawns and up to the Ring and is done in pastel pinks and blues, with a quiet Persian rug and a beautiful Oriental-looking print of ducks over the mantelpiece. Definitely easy on the digestion. But, alas, the food itself was disappointing. For starters, half an avocado or mushroom omelette. The main course was a sort of curry with fat peas, a few chickpeas and sultanas, and mostly potatoes; accompanied by huge wet chunks of marrow, carrots and more potatoes. Dessert was soya ice cream and fresh fruit, or steamed chocolate sponge with cream. This year you can have wine from their next-door winery which is not organic, and next year, if all goes well, you can sample Nash's own organic product.

They cater very well for vegans (Joyce Elsden, Nash's proprietor, is 'nearly' vegan) but more complicated, or limited, diets seem to stretch them a bit. Joyce Elsden herself is careful and very tuned in to people's dietary needs, but the manageress, who does the main running of the kitchen and the serving, was much more cavalier about such things. I had written a note prior to my arrival indicating my allergy to wheat and potatoes, but this seemed not to have registered. She laughed and said she'd remove the side-dish potatoes – fine; but what about the main course whose main ingredient was also potatoes? I know it's a lot to ask – and I live in a state of constant embarrassment and apology over my finicky diet – but if they say they can cope (which they did) they should take it more seriously.

Breakfast was better in this respect, with special rye pumpernickel as well as oatcakes, two thoughtful alternatives to wheat bread. But otherwise there was only the basic sugar-coated assortment; no muesli – which is unusual – fruit or yoghurt. The soya milk failed to appear on the tables (there were two vegans when I was there) and the herb tea took half an hour to come. The carnivores, I thought, got better service for their bacon and egg; vegetarians did next best with free-range eggs, mushrooms and tomatoes; vegans had to be patient. They weren't very busy either.

Joyce Elsden joined us in the dining room for a chat while we drank our tea. She is a very lean, impressive and charming lady, with a laid-back attitude to nature and people. If people want to eat meat, she serves them meat, believing that people will change when they're ready. She believes she's doing more towards fostering change, in fact, by gentle example and persuasion than by catering only for vegetarians and vegans. No sense preaching to the converted, as one of the other guests said. A writer most of her life, she is thoroughly involved in the Christian Healing and Spirituality movement, and makes Nash a meeting place for all kinds of weird and wonderful types. Her autumn programme of Sunday talks includes: Mental Colour Therapy, Spiritual Awakening in the West, Songs for the Spirit, Simplicity and Humility, and Touch for Health. Most of these all-day events cost £3, which includes lunch; not exactly a money-making venture.

If her head is in the clouds, her feet are firmly planted on the ground. She certainly knows how to make a vineyard grow (organically) and how to run a successful small hotel where vegetarians and vegans feel comfortable, even if the food is not a gourmet treat. Nash Hotel's simple, friendly atmosphere goes a long way and you can always take a night off for dinner. But be prepared to nag them a bit if you have food allergies.

CATERING Traditional and vegetarian; vegans catered for. Licensed – own organic wine.

SMOKING Not in evidence.

PRICE CATEGORY High.

FURTHER INFORMATION Joyce Elsden,
Nash Country Hotel,
Steyning, W.Sussex
Phone (0903) 814988

23. Number One, Brook Street

I do not write this with Karel Bergwein's blessing; in fact, if he ever gets wind of it he will have my guts for garters, or more likely, feed them, rabbit flavoured, to his Burmese Boys. But, really he shouldn't care a fig for what I write since, as he so candidly put it, 'I only do this for a joke.'

From the effusions of his brochure, you'd expect Number One to be grand. An eating club serving five-course dinners, seminars, cookery classes, etc. must be housed in a pile overlooking the sea, at least. It isn't. The real-life Number One, Brook Street is a wee terraced house in a not-so-salubrious neighbourhood across from a pub. You come in off the street into the one main room which serves as dining room, kitchen and sitting room combined. There is no separate area for guests, so unless you like interacting fairly constantly with host Karel and his Manx cat (as distinct from 'The Boys' who live up in the attic), you're out of luck.

Karel Bergwein is or was Czech, Russian and British, in what order I'm not sure. He is quite a raconteur; he regaled us with stories of romantic, political and economic adventures in half the countries of Europe; stories worthy of the pen of Eric Ambler or John Le Carré. He is now 'in' international banking, which is the reason why he cannot take bookings too far in advance, lest he should have to fly off in the middle of the night. Quite entertaining stuff, in small doses.

Never mind, he's an excellent cook, if slightly on the nervous and slapdash side. He boasts that he spares no expense on ingredients (the tariff reflects this), and dinner is certainly a long and leisured affair ('takes three hours to eat, arrange beforehand'), with wine if you wish to bring a bottle – 'or several'. For starters we had sweet corn followed by garlic mushrooms and delicious homemade caraway bread. The main course was a spicey butter bean stew with brown rice, with a salad of chickpeas and chopped raw vegetables (accompanied by bottled Paul Newman salad dressing; a joke, I think). To finish off, a bowl of huge, luscious M & S grapes. Sadly, the coffee was instant and there was little choice of tea, herbal or otherwise. And there was no milk for the Nescafé, because Karel (not vegan) runs a one-man hate campaign against kitchen appliances – refrigerators, freezers, microwaves, and even the homely toaster – the enemies of fresh food. So be prepared, when you stay with him, to get powdered milk, no butter or yoghurt, though you may get cheese, as we did. Oh dear, it's all a bit dotty (and doesn't excuse not getting in a pint of milk, refrigerator or no) but, never mind, it's all part of the Bergwein Experience.

The real problem begins after dinner as there is no separate lounge to escape to or relax in. We felt a walk would be digestive, but it was raining hard and Karel further discouraged us with tales of muggings in the neighbourhood. So we asked if there was a telly and were most generously invited to watch it up in his room, with slightly abashed apologies for the mess. Up we went to the attic room where ne'er was a door opened on a more Hitchcockesque scene. There were the Burmese Boys – a pair of huge, shiny, rippling-muscled fourteen-year-old pussies – in a room painted brown (to match The Boys?), with litter trays and food dishes the only furniture apart from a double bed and a huge TV. The Boys had had a party scratching the walls to shreds, ditto the sides of the mattress which hung in tatters. We shrugged, smiled weakly, said what an interesting room, admired The Boys and piled philosophically onto what was left of the bed. And there we sat, watching *Lolita*, for heaven's sake, with James Mason drooling and twitching subtly over his blonde bombshell-let, with The Boys sneezing out great green mucousy jets (poor dears, they suffer from sinusitis) and further expressing their views of the movie by fairly frequent visits to the loo. Everything suddenly seemed comic: the giant telly, the giant green grapes; the colour-coordinated Boys, walls, sunken bathtub (also brown, and none too clean) and dear little samples of Gentle soap covered in mould. Oh my. (But, after all, Karel's room is his own business; in ours the beds were firm and the reading lights good.)

Next day after breakfast (tea, powdered milk, good homemade toast; made in the broiler), we left Karel standing in the doorway of his rather dark front room and escaped out into the bright sunny morning, the first in a long while. Our hearts lifted. We had a fine day in Hastings, walking the cliffs and sitting in the warm sunshine. When it was time for Brenda to return to London, I apologised for the rather weird experience at Number One. 'I wouldn't have missed it for the world,' she said. By the way, children (in case you were tempted) are *not* welcome.

CATERING Exclusively vegetarian; vegan and other diets catered for.

SMOKING No smoking.

PRICE CATEGORY High.

FURTHER INFORMATION Karel Bergwein,
Number One, Brook Street,
Hastings, E.Sussex TN34 1RX
Phone (0424) 444383

24. Quendale Lodge

Quendale Lodge is a late Victorian villa in a quiet leafy street in South Croydon. Essentially it is a small, family-run B & B, though an evening meal may be provided with modest advance notice. (I was unable to try one of these.) To be frank, it is difficult to find anything very positive to commend it – or indeed to single it out in any way from thousands of other guesthouses, since its vegetarian (for thirty years) proprietor, who should be its chief claim to my or your interest, is quite prepared to cook offensive, smelliferous bacon, etc, for carnivores' breakfasts. And similarly, despite many notices begging residents not to smoke (slightly contradicted, I couldn't help feeling, by the ashtray in my bedroom), the air in the only lavatory was thick with smoke.

The bedroom I was given was depressing: drab decoration, the kind of carpets that look unappealing even when clean, a tired mattress, a coin-operated gas fire and a small (but free) black and white television with terrible reception.

There is no guests' sitting room in the house. A large bathroom has been divided into a cramped shower and cramped bath (also with desperate handwritten requests not to smoke: the effect of so many seems mysteriously to devalue them all). The dining room has a handsome bay window, filled with a huge, loud TV set which distracts you from your breakfast with its impressively garishly coloured version of the BBC's Breakfast Time. The inmates sit in rows, facing it in stunned silence. Possibly it was a mercy to be distracted from the breakfast. Avoiding the bacon, sausage, kippers, etc, I asked for grapefruit juice and scrambled eggs. The eggs were fine; the juice was sweet and syrupy.

In other words, if you want a quiet (it really is) small place to stay in South Croydon or thereabouts, where you will be left alone and undisturbed; and perhaps if you want vegetarian or vegan meals as well (the house has the Vegetarian Society's stickers and

I'm sure they will respect your mouth if not your nose), then Quendale Lodge will do you for a night or two. For myself, despite the lack of much choice in reach of central London, I don't think I shall be going there again. O.F.

CATERING Traditional; vegetarians catered for; evening meal with advance notice.

SMOKING No smoking (they say).

PRICE CATEGORY Medium.

FURTHER INFORMATION Mrs Richardson,
Quendale Lodge,
70–74 St Augustine's Avenue,
South Croydon,
Surrey
Phone 01–688 2839

25. The Rose House

I nearly didn't go to the Rose House. To start with, Mrs Nicholson has a two-day minimum booking, and – expense aside – two days were difficult to find. And when I finally persuaded her to relent, the weather was so awful by the Southern Region's delicate standards that I fully expected to spend the night at Waterloo instead. But I got to Haslemere, although the two toes with which I perched in the train for 1½ hours may never straighten again; I found a taxi, mistrusting further tests of public transport, and in due course I was dropped, with visions of well-earned crumpets in front of a roaring fire moistening my lips, in the snowy Surrey twilight outside the Rose House.

This was a bit of a shock. I don't know quite what 'The Rose House, Hindhead' suggests to you: I certainly didn't expect roses in February. But after my drive through Surrey villa country, I did think it would be a bit grander and bigger than one of a row of closely packed Edwardian detached houses, albeit on a quiet cul-de-sac perched among the trees above a corner of Hindhead golf course. The next surprise was – no Mrs Nicholson. Eventually I found the front door, which was unlocked, and had a note attached inviting 'Mr Fulsome' (I didn't know my telephone manner was *that* bad, though I confess to wheedling a bit for my one-night concession) to make himself at home. I'd only just started to do so when Mrs Nicholson reappeared from errands in Hindhead village, sat me in the warm but fireless sitting room and brought me tea: oatcakes with honey, Neal's Yard Bakery date squares, and tea with lemon but no milk (she doesn't use it, though yoghurt is acceptable).

There are entries in this book where the house, the food, the location are all important, and the proprietors are scarcely visible; and others where the people are what make the difference. The Rose House falls firmly into Category Two. Mary Cadoux-Nicholson is a distinctive personality. She is a lady of a certain class and a certain age, and she has the manners, and some of the eccentricities and prejudices of her background and her generation. That is only where she starts from: to my mind, she thoroughly transcends these; but unless that's your milieu too, you do need to adjust your normal expectations a few notches.

Supper was a splendid leek, mushroom and etcetera soup, which came as cooked, though Mrs Nicholson offered to 'whizz' it if wanted, with a Neal's Yard loaf and a huge jar of ground nuts (sunflower, sesame and pumpkin) for sprinkling: on the soup, on the salad which followed or, for that matter, on the breakfast muesli. Next was a kind of mushroom quiche-without-the-crust – a baked egg pudding, with lots of baked potatoes and a huge and splendid salad of winter vegetables. After that (and no complaints, I was full) Mrs N. said that owing to an earlier disruption she hadn't made a pudding and did we mind fresh fruit and cream or yoghurt? We didn't. (Both the latter, like the bread, had been specially fetched from Neal's Yard.) There was then a wide range of tea, herb tea, coffee or substitutes, etc.

Supper is eaten *en famille*, with Mrs N. presiding, though she pretty much only eats salad and there's quite a lot of hopping up and down. But it was a relief, since her daytime style is to talk as she walks round the house: either you follow, which is wearing and may lead you into places you aren't meant to be, or you sit and hear her fading in and out, like the Home Service before the war, as she goes from room to room. She did join me after she'd finished in the kitchen, and the other guest had gone to bed. We sat up for hours while she told me about her life. I'm not going to tell you about it, since these were genuine confidences, not hotel-keeper's chat, and I felt privileged and touched. What I can say is that despite differences in age and background, and perhaps especially in belief – she is something of a spiritualist and a follower of Krishnamurti and I am a dogged rationalist – I felt very much at home. There are testimonials in her brochure and in her visitors' book from many others; and her warmth and goodness is what they all speak of. I certainly felt it most strongly.

In other respects, the Rose House is, to be frank, not over-comfortable. The food is a bit basic and occasionally odd but nourishing and thoughtful. Mrs Nicholson eats very little herself, but she provides plenty – and it's well-balanced – for her guests. She is a vegetarian of very long standing, having given up meat as a young woman after reading Tolstoy. The bedrooms and bathroom are a bit small and uncared for, but not uncomfortable. And mostly they have, like the main downstairs rooms, little balconies looking out across the valley below: a very pretty view. The house is full of books, an extraordinary collection, mixing classics of all kinds with a wide range of mostly pre-war literature, politics, philosophy and religion. I could have spent ages with Mrs Nicholson and her library for company and lovely walks on the doorstep. If you want a conventionally comfortable, gourmet, non-intrusive guesthouse, don't go; but if you're up for something wonderful in its own way, and quite outside your normal experience, whoever you are, hurry to the Rose House. Mrs Nicholson, who is getting on a bit, is talking about giving up and moving. I doubt if it will happen in a hurry, but go while you can. O.F.

CATERING Exclusively vegetarian/vegan.

SMOKING Not in evidence.

PRICE CATEGORY High.

FURTHER INFORMATION Mrs Cadoux-Nicholson,
The Rose House,
Hindhead, Surrey
Phone (042 873) 5389

26. Tekels Park Guest House

'Tekels Park, owned by The Theosophical Society in England, is a secluded estate of 50 acres in Surrey, 35 miles from London and 15 minutes pleasant walk from Camberley . . .

Ye-es, so long as you don't attempt the journey in a snowstorm on a Friday evening in February. It took me 2½ hours, as it happened, from London: that included an hour's wait at Waterloo for a delayed (inclement weather . . .) train, another wait at Ascot, and another wait in Camberley for a taxi out to The Park. The pleasant 15 minute walk (via a footpath) was unfortunately buried in snow and anyway unfindable without a torch. Even the taxi driver was none too keen to hazard the drive up the private road which leads to Tekels Park for fear of getting stuck or doing a slide. He did get stuck, but was very theosophical about it all.

When I got there I was greeted warmly by Barbara, who seemed to be running the show (the 'real' manager is a Miss J. Francis, but I never met her). A hot bath restored my toes. Then in to dinner, which is served communally in a large, open-plan dining room. I found myself – entirely coincidentally – sharing a table with a group of young musicians who happened to be in residence that

weekend conducting workshops in Baroque performance practice.
Since I am an ex-harpsichordist, we had much to talk about over
dinner. The meal went as follows: first course was a thick
vegetable soup made with buckwheat flour – very delicious. Then
came a serve-yourself buffet: quiche and a fine assortment of raw
vegetables/salads/sprouts. Dessert was tinned peaches in jelly with
whipped cream. There was a cheese board with oatcakes and
various crispbreads and a big bowlful of homemade yoghurt; also
nuts and raisins. Finally coffee/dandelion coffee, or tea/herb tea.
Entirely vegetarian, of course; very simple and good. And they
were amazingly kind about providing me with a gluten-free menu,
to the extent that the whole dinner was (except for the quiche)
planned around my dietary restrictions.

After dinner the group played an informal concert in the small,
cold lecture room at the back of the house – evidently too far from
the source of the central heating. Afterwards there was tea and
homemade biscuits in the (warmer) dining room-cum lounge. The
guesthouse is a newish brick building on the utilitarian model,
perfectly comfortable, warm and clean but not a thing of great
beauty. The public rooms are large and light, the bedrooms are
small and simple. I would say the accommodation, in general, is
more that of a conference centre or hostel than a guesthouse or
hotel – white painted unadorned walls, green carpeting, functional
furniture, and so on. The front hallway contains a table with
literature about The Theosophical Society and a glass case filled
with related spiritual and health books.

Breakfast was also buffet-style, and also plentiful, nourishing
and delicious: big bowlsful of cereals/muesli to choose from;
stewed fruit (prunes, apricots, and grapefruit segments), yoghurt,
nuts and raisins. If wanted, wholewheat toast, with marmalade or
homemade apricot jam, followed by coffee (real or dandelion) or
tea. Nothing wanting.

While you don't have to be a card carrying Theosophist it's as
well to know that the management, and general atmosphere of the
place, are definitely on the 'spiritual' side. You may find yourself
much uplifted by it, or even converted to their cause, but in any
case, if you are not positively deterred, then good food and a
beautiful setting await you. Tekels Park has extensive gardens with

splendid trees and shrubs and it's also a wildlife sanctuary. A good place to be peaceful, to read, think, or recover from whatever or go for walks in the Surrey countryside. Possibly a better place to go singly or with friends than as a couple, although there are some double rooms, and there was a family with two children there when I stayed. They have a lot of weekend conferences, all on spiritual, or at least non-commercial, subjects. Write for their agenda. Happily for us, vegetarianism is part of their way of life, so whether or not you want to be part of one of their weekend groups, you can still enjoy the food. Don't expect a luxury hotel: it's not that. But a luxuriously simple healthy retreat, yes.

CATERING Exclusively vegetarian; vegan and other special diets catered for.

SMOKING No smoking.

PRICE CATEGORY Medium (includes full board).

FURTHER INFORMATION The Manageress,
Tekels Park Guest House,
Camberley, Surrey
Phone (0276) 23159

Other Places to Stay

CHANNEL ISLANDS

Guernsey: Itati, Le Varclin, St Martins
Phone (0481) 38754
XV guesthouse, 'quiet garden, nr bay and cliffs'.

Jersey: Argilston Vegetarian Guest House, Mont Nicolle, St Brelade
Phone (0534) 44027
XV, old Jersey farmhouse, 'unspoiled valley, nr beaches for quiet restful holiday'.

HAMPSHIRE

New Forest: Sylvia Durham
Phone (0425) 621166
XV, B & B only, NS, thatched cottage.

New Forest:
Phone (0590) 74885
XV, B & B only, NS, terraced cottage.

KENT

Dover: Kalamaki Retreat
Phone (0304) 373739
XV, B & B + EM, bungalow, 'tranquil, spiritual atmosphere'.

Fordcombe, nr Tunbridge Wells: Daneby Hall
Phone (0892) 74235
B & B + EM by arr. V meals a speciality of the house. Host conferences/groups, also take guests.

(GREATER) LONDON

Middlesex: Brightwater, Dunally Park, Shepperton
Phone (0932) 220590
XV, B & B + EM, private house.

Middlesex: Thirty Kenilworth Crescent, Enfield
Phone 01–366 6763
XV, B & B + EM, private house.

N.London: Aunties (GB) Ltd, 15 Albemarle Ave, Potters Bar, Herts
Phone (0707) 58811
Agency which books B & B (some EMs) in N.London suburbs for vegetarians and vegans. Price category L. Watch out, not all Aunties XV.

N.E.London:
Phone 01–989 5123
XV, B & B or self-catering, private house nr underground.

Walthamstow (E.17):
Phone 01–521 6204
XV, B & B + EM, women only, private house.

SURREY

Nr Gatwick:
Phone (0293) 885615
XV, B & B + EM by arr, transport to airport.

Godalming: Mr and Mrs Noakes, Prospect House, Upper Manor Rd
Phone (04868) 22302
XV, B & B. 'Panoramic views; maps provided for walks.' Not very welcoming on phone.

SUSSEX

Bexhill-on-Sea: 10 Deerswood Lane
Phone (04243) 5153
XV, B & B only.

Coolham, nr Horsham: The Blue Idol
Phone (040387) 241
T-V (prop V), old timbered guesthouse.

Brighton: Rozanne Mendick, 14 Chatsworth Rd
Phone (0273) 556584
XV, B & B only, quiet street.

Brighton: Little Wholefoods Guest House (M. Turner)
Phone (0273) 25138
B & B only; prop 'almost vegetarian – Assoc. Member Veg'n Society'.

Brighton: 'The Only Alternative Left', 39 St Aubyn's, Hove
Phone (0273) 24739
V-T, B & B + cook your own. Price category VL.

Rye: Half House, Military Rd
Phone (0797) 223404
V-T, B & B only.

Places to Eat

HAMPSHIRE

Portsmouth: Barnabay's Restaurant, 56 Osborne Rd. Phone (0705) 821089.

Ringwood: Gracious Goodness (XV), 34b Christchurch Rd. Phone (042 54) 3134.

Southampton: Oscar's Restaurant, 8a Commercial Rd. Phone (0703) 36383.

Southsea: Country Kitchen Wholefood Restaurant, Marmion Rd. Phone (0705) 811425.
XV, but watch out for the tuna fish!

ISLE OF WIGHT

Newport: God's Providence House Upstairs Parlour, 12 St Thomas Square. Phone (0983) 522085.

KENT

Dover: Must Be Nuts (XV), 40 Castle St. Phone (0304) 204736.

Folkestone: Nature's Way (XV), 80 Sandgate Rd. Phone (0303) 45210.

Folkestone: Websters Health Food Restaurant (XV), 45 Bouverie Rd W. No phone.

Hythe: The Natural Break (XV), 115 High St. Phone (0303) 67573.

Tunbridge Wells: The Pilgrims (XV), 37 Mount Ephraim. Phone (0892) 20341.

Tunbridge Wells: Wholefood Health (XV), 15 Ritz Buildings, Church Road. Phone (0892) 20476.

[GREATER] LONDON: Note: There are simply too many restaurants and cafés to list in metropolitan London. See *Where To Eat If You Don't Eat Meat* or *The Vegetarian Handbook* for comprehensive lists and descriptions.

SURREY

Croydon: Hockneys (XV), 98 High St. Phone 01–688 2899

Croydon: Munbhave (XV), 305 London Road, West Croydon. Phone 01–689 6331.

Croydon: La Vida (XV), 164 Cherry Orchard Rd, East Croydon. Phone 01–681 3402.

Guildford: Perrotts Vegetarian Restaurant (XV) (NS), 8–9 Jeffries Passage. Phone (0483) 35025.

SUSSEX

Bexhill-on-Sea: Corianders (XV), 66 Devonshire Rd. Phone (0424) 220329.

Bognor Regis: Harvest (XV), 6–8 York Rd. Phone (0243) 864613.

Brighton: Food For Friends (XV), Prince Albert St, The Lanes. Phone (0273) 202310.

Brighton: Nature's Way (XV), 35 Duke St. Phone (0273) 21574.

Brighton: Saxon's (XV), 48 George St. Phone (0273) 680733.

Brighton: Slims Health Food Restaurant (XV), 92 Churchill Sq (lower level). Phone (0273) 24582.

Chichester: Clinch's Salad House (XV), 14 Southgate. Phone (0243) 788822.

Chichester: Beanfeast (XV Takeaway), Southgate. Phone (0243) 783823.

Eastbourne: Ceres Health Food Restaurant (XV), 38a Ashford Road. Phone (0323) 28482.

Eastbourne: Nature's Way (XV), 196 Terminus Rd. Phone (0323) 643211.

East Grinstead: Thanks (XV), 61 High St. Phone (0342) 21976.

Forest Row: Seasons Kitchen (XV), Ashorne House, Lewes Rd. Phone (034282) 3530.

Hastings: Brants Health Food Restaurant (XV), 45 High St. Phone (0424) 431896.

Hove: Nature's Way Coffee Shop (XV), 122 Church Rd. Phone (0273) 729774.

Worthing: Nature's Way Coffee Shop (XV), 130 Montague St. Phone (0903) 209931.

III
THE GREAT EMPTY MIDDLE

Includes Avon, Berkshire, Bedfordshire, Buckinghamshire, Cambridgeshire, Derbyshire, Essex, Gloucestershire (*except Forest of Dean*), Hereford and Worcester (*Worcester half*), Hertfordshire, Leicestershire, Lincolnshire, Norfolk, Northamptonshire, Nottinghamshire, Oxfordshire, Shropshire (*except Border country*), Staffordshire, Suffolk, Warwickshire, West Midlands, Wiltshire

If the West Country is well supplied with providers for alternative lifestyles, and London and the south-east are prosperous enough to cater to all tastes in food as well as in anything else you fancy, something odd happens north of Watford and west of Uxbridge. We've managed to put together a reasonable collection of places to stay and to eat, but only by combining the huge list of counties above into an area almost the size of Scotland. We are tempted to call it Roast Beef (of Olde England) country: more accurately, perhaps, it's the heart of burger-and-chip land, apart from a few rural retreats and some islands of decent diet mostly in university towns.

Places Reviewed

27. Coney Weston Hall, Nr Bury St Edmunds, Suffolk.
28. Lapwings, Apley, Lincs (XVgn)
29. Old Engine Farm, Ashover, Nr Chesterfield, Derbys
30. The Old Schoolhouse, Saxtead, Nr Framlingham, Suffolk (XVgn)
31. Parkside Guest House, Bath, Avon
32. Reddings Guest House, Burleigh, Stroud, Glos
33. Runnings Park, W.Malvern, Worcs
34. Trinity House Hotel, Coventry, W.Midlands

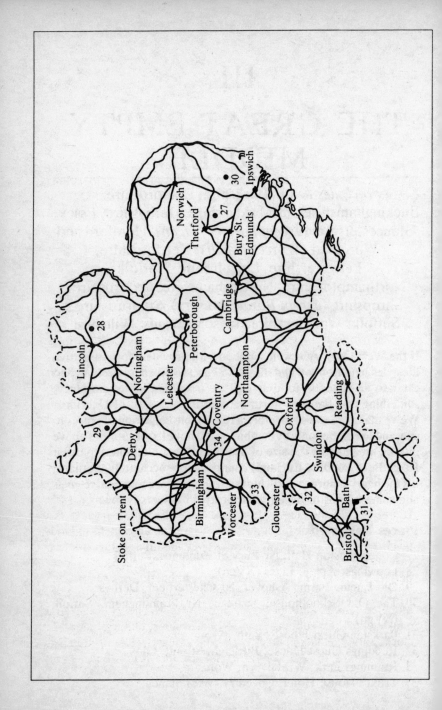

27. Coney Weston Hall

Coney Weston Hall is a fine ('definitive' says Ashley Courtney) Queen Anne country house with no head waiter, no bar (drinks will be brought to you) and no background music. It's set in twenty-six acres of farmland on the Norfolk/Suffolk border and surrounded by grazing animals, an arboretum of exotic trees, lakes, professional nurseries, huge kitchen and flower gardens, and a former swimming pool in which many forms of flora and fauna other than human thrive.

We arrived in the middle of an early September downpour to be greeted by a bear-like dog and our host, David Backhouse, in long garden mac, with a wicked, toothy grin very like Alistair Sim's in *The Ladykillers*. 'I have just been picking your dinner,' he said, as if he might have more than leeks up his sleeve. He showed us to our room – a bedroom the size of a large drawing room, with en suite bathroom the size of a decent bedroom. The sink could have bathed a two-year-old. All very pink, with circular bay, Adam-style fireplace, plain good green wool carpet, excellent firm bed with good cotton sheets and blankets. On one wall hung the complete works of Brueghel in miniature and on another a contemporary oil depicting a bomber wreathed in pink and grey clouds. The central heating system, in general, leaves something to be desired (it would take a richer man than our host to heat the Hall fully) but the electric fires were very efficient, especially the one in our bedroom. On its windowsill was an ancient sit-up-and-beg telephone, with push buttons and identifying tags for the various quarters: Lady B, Sir R, Library, Kitchen, etc. Very period. Ditto David Backhouse's vintage beetle-backed Alvis.

The public rooms are, as you can imagine, gigantic, with high moulded ceilings and floor-to-ceiling windows. The hallway sports a fake giant brass rubbing of a knight in armour, plus a grandfather clock, a marble lady in an alcove and a vast collection of drawings and paintings of World War II planes, pre-Raphaelite kitsch, horses; as well as medals, mounted rifles and other memorabilia. There is a giant dining room, a huge and a modest sitting room, and then the library, where we sat before and after dinner. It's a splendid warm room, complete with red walls, leather furniture, steaming dog (Blitz) warming himself by the fire (electric, alas), books by the yard (real), fabulous red and gold damask curtains, and so on. The books are mostly of a certain generation – Buchan, Spillane, Woodhouse, etc – but there are also a good few classics, gardening and nature books, and general interest titles. The dining room sports a whopping great chandelier over the polished 15 foot mahogany table, which is much cheered up by vases of roses from the garden, marble fireplace (with glow-effect electric fire), a collection of china and an assortment of Dutch and Impressionist reproductions.

We were served by a young girl from the village, frequently overseen by Backhouse himself ('This is where I'm supposed to ask if everything is all right,' he announced, not waiting for the reply), who sandwiched in some determinedly informative chat between courses. He makes rather a to do about the food he serves – pure, simple, straight-out-of-the-garden and untreated by artificial fertilisers; only traditional methods of cultivation used; only the freshest ingredients bought in; the greatest care and attention taken over preparation; fresh fruits and vegetables in season, bread made with wholewheat flour, etc, etc, etc. Such care is taken that the menu has to be limited. Well, for four of us I counted at least five starters, three main courses and six desserts on the menu. This is limited?

Choice of starters included vegetable pâté, avocado stuffed with vegetable puree, melon boat, gnocchi romaine and noodles neapolitain. I had the melon boat, which was fine as far as the melon went, but was rigged out to look like a Venetian gondola, with skirted toothpicks and orange slices – too cutesy for my taste, unnecessary, and, more to the point, out of keeping with a policy of good, simple, fresh food. Oliver had the gnocchi (mostly mashed potates and cheese), with fresh tomato sauce, which he reported as good, but again rather an elaborate effort for what it was. For the main course, one of us had vegetable hot pot, which was a stew with aubergines, carrots, courgettes, onions and tomatoes; the other had the vegetable rissoles, which were a bit stodgy but good. The accompanying vegetable platter was big enough for the Christmas turkey (pardon me) and contained every vegetable out of the garden – and then some – plus two peppers stuffed with aubergine puree. The parsnips, brussels sprouts, broad beans, carrots, mashed potato, mushrooms, green beans and 'American' potato (a knobbly but marvellously tasty specimen) were, as advertised, fresh and delicious, but there were just too many and the dishes were too repetitive. For dessert I had fruit compote, which I'd hoped would be fresh fruit but was soaked, dried fruits. There was only dairy cream, no soya milk or cream to go with. I would have preferred a plate of garden peaches, plums and grapes, which were only brought in after dessert. There was also rice pudding made from very special (white) 'Lima' rice which comes from the Camargue. (Mr B never uses brown rice, he explained, since the husk gets and retains the chemical sprays, even when advertised as 'organic'.) There was a wide selection of coffees and teas – real, decaf, herbal. I was tempted by a coffee substitute called 'Carousel' which was very good indeed, but no use trying to buy it, you can only get it in Switzerland.

Hard to sum up, but I'd say that while the ingredients were certainly freshly picked, the presentation was not all that simple. Somewhere along the line, I suspect, the chef has been to catering school, and just cannot resist plunking an umbrella onto the melon or getting out the old nozzle to pipe curly mashed potatoes. As well as being over-elaborate, it's also a rather expensive meal – £10.50 in 1986 – with no cheese course included for the lactos. I don't mind paying this for something wildly special, but I didn't think this was. I would also have appreciated more real attention to diet. When I booked, saying that I was vegan and allergic to wheat and potatoes, Mr Backhouse sang into the phone, 'Oh yes, yes indeed, no problem, we're rather good at that sort of thing here.' Well so they may be, but the breakfast muesli had wheat flakes in it, and there was no soya milk, though it was brought when I asked for it. Fortunately there was a bowl of fruit, and during our walk around the orchard I managed to liberate an apple and a couple of plums, which were very good indeed. For the non-vegan, cooked breakfasts were on offer.

Coney Weston is by no means exclusively vegetarian. (David Backhouse, who is the former owner of Hofels health food products and, as various clues imply, an ex-fighter pilot, boasts that he smokes a pipe, drinks and overeats carnivorously.) Our fellow guests in the dining room were also vegetarian, but, as we left, there was a distinct smell of Sunday roast. If this doesn't put you off and if you're looking for something quietly and tastefully luxurious with more than a touch of vegetarian and organic-farming know-how, then do give it a try. Definitely worth going for a lark, if you can afford it.

CATERING Traditional and vegetarian. Restaurant open to the public. Licensed.

SMOKING Smoking restrictions.

PRICE CATEGORY Very High.

FURTHER INFORMATION Mr David Backhouse,
Coney Weston Hall,
Coney Weston,
Bury St Edmunds, Suffolk IP31 1HG
Phone: (035 921) 441

28. Lapwings

'Unflat Lincolnshire' is how one of Margaret and John Crompton's advertisements begins. And so it is, hereabouts at least. It's a negative description which troubles me slightly, especially since Margaret likens the Lincolnshire landscape to Lapwings' firmly vegan diet: subtle and unflashy, needing love and attention to enjoy it, yes, but I hope something more than 'unmeaty'. There is, I think, just a touch of defensiveness – or do I mean defiance? – in her attitude to both, and neither is justified. Lincolnshire has real beauty, and the vegan way of life both a philosophical appeal and a pleasure, which are thoroughly positive.

Apley, which is about 7 miles due east of Lincoln – the last 2 miles being winding lanes – is a *very* small village. Two hands will do to count the houses: aside from Lapwings, there is a manor house (rather ugly); High House (rather beautiful); two farms, four or five modern houses, a chapel and that's it. But otherwise nothing but rolling wheatfields, plenty of woods and copses to break up the view (and to walk in) and way off in the distance a sugar beet factory across the fens, and perhaps on a clear day Lincoln Cathedral. Traffic is negligible.

Lapwings itself is a modest-sized house (distressingly so when you learn that it was once three farmworkers' cottages) of two shades of local brick. John and Margaret moved in in the late summer of 1984 and were still improving both house and garden when I visited a year later. But much of the food was already home grown, despite the worst season in years for turning a hayfield into a vegetable plot, and the house was already thoroughly comfortable. There are three bedrooms if you count, as the Cromptons do, their own room, out of which they moved for my benefit as the fifth guest; one bathroom with bath and shower and an extra loo downstairs. They are simply decorated, mostly in strong but not aggressive colours, and all face south. My bed was excellent and I slept well. Downstairs (and you need a little care if you're over average height) there is a smallish guests' sitting/dining room, lined with wonderful books: English and world literature (classics and modern), philosophy and religion, social work, local interest; something for almost anyone. Also a piano. With the dining table as well, it doesn't leave a lot of space for many people to sit, but the night I was there, with five guests in residence and an evening visitor expected, we were all invited through to the Cromptons' own sitting room to spread ourselves and drool over the other half of the library. (On quieter nights you may expect one or both the Cromptons to join you in *your* sitting room for a bedtime hot drink and a chat.)

I don't feel able to be very objective about the Cromptons as hosts. Both are Quakers, and so are some of my family; both are very early retired ex-academics, and John is in my subject; both are writers. It quickly became very odd that we hadn't met long ago and in the morning my intention to leave after breakfast faded imperceptibly, and I only hauled myself away at two o'clock with the greatest difficulty. I can't promise that kind of instant familiarity to everyone who visits, but the Cromptons are such warmly interesting, and interested, people that it's hard to imagine anyone who wouldn't make a personal connection.

And the food? Well, that too is difficult. When I arrived John was away for the day and Margaret had had a bruising afternoon at the dentist. What we had was plain and good: a casserole of vegetables based on chickpeas but with lots of other garden goodies, brown rice and a very fresh salad; followed by Gainsborough pie (the nearby town, not the painter) – mostly coconut and jam in a pastry case. I didn't, to be honest, think them very inspired, in fact a bit plain and underseasoned; but it was an unpropitious day and I was probably influenced by rather a lot of wingeing from two distinctly carnivorous teenage fellow-guests. Certainly nutritious, thoughtfully varied and filling: no worries for any non-vegan doubters about surviving on this for a week. Breakfast was comprehensive: muesli and conventional cereals, lots of additions (nuts, raisins, coconut, etc.) fruit juice and fresh fruit, bread and delicious homemade jam. Soya milk only, of course – the house really is 100 per cent vegan – and tea or coffee if you don't mind it black. The children had some appetising looking, fresh, homemade limeade.

In conclusion, don't be put off by the negatives: the advertising is rather full of them (no smoking, no alcohol, guide dogs only . . .). If you are a vegan, rejoice in and support an uncompromising vegan place, and if not, relax: you'll enjoy it. Come for quiet walking or cycling (but you'll need some gears on your bike – Holland it ain't); or drive gently around in quiet lanes and enjoy astonishingly unspoilt towns and villages. You won't need books with you, either; there's plenty to occupy the evenings between the library and your hosts' conversation. I'm planning my next visit already. O.F.

CATERING Exclusively vegan.

SMOKING No smoking.

PRICE CATEGORY Very Low.

FURTHER INFORMATION John and Margaret Crompton,
Lapwings,
Apley, Lincolnshire LN3 5JQ
Phone (0673) 85801

29. Old Engine Farm

Old Engine Farm is no longer a farmhouse, though you will first
spot it by its huge green silo on the horizon. (The land is still
farmed, but the farmer, I presume, now lives in a sensible
bungalow down in Matlock or Ashover, out of the worst of the
weather.) It perches high on a crest overlooking the whole of
Matlock and Darley Dales, in the south-east corner of the Peak
District, within easy reach of the M1 and main line trains at
Alfreton or Chesterfield, and with plenty of good walks on the
doorstep, and Haddon Hall and Chatsworth House close by. (The
Community Programme has produced some excellent leaflets
about Ashover village and the walks around it, which you can
borrow or buy from the Preslands.) Set in a wild and dramatic
place (which gets a lot of weather), Old Engine Farm is a
splendiferously modernised house. The Preslands have done a
good job, with the help of a herd of architects and designers, to
insulate it from the outside world. It's a very snug – nearly tropical
– modern eyrie inside.

We were met at the back entrance by Lynn and Bryan Presland,
their barky but friendly labrador bitch, Brandy, and their two cute
children, Christopher and Emma. To get to the guest wing, you go
through the kitchen/family room to a spotless piece of design-for-
living. In the guests' dining room and lounge any resemblance to
the original farmhouse is purely coincidental. (The outside of the
house, apart from being very much cleaned up, is lovely and quite
unspoiled.) The dining room is a rectangular box, decorated in
greens, with a modern, light wooden table and sideboard and
that's it. The curtains do not actually open or close, or indeed
cover the window; that's done by a blind. I thought it looked more

like a Habitat display than a place where people actually ate. Its view – out over the valley – could be spectacular, but is not since a large barn entirely blocks it. The next door lounge is the glory of the house, though uncompromisingly late twentieth century in spirit, and not, in my opinion, in keeping with an old farmhouse. That aside, it's quite sensational: light and airy with lots of glass and huge pitch pine beams, both horizontal and vertical. The details – lighting (both direct and indirect spots), wood ceiling trim, fireplace, and so forth – are all very swish and expensive. The decoration is quite lovely if you like that kind of thing: pale pastel wallpaper and matching (correlated, I believe, is the current word) curtains, thick nubbly ivory rug, custom floral-print three-piece suite, and one large potted plant. Very sparse and elegant; very American. Only the cat, done in orange and black tortoiseshell, didn't quite correlate. Pity, that. I enjoyed curling up after dinner with a magazine in one of the plush chairs, fancying myself a designer-designed lady, but it didn't take for long. After a while the room began to seem rather oppressively cold and character-less: not a book in sight, one soppy designer picture chosen to match the decor. I had the distinct impression that the room belonged to no one so much as the designers.

The rest of the house is more ordinary. The hallway has walls which look like they've been plastered with cream cheese laid on with a palette knife. The upstairs guest bathroom, with its matching silver birch wallpaper and curtains, and shelves bare but for one empty vase, is elegant and spotlessly clean but rather gruesomely unlived-in. Ironically, for all its modernity, the shower was a tepid dribble, though this might have been a bit of one off bad luck. The bedroom was modern nondescript, with white melamine built-ins and a not very comfortable bed, though the sheets (top and bottom) were cotton, with a cotton-covered duvet.

As for the food, it was real, simple, fresh, tasty and nice to look at, presented by Bryan Presland with the help of slightly shy Emma (about six), while little Christopher floated about starkers practising his swimming. (That tells you how warm the house is.) The first course was avocado stuffed with chopped chives, toma-toes and cucumber, accompanied by slices of wholewheat (com-mercial sliced) bread and a big jug of spring water with lemon slices. The main course was brown rice with peppers, celery, cashews and mushrooms – perfectly plain and delicious. The salad had an interesting, slightly sweetish, dressing. Dessert was a huge fruit salad, packed with interesting fruits; cream to go with. Drinks were limited to coffee or ordinary tea. It's possible – if you're a no nonsense lacto-vegetarian – you'd get more elaborate food, but it's hard to imagine it better.

Breakfast was on the thinnish side for me – Scott's porridge oats and fresh fruit and soya milk – but good and as much as I wanted. Mrs Presland, who does the cooking, has only been vegetarian for four years and is pretty inexperienced when it comes to vegans. I was her first vegan guest. She has some things to learn – about herb teas, vegan margarine, alternatives to wheat bread, and so on – but she is very eager to learn and I'm sure she will in time. There were ordinary muesli and toast and cooked breakfasts on offer.

It's a hard place to summarise, such a curious combination of wild exterior with over-tame interior. There's a stronger feeling of staying in somebody's house than in many guesthouses, possibly because you have to go through their kitchen, but that's not meant as a criticism, merely a warning. Lynn Presland is friendly, her kids are cute, and her food is lovely. The style of the decor might put some people off, but then again it might appeal to those who value their creature comforts. (Perhaps there will be more hot water when you go; I hope so.) But for God's sake, if you go, don't forget your lounge lizard gear; I'd hate to think of you clomping around on their elegant ivory carpet in your muddy hiking boots.

CATERING Vegetarian and traditional.

SMOKING No smoking.

PRICE CATEGORY Low.

FURTHER INFORMATION Mrs Lynn Presland,
Old Engine Farm,
Holestone Moor,
Ashover, Nr Chesterfield,
Derbyshire
Phone (0246) 590513

30. The Old School House

Jeff Tarlton doesn't have a brochure, so nothing really prepared me for The Old Schoolhouse at Saxtead. It's not the easiest place to find: the roadside trees concealing it are so thick in summer that I'd driven past before I had time to see the sign. When I'd turned and come back I found I could drive in and park on what's left of the playground, overlooked by the big end window of the classrooms, which is adorned by a cheerful collection of vegetarian, anti-nuclear and pro-Nicaraguan and pro-Mozambican stickers.

There was a sign saying 'This Way' propped against some bales of straw: I followed it round the back of the house, past a pile of bricks and two oil tanks, one bearing the slightly ambiguous inscription JEFF WOZ ERE. There was a little brick sitting-place (patio sounds much too twee) which, as it turns out, gets the sun for most of the day, and beyond it a garden area with several fruit trees, some quite young and cheerful, lots of nettles, a healthy potato patch at one end and the remains of at least six 2CVs at the other. (There were also two rather less moribund ones on the playground, one missing a wheel and one looking really quite lively.) There was a plastic-draped shed, and another plastic-covered structure which seemed to be a large geodesic dome with two large television sets, one in best 1950s style, standing at its door. Beyond were open fields.

When I'd absorbed all this, I turned to the house and knocked on the only door in sight. Jeff Tarlton emerged to offer me an apologetically oniony hand. The only way into the main living and eating part of the house is through the kitchen, which is an astonishingly crowded little room, with every available surface – including several tables which just about trap Jeff in his cooking corner – covered with fresh food, dry ingredients, herbs and spices and so on; even the floor was full of utensils and rows of demijohns of newly made wine. In someone else's hands it might have been a bit alarming, but there was something immediately reassuring

100

about Jeff, who was cooking up a storm, preparing twenty or so lunches for a party the next day, and I relaxed.

The living room, anyway, is a bit less cluttered. It was one of the two classrooms – the other is now Jeff's bedroom and storeroom – while the rest of the house, apart from what Jeff has built on, is the old schoolteacher's or curator's quarters. The classrooms are divided by a tall pitch pine and glass screen, originally panelled in wood to waist height and with windows above, but a nervous schoolteacher had had the bottom row of glass panes replaced by plywood panels, lest the larger children should make faces across the partition, I presume; this rather spoiled the look and the proportions. But the partition rises to the pitched roof, 15 feet or so above you, with its beautiful heavy pitch pine rafters exposed to view like a church; a lovely shape for a room, and with white walls and high windows (no distractions for the children from outside either) looking out onto the trees, it has a lovely soft, cool, filtered light. There is a pretty Victorian fireplace in which Jeff offered to light a fire (even in early September the light and the air were cool) and the room is beautifully furnished – a big dresser stacked with piles of china that reminded me of my grandmother's collection, a huge sideboard, big dining table, double bass case against the wall, two comfortable sofas, an armchair and a coffee table. On it and on the sideboard were vegan, vegetarian and Greenpeace literature and magazines, and two copies of *Architectural Review*. Even before I found them, I'd felt that I was in the home of someone with a feel for space and light; I wasn't surprised to learn that Jeff did an architecture degree in the early 1970s, and though he's never bothered to qualify fully he does some work as a designer between running his guesthouse and playing bass two or three nights a week with local jazz bands.

The rest of the house has the same quality about it. The bathroom, which Jeff built onto the back on the ground floor, is a big space with nice old fixtures, including a proper cast-iron bathtub which he's panelled, and a bidet, as well as a splendidly eccentric armchair, apparently mostly wrought iron but with thick cushions, a copy of *Cold Comfort Farm* on a spindly table next to it, a purple hatstand, and a tailor's dummy wearing a rather fifties summer skirt, hat and fan. It has a big, curtainless picture window looking out at the lovely colours of the crumbling whitewashed brick wall on an outhouse. Upstairs, my bedroom was an equally interesting shape, high up under the eaves, with thick green leaves outside at window height – completely masking the noise of the not-too-busy road outside – and plants inside to echo them, a jug of dried herbs on the mantelpiece of the tiny cast-iron fireplace, an old washstand, a tiny basin with hot and cold (handy since the loo is downstairs), a big old chest of drawers painted in soft green, and a double bed with bright red sheet and duvet. Above the bed was another poster for Mozambique. Extraordinarily symphonic and restful; and the bed (which had an electric blanket) was exceptionally comfortable, as were the sofas downstairs. Funky the place may look, but don't be deceived: you certainly aren't slumming it.

Dinner made that point very well. When I got in from a stroll round the local lanes in the setting sun, I found my simple place-setting, with a glass of apple juice and a bottle of spring water beside it, laid on a spotless linen table cloth with a jug of orange zinnias at the other end for balance. To start with, Jeff brought me a bowl of incredibly fresh-tasting hummus, full of good olive oil, lemon juice and parsley, thin fingers of toast to eat it off, and a huge lemony salad with lots of crisp vegetables in it. I'd have settled happily for that, but made the right deduction from the number of knives and forks and found myself next facing a big round 'aduki burger' – a ball of aduki beans, sprouted beans and sprouted grains, nicely seasoned, rolled in sesame seeds and deep fried. It came with a huge mound of mashed potatoes just cooked in their skins, lots of lightly steamed broccoli and a rich, brown mushroom sauce. I wished I'd been twice as hungry. Then, after I'd had another go at the salad which had been kindly left for me, there was a baked apple stuffed with lots of raisins. I washed it all down with herb tea. Altogether a superb meal, beautifully presented if slightly daunting in quantity. But I found it quite irresistible.

I don't really need to describe breakfast after that: it was as good as you'd expect and complete with a huge bowl of all kinds of fresh fruit to fill in any corners. The best part was Jeff's homemade marmalade, made with Barbados sugar in moderation, and tasting wonderfully strong and bitter. If he ever sold it he could make a fortune.

When I arrived Jeff recommended the pub in the next village, a couple of miles away, which he says has good live music (and he should know); but I didn't feel like more walking or driving, so I sat and read quietly (in comfort and with excellent light) and then talked to Jeff when he joined me after finishing his preparations for the next day. I was given the new vintage of elderflower wine to try, and found it excellent and quite potent: I slept extremely well. But not before some enjoyable conversation. I liked Jeff Tarlton very much. I suppose you could call him an aging – and greying – hippy, living a determinedly unexploitative (of people or the environment) life. He doesn't go in for money much, as his near-giveaway prices serve to illustrate. He is a serious vegan, with the one exception that he has (keeps is quite the wrong word) three chickens: one extremely handsome cock and two hens, of which one hardly ever lays and the other goes broody for weeks. It's hard to imagine a happier life for an animal liberationist to wish for them, and I can't think there are ever many eggs for breakfast. He is also strongly committed to environmental politics: his bass is well covered with anti-nuclear stickers to tease the Sizewell engineers who can't resist his music, and he talks sadly about the destruction of the Suffolk countryside. But he's not at all a sad person: I'd enjoy spending more time with him. He has his own sitting-room, so whether you'd see as much of him if you came with a friend as I did on my own I can't be sure; but it would be hard to object. The Old Schoolhouse is not for everyone: it's not your country house luxury, nor yet a tidy modern home, and you need to be as young in spirit as Jeff Tarlton is (he's past fifty in calendar years) to enjoy it. I could easily stay for days, with a bike to ride around the lanes and villages or just strolling around the (to my eyes) still unprairiefied woods and fields. O.F.

CATERING Vegan (cow's milk provided if requested).

SMOKING No smoking (and London Transport bus posters to remind you).

PRICE CATEGORY Very Low.

FURTHER INFORMATION Jeff Tarlton,
The Old Schoolhouse,
Saxtead,
Woodbridge, Suffolk IP13 9QP
Phone (0728) 723887

31. Parkside Guest House

Parkside Guest House is a large Edwardian semi on a lane about a hundred yards outside Bath's Royal Victoria Park. It's a convenient location – 10 minutes' walk to the city centre – and fairly quiet, with views to the front of the city's allotments and to the back of its own and its neighbours' substantial gardens. Parking is no problem, either on the Lane itself or in the Park.

The house itself has large, sunny rooms with huge windows and original cornices and mouldings. But, like many another guesthouse, it's spoiled by over-colourful carpets, and a mixture of modern tackiness and mid-century nondescript furnishings. My bedroom, for example, was of grand proportion with an ornate Edwardian tile fireplace, but was spoiled by a plastic shower cubicle butting up against it. Understandable, perhaps, when the Parkside and many another like it are forced to compete with the big, posh hotels in what are euphemistically called 'amenities', by lumbering their loveliest rooms with hideous specimens of modern British plumbing – but a pity, especially when they don't work very well. The one I had alternately scalded and froze me.

Parkside offers dinner, both traditional and vegetarian (in that order); also 'light meals' and packed lunches can be arranged. I had an early light meal which consisted of salad (raw courgettes, cucumbers, lettuce, tomato, celery and nuts) with 'French' dressing, a tiny piece of vegetarian cheese, two pappadums (an imaginative bread substitute, though made with 'edible' oil) and a fresh fruit salad. Apple juice was extra. They coped admirably with my perverse grain-free diet, but I cannot say the meal was a gourmet treat. While they are reasonably conscientious about serving vegetarian products (e.g. Granose margarine, vegetarian cheese), they are not purists (thus the pappadums), and possibly have limited tolerance for people who read the fine print on packets.

Breakfast was serve-yourself juice, muesli or other packet cereals, and stewed or fresh fruit, yoghurt and soya milk available, followed by a cooked breakfast of mushrooms and tomatoes on toast (commercial-type wholewheat). I shared a table with a bacon and egg eater who was very nice even if her bacon wasn't.

On the whole Parkside is a very comfortable place to stay if you're in Bath: clean, warm, light and sunny. On a fine summer day, the garden would be very welcoming. There's a large TV in the lounge and lots of brochures and tourist information lying about. The proprietors are both cheerful, friendly ladies and will do their best to cater for your vegetarian/vegan dietary preferences. But don't expect magic. Depending on how long your stay is, you might want to treat Parkside as a B & B and have dinner at Huckleberry's, Bath's vegetarian wholefood café, or one of the non-exclusive but interesting sounding restaurants which offer vegetarian and vegan choices.

CATERING Traditional and vegetarian; vegan and other diets catered for.

SMOKING Smoking restrictions.

PRICE CATEGORY High.

FURTHER INFORMATION I. Larman,
Parkside Guest House
11 Marlborough Lane,
Bath, Avon BA1 2NQ
Phone (0225) 29444

32. Reddings Guest House

I am, to be honest, flummoxed by Reddings Guest House. Its enticing little hand-lettered and -drawn brochure advertising homemade bread and yoghurt, and a crenellated house high up on Minchinhampton Common overlooking the Cotswolds, made me eager to visit. But reality proved rather less attractive. Despite its fine position, the house is grimmish with large, barren, cold rooms, though it could have been made more comfortable and appealing had more attention been paid to decor and furniture. It has a large, lawned garden but its potentially panoramic view of the valley is blocked by surrounding conifers. Added to this, Mrs Lewes, the proprietor, is not overfriendly. She didn't offer any pleasantries and I felt discouraged from chipping in with any of my own. She was quite willing to cater for my vegan/wheatless diet, but she required precise written instructions beforehand.

The food itself wasn't too bad. Dinner was bean soup and homemade bread (yeasty and heavy but good according to Oliver), followed by a nut loaf casserole (too rich), carrots and black-eyed beans, rice with broad beans, and potatoes, both boiled and fried. Dessert was fruit salad. Though it might sound interesting and plentiful – and in another context might have been enjoyable in spite of its imperfections – I found it rather unattractive and indigestible. It certainly proved the importance of presentation and good atmosphere. Nor was breakfast an improvement: cornflakes or muesli, commercial bread (what happened to last night's homemade loaf?), no yoghurt (what happened to that?), not a piece of fresh or dried fruit. Two rice cakes for me. Fortunately, we had some fresh fruit in the car to get us through the morning until we got to Cheltenham.

The house is full of nondescript furniture placed at random, without much warmth or interest. The beds in our room were frankly awful; the cold water was hot, and the trickling shower (down the hall) either burnt or froze. The dining room was painted orange, with bare wood floor and chairs lined up institutionally against the walls. There were plants and some rather nice over-sized ceramic bowls on a table by the window, but they couldn't, by themselves, enliven the atmosphere. The lounge looked so dreary, I was not tempted to sit in it. Fortunately the evening was fine, so I went for a walk instead. The house is full of interesting books, but I didn't feel entirely welcome to browse through them.

Reddings, I'm afraid, is not my idea of the perfect veggie stay. The food was plentiful and Mrs Lewes went to some trouble to cater for my special diet, but I did not find it inspiring. It was also on the expensive side for what you got. Afternoon tea alone was £1.50 (one pot of weak elderflower and a few commercial biscuits). I couldn't help comparing that with my previous night at Holway Mill: two kinds of tea and delicious homemade biscuits for 40p.

That part of the Cotswolds is really lovely, with its golden stone and steep valleys. I would like to go back some time, but I doubt if I will stay at Reddings again. I hope by then there will be an exclusively vegetarian place with a more inviting ambience.

CATERING Traditional and vegetarian; vegan and other diets catered for.

SMOKING No known rules.

PRICE CATEGORY High.

FURTHER INFORMATION Mrs Lewes,
Reddings Guest House,
Burleigh, Stroud,
Gloucestershire.
Phone (0453) 882342

33. Runnings Park

Originally a dairy farm, Runnings Park has been converted and expanded to form a hotel, conference and riding centre. The half-timbered, rambling building is set in 17 acres of hilly land on the western slopes of the Malvern Hills – a very romantic spot, lush and green in spring, with views across to the Black Mountains. A good place to get away from it all, whether you're an active walker or rider, a semi-mobile tourist, or a slug-like lounge lizard. Even if you're none of the above, you can still swim (there's a small heated indoor pool), take saunas, read, eat and drink.

The food at Runnings Park is excellent. Although not exclusive, the emphasis is definitely on vegetarian – two vegetarian main dishes to one non-vegetarian. The proprietors (themselves vegetarian) do both, partly for economic reasons but also because they enjoy making converts – which I'm sure they do. For starters there was fresh tomato soup or artichokes with a light mayonnaise dressing. Main courses included lentil bake, cauliflower cheese, celery and cheese pie, mushroom croustade; plus assortments of fresh, wonderful vegetables. For dessert there was a not-too-sweet lemon sorbet stuffed into a big, handsome lemon (wonderful!), apple crumble with real custard, fresh fruit salad (including strawberries, cherries and pineapple) with gobs of thick yellow cream (sigh). All this followed by coffee, tea or herb tea. The house wine was very drinkable too.

The decor is modernish and tasteful, with oatmealy carpets and white walls. The lounge is large with good old-fashioned sofa and fantastically comfortable modern swivel chair, with telly and lots of books, though mostly on spiritualist subjects. The dining room is done in simple café style, with a very low-profile bar (basically a counter where you can order drinks). The bedrooms are dormitory style, but cosy, comfy, warm and clean, with kettles and basins in every room. There are two bathrooms for each floor and plenty of hot water for baths. Unfortunately, you have to walk through the swimming pool room to get to the lounge or bedrooms, so that you are repeatedly wading through thick steam.

The owners of Runnings Park are seriously interested in spiritualism, health and healing, and they host a large number of conferences on these subjects throughout the year. We were there during one attended by aged Anglo-American Christians of some fundamentalist breed, our delicious dinner being frequently punctuated by pink-cheeked, white-haired enthusiasts waving their forks, exclaiming, 'Up to the hilt with Jesus!' Wailing psalms wafted in just as I was relaxing in the sauna. The front hall sported a display of Nature's Own vitamin products – the business of one of the owner/partners – and the library consists almost exclusively of books about Stonehenge or on Egyptology; ditto the prints on the walls. All in all, the health and healing business is as much in the air as the steam.

If such things interest you, write for their schedule; if not, I'd recommend going during a free week or weekend, not only because the conferees in their numbers and solidarity can be intrusive to an otherwise restful holiday (even offensive if you don't go for their kind of preachiness), but simply because it's rather weird to be one or two among a hotelful of likeminded devotees.

But all in all, I thoroughly enjoyed my stay. The food, comfort, sport and space were good, wholesome and refreshing, and the people who run Runnings, religious views aside, were extremely kind and friendly. With some caveats, I do recommend it.

CATERING Vegetarian and traditional. Licensed bar.

SMOKING Smoking restrictions.

PRICE CATEGORY Very High.

FURTHER INFORMATION Runnings Park
Croft Bank,
West Malvern,
Worcester WR14 4BP
Phone (06845) 3868/65290

34. Trinity House Hotel

If you have to stay overnight in the Midlands, and despair of finding a decent night's rest and a genuine vegetarian meal, go to the least obvious place – Coventry city centre – where you'll find both together. The hotel is like many modest family hotels – a large terraced house that has been saved from the alternative fates of becoming student flats or part of the foundation for the nearby dual-carriageways. The approach is not inspiring: a cul-de-sac off the inner ring road, close to huge shopping malls and their boarded-up predecessors. A phone call to the information desk at the National Exhibition Centre – 15 minutes' drive away – yielded this solitary address for the benighted vegetarian, but it's good, which is just as well when there's no alternative.

This is a place for those who like to be treated with friendly deference; you won't be invited to help shell the peas or milk the goat, but the owners and staff will make you feel very welcome and clearly want to provide a professional service. The general impression is one of informal competence: I was shown my room by one of the owners, still wearing his chef's uniform because he had been called from the kitchen, and was made to feel welcome even though I had arrived at a busy time. The room was spacious and comfortable in a domestic sort of way, with coffee and tea making facilities and a black and white TV. It was also clean and well-aired. The hotel has a large lounge and television room for residents, a restaurant – 'Herbs' – that doubles as the hotel dining room and breakfast room, a compact bar, an outside area too large to be called a yard and too small to be called a garden, and a lounge for diners who like to linger over their after-dinner coffee. The bar is very small, but well-stocked and the snacks put out for guests included wholefood brands. Smoking is allowed in the bar, but not in the restaurant itself.

The restaurant was, for a Monday night, surprisingly full by an early hour, and full of people who were clearly enjoying their food. It's obviously a place for an evening out with friends, and there were several parties that included carnivores who had been cajoled into trying vegetarian food and were pleasantly surprised at the quality and diversity of the menu. As for the menu and the preparation of food, the principle seemed to be to offer an interesting and reasonably exotic choice, prepared in such a way that individual ingredients could be tasted; nothing was over-cooked or swamped in sauce. Fresh vegetables formed healthy salads to accompany main dishes, with optional jacket potatoes. The menu changes on a monthly basis. The choice of starters during my stay included crunchy deep-fried brie, chilled melon with cucumber sorbet, and a sweetcorn and Madeira soup that was so good I had it the next evening too. The main dishes all sounded (and looked) equally tempting. The cashew nut and red pepper loaf was excellent: the cashews were cooked *al dente*, and there was a judicious use of herbs to season a very superior nut loaf. A salad of fresh vegetables added further bite. Also available were broccoli and mushroom country pie, ratatouille cheese crumble and a grandly named spinach roulade provençale. There were several sweets, with a leaning towards fresh pies and fruit and cream, but I settled for biscuits and cheese, not on the menu but provided without hesitation. Coffee was hot and fresh: could you ask for more?

Breakfast next morning in the transformed restaurant – service-able brown tablecloths instead of the crisp decorations and candle light of the night before – was for most people a traditional English breakfast, including bacon and eggs, since many of the residents were not vegetarian. The alternative was a satisfying sequence of fruit juice, muesli, toast, coffee and a generous basket of fresh fruit.

The verdict must be that this is a very reasonably priced and worthwhile hotel, with a restaurant recommended for an evening out. I was particularly impressed by the questionnaires placed in rooms and in the restaurant for guests to evaluate the service: it even seemed likely that they would be read by the management. For visitors to the National Exhibition Centre, or to the newly opened National Centre for Organic Gardening, Ryton Gardens, this hotel is ideal. In addition it's 3 minutes' walk from Coventry's

Belgrade Theatre, some fine churches, and a street full of preserved medieval buildings rescued from other parts of Coventry. Be sure to book in advance: it seemed very popular. D.G.

CATERING Exclusively vegetarian dinner (at Herbs Restaurant); traditional and vegetarian breakfast at the hotel. Licensed bar.

SMOKING Smoking restrictions.

PRICE CATEGORY Medium.

FURTHER INFORMATION Trinity House Hotel,
28 Lower Holyhead Rd,
Coventry, W.Midlands
Phone (0203) 555654

Other Places to Stay

Avon: Abbeywood, Weston-super-Mare
Phone (0934) 416024
XV, B & B + EM.

Avon: Bath
Phone (0225) 310143
XV(?), B & B + EM.

Berkshire: Westridge Centre for Arts and Healing, Andover Rd,
Highclere, Nr Newbury
Phone (0635) 253322
V-T. Healing and arts centre. See Chapter X.

Derbyshire: Joan Harvey, The Manse, Wetton, Manifold Valley,
Ashbourne.
Phone (0335) 27259
XV/Vgn, NS. Peak District, log fires, home baked bread. Price category VL.

Essex: Chelmsford
Phone (0245) 59273
XV, B & B + EM.

Gloucestershire: Oak Cottage, Gretton, Cheltenham
Phone (0242) 602570
XV B & B + EM. Artist/potter. Also do pottery and art tuition and V cookery demonstrations. Price category L. See Chapter X.

Lincolnshire: Manor Farm Retreat, Church Lane, S.Witham, Grantham
Phone (057 283) 500
V-T (props 'almost 100 per cent V'). Retreat, health care, diet, stress-management, relaxation, holiday. Price category M.

Norfolk: Chandlers, Horning, N.Walsham
Phone (069 260) 504
XV? B & B + EM.

Norfolk: Travellers Cottage, Horningtoft, Dereham
Phone (0328) 700205
V-T (prop 'almost' V), 'vegetarians welcome'. B & B + EM by arr (not normally). Price category L.

Norfolk: The Vicarage, Bacton-on-Sea
Phone (0692) 650375
T-V guesthouse. Homemade bread, farm produce. Price category L.

Norfolk: Nancy Brown
Phone (026 370) 635
'Wholefood/veg [XV?], NS adults, B & B + EM by arr, area of outstanding beauty, quiet location.'

Norfolk: North Coast
Phone (0263) 823690 evenings
XV, NS B & B + opt EM.

Oxfordshire: Dappers Guesthouse, 16 Reading Rd, Henley-on-Thames
Phone (0491) 578490
XV restaurant with one room above.

Oxfordshire: Earlmont Guesthouse, 322 Cowley Rd, Oxford
Phone (0865) 240236

XV, B & B only. We booked to stay but were refused entry at 10 p.m. after a concert. Prop very rude.

Suffolk: Western House, High St, Cavendish
Phone (0787) 280550
XV, B & B + EM by arr. Large garden, wholefood shop.

Warwickshire: Ashburton House, 27 Evesham Pl, Stratford-upon-Avon
Phone (0789) 292444
T-V. Pre-theatre dinners. Price category M.

Wiltshire: Harestock Cottage, Southampton Rd, Whiteparish
Phone (07948) 370
T-V guesthouse. Own produce; bees, goats, etc. Small, friendly but on busy main road.

Worcestershire: Malvern Nature Cure Centre, 5 College Grove, Gt Malvern
Phone (06845) 66818
XV guesthouse in Malvern Hills but nr town. Restful, walking holidays or/and naturopathic care. See Chapter X.

Places to Eat

AVON

Bath: Huckleberry's (XV), 34 Broad St. Phone (0225) 64876.

Bristol: McCreadies (XV), 26 Broad St. Phone (0272) 25580.

Bristol: Pushpanjli Pure Vegetarian Restaurant (XV), 217a Gloucester Rd. Phone (0272) 40493.

Bristol: Wild Oats II (XV), 85 Whiteladies Rd, Clifton. Phone (0272) 734482.

CAMBRIDGESHIRE

Cambridge: Nettles (XV), 6 St Edwards Passage (nr Arts Theatre). No phone listing.

DERBYSHIRE

Derby: The Lettuce Leaf (XV), 21 Friargate. Phone (0332) 40307.

ESSEX

Chelmsford: Melissa Wholefood Restaurant (XV), 21 Broomfield Rd. Phone (0245) 353009.

GLOUCESTERSHIRE

Cheltenham: Chives (XV) 226 Bath Rd. Phone (0242) 516676.

Cheltenham: Fruit and Nut Restaurant (XV). Phone (0242) 520577.

Stroud: Mother Nature (XV), 2 Bedford St. Phone (045 36) 78202.

HEREFORD AND WORCESTER

Worcester: Millwheel (XV though sometimes fish), 17 Pump St. Phone (0905) 23353.

LEICESTERSHIRE

Leicester: Aarti Restaurant and Chaat House (XV), 108 Belgrave Rd. Phone (0533) 660513.

Leicester: Blossoms Wholefood and Vegetarian Restaurant (XV), 17b Cank St (nr market). Phone (0533) 539535.

Leicester: Bobby's (XV), 154 Belgrave Rd. Phone (0533) 660106.

Leicester: Bread and Roses (XV), 70 High Street. Phone (0533) 532448.

Leicester: The Good Earth (XV), 19 Free Lane. Phone (0533) 26260.

Oakham: Oakham Gallery (XV?), 17 Mill St. Phone (0572) 55094.

NORFOLK

Norwich: The Café at Premises (XV), Reeves Yard, St Benedict's St. Phone (0603) 660352.

NOTTINGHAMSHIRE

Nottingham: The Beehive (XV), 23–7 Heathcote St, Hockley, Phone (0602) 476922.

Nottingham: Maxines's Salad Table (XV), 56 Upper Parliament St. Phone (0602) 473622.

OXFORDSHIRE

Henley-on-Thames: Dappers Wholefood and Vegetarian Restaurant (XV), 16 Reading Rd. Phone (0491) 578490.

Oxford: Holland and Barrett Health Food Restaurant (XV), 3 King Edward St. Phone (0865) 24307.

STAFFORDSHIRE

Cauldon Lowe: Lindy's Kitchen (XV), Staffordshire Peak Arts Centre, The Old School. Phone (05386) 431.

SHROPSHIRE

Shrewsbury: Delany's Vegetarian Restaurant (XV) (attached to St Julian's Craft Centre), St Alkmunds Sq. Phone (0743) 60602.

Shrewsbury: The Good Life Wholefood Restaurant (XV), Barracks Passage, Wyle Cop. Phone (0743) 50455.

SUFFOLK

Bury St Edmunds: Beaumonts (XV), 6 Brentgrovel St. Phone (0284) 706677.

Bury St Edmunds: Chalice Restaurant (XV), 28–9 Cannon St. Phone (0284) 4855.

Ipswich: Marnos (XV), 14 St Nicholas St. Phone (0473) 531006.

WARWICKSHIRE

Leamington Spa: Rainbow Vegetarian Restaurant (XV), 9 Regent Place. Phone (0926) 311056.

Birmingham: Whitakers (XV), 158 Broad St, Five Ways. Phone 021–632 5590.

Birmingham: Wild Thyme Vegetarian Restaurant (XV), 422 Bearwood Rd, Bearwood. Phone 021–420 2528.

Birmingham: Wild Oats Vegetarian Restaurant (XV), 5 Raddlebarn Rd, Selly Oak. Phone 021–471 2459.

Coventry: Herbs Vegetarian Restaurant (XV), 28 Lower Holyhead Rd. Phone (0203) 555654. *Also Trinity House Hotel; see review.*

WILTSHIRE

Avebury: Stones (XV), High St. Phone (067 23) 514.

Salisbury: Mainly Salads (XV), 18 Fisherton St. Phone (0722) 22134.

Warminster: Jenners Wholefood and Coffee Shop (XV), 45 Market Pl. Phone (0985) 213385.

IV

YORKSHIRE AND THE NORTH-EAST

Includes Cleveland, Durham, Humberside,
Tyne & Wear, and North, South and West
Yorkshire

Places Reviewed

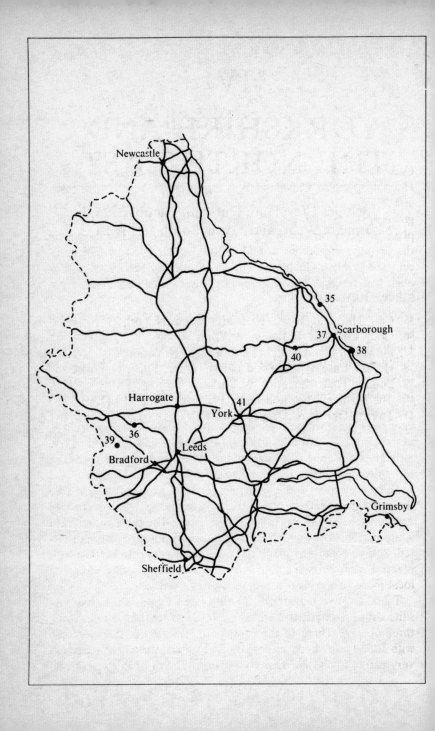

35. Crag Hill

Crag Hill looks from the height of Ravenscar across to Robin Hood's Bay. The Cleveland Way edges cliffs covered with birds and flowers – in May primroses, violets and marsh marigolds – and grazing sheep and goats, while the rocky beach provides a platform for dozens of brightly anoraked schoolchildren exploring the sea-life and geology around mysterious Boggle Hole. Ravenscar itself is a tiny village in a cul-de-sac midway between Scarborough and Whitby. The only public transport is a bus service from Scarborough.

Crag Hill is a four-square house in its own garden, with a good sized car park and a little terrace overlooking the sea. June and Philip Robinson welcomed their first guests at Easter 1986, fulfilling June's three wishes: to live in the country, to cook and to look after people. During our brief stay in May 1986 we enjoyed her exclusive attention, culinary and social, from the offer of tea when we arrived to the sample of delicious cake given as we left for later enjoyment with our picnic. The house is as fresh and bright as new paint and carefully chosen furnishings can make it. The welcome from June is complemented by the cheerful luxury of the red patterned carpet in the hall and on stairs and landing.

The dining room and lounge give generous views of the sea. The dining room is neat and attractive, its plain parquet floor and white walls enriched by deep rust rugs and frieze. The tables have fresh white cotton cloths over rust 'petticoats'. Smoking is not permitted. A high chair is available. The lounge is very comfortable with plenty of armchairs, a colour television and many books, including local maps. There is a downstairs cloakroom.

There are five bedrooms, all with open views. Three have en suite shower rooms, the others wash basins; two have twin beds, three double. Three of the rooms are classified as family rooms with added bunk beds and/or cot as required. Colour schemes are very carefully chosen. Our room was a luxury of deep pink and cream with flowered duvet and pillowslips, two large, soft towels each, two wardrobes, an armchair, reading light, tea/coffee-making equipment and a digital alarm clock, plus a neat packet of information about meal times and local events. The bed was brand new and firm.

All the bedrooms and bathroom are on the first floor; while the second floor contains a most unusual feature, admired but not tested by us – a gym, complete with transports of delight or instruments of torture, depending on your attitude. Prospective guests should know that a pre-breakfast circuit is not obligatory, though some may like to limber up for a round on the local golf course. The brochure also refers to the availability of tennis courts, outdoor swimming pool, garden centre and pony trekking nearby and offers to lend 'tennis rackets, kites, skipping ropes, etc'. We forgot to enquire about the 'etc', but learned that guests' dogs can be safely accommodated at kennels recommended by the Robinsons three miles away.

Catering is excellent. June is herself vegetarian and advertises as serving wholefood. She hopes before long to provide only vegan/vegetarian meals but, while establishing the guesthouse, could not refuse to receive omnivores, although she offers less choice to meat eaters than to vegetarians. She had prepared a complete menu especially for us vegans and we sampled almost everything. Helpings were so generous that we easily halved and shared each other's choices. We were offered hummus and pitta bread or lentil soup and roll for starters; then hazelnut pâté or mushroom and cashew nut flan, with baked potatoes, broccoli, bean salad; for dessert, rhubarb crumble, fresh fruit salad and almond cream or baked banana Hawaiian. We had herb tea (full range of drinks available); wine is available.

For breakfast we had a choice of fruit juice and served ourselves from a range of cereals and muesli, and also a delicately arranged fresh fruit salad including kiwi fruit, grapefruit and orange. We did not try a cooked course but filled any corners with wholemeal bread, marmalade and jam. Soya margarine and milk were also provided. Later we became June's first coffee customers of the day, enjoying a good, strong Rombouts before our walk. June serves marvellous homemade cake with morning coffee and afternoon tea and an interesting vegetarian lunch including, for example, baked potatoes with various toppings and salad.

We should certainly like to return to Crag Hill and have no reservation about recommending it in every way for people of any age. Our only regret was that smoking is not completely banned and that some meat is served. M. & J.C.

CATERING Vegetarian and traditional; vegan and other diets catered for. Licensed.

SMOKING Smoking restrictions.

PRICE CATEGORY Medium to High.

FURTHER INFORMATION June and Philip Robinson,
Crag Hill,
Raven Hall Road,
Ravenscar,
Scarborough, N.Yorkshire YO13 0NA
Phone (0723) 870925

36. Craig End Lodge

Craig End is a detached Victorian stone house, perched at the top of a hill where Ilkley ends and the moors begin. Our bedroom (which had beds for a family of six) had a spectacular aerial view of the surrounding houses and moors beyond, as did the sitting room below. Inside, Craig End is done out in purples and pinks, and the motley collection of patterned carpets and wallpapers can be just a bit dizzymaking. Like its proprietor, Craig End is rather Gothic and eccentric.

Mrs Hunter herself adds quite a bit to the sense of spin about the place. She is an endearingly scatty lady of considerable years who – though she worrits and fusses a good deal – actually has things pretty well under her thumb. She may not remember when you made your booking, what time you are due to arrive, or even your room number, but in the end things seem to sort themselves out. When a couple arrived late, for example, she dealt with them by chirruping gaily, 'Oh, it's OK, we haven't fed the dogs yet.' Giggles, apologies: generally a cheerful sense of disorganisation.

The food was plentiful, healthful and good, though not enormously attractively presented, and very rushed because Mrs Hunter had to get away that night to see *Educating Rita* at the local theatre. The dishes came and went in rather a blur. However, I believe there was a delicious blended vegetable soup, followed by a lentil hotpot and baked potatoes. The salad really looked pretty forlorn, scattered in compartments of a tin serving tray. Dessert was fresh fruit, including grapes. Drinks (help yourself) from a caddy assortment of instant coffees (including ideologically sound stuff) and ordinary and herbal teas. Breakfast was delicious: homemade bread and muesli, and stewed fruit.

We were there on a Bank Holiday weekend. Except for us, our fellow guests seemed to be either geriatric or adolescent. Conversations tended towards the Pinterish: Where have you come from? Where are you going? Do you remember Mrs Smith from Silverdale? No, I don't suppose you would, that was thirty years ago. She's dead now. And so on. Interspersed with Mrs Hunter doing her plate juggling act: 'I don't mean to rush you but . . . Things aren't usually like this . . .'

Still and all, I would recommend it. If you are vegetarian, have a good sense of humour, and have reason for stopping in Ilkley (aparently there are many), then by all means do go and stay at Craig End. However, if you are ageist or clinically fastidious, you'd better not go. 'No, you can't come into the kitchen, it's too messy,' scolded Mrs Hunter, shooing me out. And it was, but I didn't care. I liked Mrs Hunter a lot and enjoyed staying at her establishment for one night.

CATERING Exclusively vegetarian; vegan and other diets catered for.

SMOKING Smoking restrictions.

PRICE CATEGORY Low. Dogs very low (30p).

FURTHER INFORMATION Mrs E. Hunter,
Craig End Lodge,
Cowpasture Road,
Ilkley, W.Yorkshire
Phone (0943) 609897

37. Flower in Hand Hotel

The Flower in Hand is a one-time fishermen's inn half-way between Scarborough Castle and the old harbour in a quiet cul-de-sac. As in a boat, much use is made of small space. Our bedroom seemed tiny but soon expanded as we stowed luggage in the curtained cubby holes above the wardrobe and under the long cushioned bench-seat which makes cunning use of the narrow end wall. A chest of drawers, double bed, two chairs, bed light and electric heater complete the equipment and this room also had a shower, WC and tiny washbasin in a walled and curtained corner. Bedding was pretty patterned polyester-cotton sheets, pillow cases and duvet. We slept with open curtains for the first-light view of the sea.

Throughout the house the decorations are clean and attractive, with plain colours on woodchip paper. In our bedroom, cream separated from white ceiling and upper wall by a frieze of red-brown and buff; the bedspread was yellow, the bench-seat cushions gold, curtains at windows and covering cupboard space brown and cream with tiny pattern of birds and flowers.

We needed a rainy day to explore the many pictures on every wall. We grew fond of the soulful maidens engaged with lambs and chickens above the bed. The dining and sitting rooms are decorated with sketches and paintings by the owner, Jean Hobson. A panoramic view of the harbour faces the harbour itself, visible through all windows, while a portrait of Jean's partner, Barry, on a motorcycle beams down at you as Barry himself brings yet more coffee. Barry is a musician and author and evidence of his interests appear as souvenirs of Little Richard, the rock & roll star. Jean and Barry radiate welcome and cannot, as another guest said (and we confirm), do too much for you.

The sitting room is equipped with large colour television, books, dominoes, table and neat, cushioned bench-seats. The dining room has American-cloth covered tables for two and four and bright curtains. A high shelf surrounding the room is crammed with fascinating objects. A tiny, private bar, to which smoking is confined, is available for residents.

The hotel is not exclusively vegetarian and, although vegetarian herself, Jean would not wish to exclude omnivores, even if she could afford to. During our first stay of four nights (we returned again for one night), we enjoyed excellent vegan dinners, partly influenced by Sarah Brown's vegetarian restaurant in Scarborough where Jean had attended a course. On one evening the menu was grapefruit juice, wholemeal pastry cashew nut and mushroom flan, broccoli, scalloped potatoes, fruit cake (a large chunk), and coffee (plentiful). Jean does not stock herb teas but was always willing to make pots from our own teabags.

The menus were varied, interesting, tasty and filling. Vegetables are bought from the nearby market, fresh from local growers.

Breakfast at nine (or earlier on request) was fruit juice; toast with tomatoes or baked beans (vegetarians would have more choice); toast (as much as we could consume before a day's walking), and tea or coffee. Soya milk and margarine were especially supplied. Packed lunches and hot evening drinks can be supplied at extra cost. Although other guests were not vegetarian, we were not troubled by their carnivorous dishes, partly because our table was at the end of the room. No unpleasant smells issued from the kitchen.

We were slightly troubled by some guests smoking but Jean assured us that this is generally confined to the bar. Meals are accompanied by cheerful background music, not to our particular taste but, in the context of the whole house, pleasant, and all part of making people feel looked after. Guests at non-peak times preferring silence would, we feel sure, only have to mention this to Jean.

The other guests all seemed extremely contented. A family

taking a half-term break had found the hotel by accident but would, they said, return. A retired businessman attending his firm's conference had come at the recommendation of his former secretary and was soon completely at home. And an artist and his wife (a teacher and musician), refugees from one night in a sea-front horror, settled with happy relief into their new haven, Colin to sketch from his room and Catrin to relax. We followed our first visit in October with a brief return in May, enjoying the warm welcome, undemanding attention and huge, tasty dinner.

The hotel is within very easy reach of all parts of Scarborough, a delightful town which itself gives access to the North Yorkshire moors and the wonderful coast. It is not ideal for people with walking difficulties as staircases are narrow and twisty and Scarborough itself is hilly. It would be an excellent place for children, as the bright faces of Jean's two daughters testify. The Flower in Hand offers excellent value. Although we would have preferred no smoking and no meat anywhere, we've already been back once and we're looking forward to the next visit. J. and M.C.

CATERING Traditional and vegetarian; vegan and other diets catered for. Licensed bar.

SMOKING Restrictions.

PRICE CATEGORY Low.

FURTHER INFORMATION Jean Hobson,
Flower in Hand Hotel,
Burr Bank,
Scarborough YO11 1PN
Phone (0723) 371471

38. Heart's Ease Whole Food Guest House

Heart's Ease is a tall terraced house facing bow-windowed Georgian holiday flats, as gentle and pleasant as its owners, Alan and Mary Norris. Filey, in May at least, is gentle and pleasant, too, a short, elegant promenade bounded at each end by open green, a compact shopping centre with an Aladdin's cave ironmonger full of odd flowery saucers, Chinese iron frying pans and reduced plastic dishmops, and Filey Brigg, the long spur of cliff to the north. The neat green and white Heart's Ease brochure describes Filey as 'a small, peaceful family resort with a splendid bay and beach that stretches for several miles'.

Fortunately we chose a date between busy periods and had Heart's Ease, the Norrises and the window table – indeed, all four tables – to ourselves. You can just see the sea from the dining room. Opposite the bay is another window – a painting with a cat on a sill – and a little model cat sits on the mantelpiece under paintings of herbs, green and purple. (Later the real cat of the house joined us in the first floor lounge.) The cool white and green of decorations, curtains, table linen, crockery and an enormous plant was echoed in the freshness of narcissi on each table and enlivened by scarlet Busy Lizzies on the window sill. In fact, everything is fresh and clean. Smoking is not permitted in the dining room. Our meal was accompanied by a tape of light classical music, Mary thoughtfully asking if we would like to hear the second side.

The good sized lounge is furnished with very comfortable armchairs and settees, a green carpet and a large shaggy white rug, floor length brown curtains, pictures, books, magazines and an enormous red geranium in the bay window. The Norrises removed the television because guests seemed to prefer to talk to one another. Instead, colour televisions with 50p meters are supplied in the bedrooms. We did not try the meters (we preferred to read or talk with the Norrises), nor the mending and shoe cleaning kits and drink making equipment. But we did use the washbasin and towels (one each, good size), and the excellent bed in our second-floor room, enjoying the pretty matching curtains, cover and firm mattress. We took proper note of the wash basin, wardrobe, drawers, two chairs, hall stand, small table, waste paper bin and bedlight before falling quickly asleep after a day of seaside air and the delicious filling dinner prepared by both Mary and Alan.

Catering is excellent: well planned and attractively presented. Our vegan dinner comprised homemade soup and roll, cauliflower crumble (especially devised for us), baked potatoes, cooked vegetables, beetroot and sweetcorn salad, whole baked oranges with apple and almond sauce, and coffee (full range of drinks available). Of the three possible breakfasts we chose the 'Vegetarian', which consisted of fruit juice/grapefruit, muesli (soaked and unsoaked), wheatgerm, raisins, fresh and dried fruit, sunflower seeds, Farmhouse Bran (for vegans milk and yoghurt were replaced by soya milk), homemade rolls/toast, soya margarine (butter), honey, tahini, jam, marmalade and coffee (choice of drinks including herb teas). Mary also serves an 'Alternative breakfast', which consists of fresh fruit/grapefruit, chopped fresh fruit, cereal, toast with choice of eggs (scrambled, poached, boiled), baked beans, fresh tomatoes or fresh mushrooms, toast and spreads and drinks.

'English breakfast' with bacon, egg and sausage is also available and meat dishes are served at dinner on request. Mary and Alan would prefer to restrict catering to vegan/vegetarian but in 1986 were not yet able to refuse meat eaters. They were delighted at the increasing number of bookings by vegetarians and hope that this will continue although they would not exclude faithful omnivores who visit regularly.

We have no hesitation in recommending Heart's Ease. The standard rate is excellent value and groups of twelve to fifteen can obtain special rates out of season. We hope to return and to explore Filey and the glorious Yorkshire coast more thoroughly.
J. and M.C.

CATERING Vegetarian and traditional; vegan and other diets catered for.

SMOKING Not in evidence.

PRICE CATEGORY Low.

FURTHER INFORMATION Heart's Ease Whole Food Guest House,
23 Rutland Street,
Filey, N.Yorkshire
Phone (0723) 512379

39. Ponden Hall

Ponden Hall conjures up Brontë country. It's a short 3 miles from Haworth, where the Brontë parsonage, now a museum, stands. Ponden itself is reputed to be the elegant Thrushcross Grange of *Wuthering Heights*; possibly the ghosts of Cathy and Heathcliff wander the gardens behind the stone wall bearing the sign 'No Admittance' on its gate. If you are a walker it will conjure up the Pennine Way and the Brontë Way. Ponden Hall is in fact a rare haven for walkers, as Wainwright tells us, as it is one of the few places actually on the Pennine Way offering food and accommodation.

On foot, coming north on the Pennine Way, it would make a fairly modest walk (a mere 10 miles or so) from Hebden Bridge, crossing the high moors above Haworth and passing the ruins of Withins Farm, where Heathcliff is said to have lived; a small detour would take you to the Brontë Bridge and Brontë Waterfalls, and you can tank up with a pint at the Old Silent Inn down the road. If you have the nerve to arrive by car (I did), you drive across Ponden Reservoir and turn right up a track, go past a dead bus and up a steep, very rough track, turn to the left, and there it is. 'It' is actually a number of buildings: the noble Hall itself, a cottage, a bunkhouse, and various other farm buildings. The Hall is long and low, with mullioned windows and is made of the local blackish gritstone. It has a deep courtyard leading to the main entranceway, with a carved inscription over the door to say it was built by Robert Hootten in 1682 and rebuilt in 1801. The front door creaks atmospherically as you enter a slate-floored hallway hung with woven rugs and shawls, relics of the now-defunct Brontë Hand-Loom Weavers (a room at the top of the house is still filled with hanks of wool, bolts of handwoven fabric and ghostly, mouldering Brontë capes). You pass through a gateway; you ring a bell and someone admits you into the inner sanctum of the house. The hallway therein is flanked by a redoubtable collection of capes, macs, cagoules and other kinds of rain gear suggestive of intrepid (living and dead) souls bent against the weather. They get a lot of it up there. Go in the winter (or even the summer) and you begin to understand about Heathcliff. My host was perfectly friendly, but he was not one to waste words.

The guest lounge/dining room is large and square with the original slate floor, wide stone fireplace, huge oak beams and mullioned windows. Then there's the billard table with an accordion sitting on top, an abstract print, and a keg of home brew. Round the coal fire are two long sofas, built to accommodate rows of tired walkers who would normally be lounging about after their day out on the moors. The refectory table seats eighteen. My bedroom, next to the lounge, was also a huge room with its windows painted turquoise and festooned with thick wires. The floor was three-fourths covered with new pine boards (raised up from the original floor) and a pine bed was suspended from the ceiling. Then there was the one corner with slate flooring, old stones peeking through the plasterwork, a well-used stone fireplace, and a huge slab of millstone grit – looking like a tombstone – leaning against the wall.

The old and the new made an odd, split-level design perhaps meant to show something of the original room. A strange house altogether, with its fabric from the past co-existing somewhat uncomfortably with the jumble of things from the present. Not that I would know how to furnish a seventeenth century house in the manner to which it must have been accustomed, nor do I think it necessarily desirable. Ponden Hall is very much alive with family, farm and guest life (and their gear); I hardly advocate mummifying it into a museum like Haworth, though it would be interesting to see what it looked like in the days of its old elegance. Mr Taylor did mumble something about a restoration fund, so it may be that by the time you read this, Ponden Hall will have been restored to its former glory. (What on earth will they do with all those wellies?)

I went for a pre-dinner stroll up the farm track and at a farmhouse junction veered left onto the Pennine Way, trying to behave nonchalantly in spite of three dogs doing a reasonable imitation of Heathcliff's snarling, coughing canine beasts, their fangs flashing at me through the moor's mist. Don't worry, they were chained up (always are, I hope). I veered off the Way, which was ankle deep in mud, and took the more appealing (to me), domesticated Brontë Way a few hundred yards up onto the moor, and looked around. It was warm and still and very beautiful with its steep valley, fields and moorland above and the silhouettes of scattered houses and trees in the hazy setting sunshine. Of course, returning to the Hall I felt like a fraud and a cheat: it's the kind of place one ought really (and I'm sure most do) arrive with thirty pounds of mud on one's boots, a vast pack, and having done at least thirty miles that day (well, fifteen anyway). Maybe next year.

Dinner is certainly geared to the active person's appetite. There was a very nice spinach soup, though it was spoilt, in my opinion, by a huge island of yellowy stuff (condensed milk?) floating on it. Then there was a vegetable crumble (root vegetables and oatmeal) and huge jacket potato; a salad of lettuce, tomatoes, peppers and raw onion (ugh!), with a dish of salad cream to go with it. For dessert there was apple snow with hazelnuts. Bread was a granary loaf accompanied by what looked like butter but wasn't; though what it was I couldn't tell you.

Breakfast consisted of orange or grapefruit juice (help yourself out of a carton); choice of muesli/Weetabix/cornflakes. While I was still working on my muesli, a cooked breakfast appeared – fried egg, mushrooms and tomatoes on greasy bread – at which I blenched and Mr Taylor apologised at being 'a bit previous'. Weakly I accepted it, but after he left I took a deep breath, marched into the kitchen and returned it to Mrs Taylor (she seemed more approachable). I apologised; she said it was quite all right, she would keep it hot for the next diner. Why not ask first if people want a hot breakfast?

Ponden Hall is not the sort of place you forget, even if the memories are not all ecstatic. I was not honestly thrilled with the food or the sleeping arrangement (the single bed had a sort of envelope affair over a nylon sheet), but I was impressed by the Hall's moor-top setting, its history, and the literary ghosts it conjured up. It was quite a sight in bright moonlight. I left in the morning glad to get away from its rather wuthering atmosphere, but full of feeling for it. A strange, lonely place; no doubt transformed by rafts of friendly walkers in summer. There is no summarising such a place. Some will love it and some will hate it. I doubt if it's the place for a honeymoon (unless you're marrying your boots) or for a gourmet holiday. Mrs Taylor, though herself vegetarian, doesn't seem to mind cooking and serving other people meat; in fact, most of her guests, she says, are carnivores. So take it from there. A good place for hearty types with hearty appetites to rough it; a must for not over-delicate Brontëphiles. Big, hot bath and home brew are added attractions. You can see a picture of Ponden Hall in Wainwright's *The Pennine Way*.

CATERING Traditional and vegetarian. Licensed.

SMOKING Allowed.

PRICE CATEGORY Very Low.

FURTHER INFORMATION Brenda Taylor,
Ponden Hall,
Stanbury,
Keighley BD22 0HR
Phone (0535) 44154

40. The Stables

Guests at the Stables in Thornton Dale eat in what used to be the piggery; the troughs have been replaced by an elegant, round table furnished with gleaming cutlery, fresh flowers and delicate china. The spacious room, blue, white and grey, encourages one to lounge in the comfortable settee and chairs, browse through the shelves of leaflets and books on the locality, or watch the large colour television.

Six guests can be accommodated in single or twin bedrooms well supplied with blankets, pillows, quilts and electric blankets. Our ground floor room had a large wardrobe with plenty of hangers and one drawer, an armchair, a small table, a cyclamen and plenty of Agatha Christies. A long, deep bay with full length velvet curtains provided both a large shelf space and a view of the quiet, tree-bordered garden. An excellent night's sleep was disturbed only by the local church clock, echoed by a sweet chiming clock indoors. Both the bathroom upstairs and the WC and basin downstairs are, like the rest of the house, immaculate. Water is really hot and plentiful, the towels fluffy and large. The ground floor WC and bedroom would make this an excellent house for people who cannot climb stairs. Efficient central heating maintains a steady temperature throughout (we visited in October). Further accommodation is provided in two nearby cottages, available for self-catering or with meals at the Stables.

The house, secluded in a lovely garden, is well placed for gentle pottering into the pretty village of Thornton Dale and for longer expeditions into Yorkshire, including the nearby towns of Pickering and Malton, further off York, the moors and the coast. George and Esme Carnes, the owners, are both vegetarian and keep a completely vegetarian kitchen. We had asked in advance for vegan meals and Esme had explained that this was not always possible when non-vegan guests were staying. However, she prepared an excellent vegan dinner for all four of us and the vegetarian couple evidently did not feel deprived of cheese or eggs. The dinner, beautifully served at 7 p.m., with George waiting on us, comprised tomato juice with parsley, vegan pâté, turnip, carrot, baked potato, sauce, fresh fruit salad, tea, coffee and a selection of herb teas (served in pots). For breakfast we served ourselves from a side table laden with bowls of prepared muesli (including cooked apple), cereals (e.g. All Bran, Bran Flakes and Granola). A separate jug of soya milk and a dish of soya margarine were supplied especially for us. Before our cereal we ate bowls of apricots and filled any corners with toast. Various hot drinks were served in generous quantities.

From George's warm welcome with a tray of tea (no extra charge) to Esme's friendly farewell, our stay was comfortable and happy. George and Esme aim to make their guests feel at home and to offer a service to both vegetarians and vegans. We'll go again to enjoy the peace, comfort and excellent catering. J. and M.C.

CATERING Exclusively vegetarian. Vegans not always catered for if non-vegans present.

SMOKING No smoking.

PRICE CATEGORY Low.

FURTHER INFORMATION George and Esme Carnes,
The Stables,
Church Hill,
Thornton Dale,
Nr Pickering, N.Yorkshire
Phone (0751) 74771

41. Twenty-One Park Grove

Twenty-One Park Grove is a Victorian town house, the last of a long terrace of red brick houses with yellow façades, on a quiet street about 10 minutes' walk from York Minster and the centre of town. The street is a mixture of larger houses with bays on one side and later flat-faced 'working men's' houses on the other. Many still look like boarding houses, which is indeed what they were when my mother-in-law went up and down these streets looking for rooms for young people from the Cocoa Works, and some look like they've been tarted up.

Number 21 is one of the larger ones, with bay window and pocket-sized front garden; it's a pleasant enough looking house to those who don't find yellow brick one of the ugliest building materials ever invented (to be fair, most of the house is red brick and only its façade is yellow). The Moores have apparently done just about everything it's possible to do to fix up a 100-year-old house and make it last for another hundred years. When I was there they'd only recently opened, having finished redecorating from top to bottom.

They've done it in high Victorian style, with embossed wallpaper and repro three-piece bathroom suite, complete with brass taps and panelled mahogany bath surround and potty seat, but otherwise it still has a lot of this century's less fortunate boarding housey furniture; as, for instance, the monumental green and gold velour three-piece suite in the lounge, which is otherwise quite a nice room, with its maroon painted dado, Victorian curly maple upright piano and extraordinary octagonal oak mirror with bevelled glass and painted flowers. The dining room is smaller and seemed a bit grim when I was there, but that was I think because of the scaffolding outside the window (they were still working on the roof) and the ecru patterned lace curtains and dark wine drapes. Without the scaffolding it will be lighter, with a splash of green from the back garden. It won't ever be a very light room, but it's

136

comfortable and snug. Mrs Moore is as generous on the central heating and hot water as she is on her portions, not your typical boarding house characteristic. Although I was there in August, it was one of those bitter, windy days, and the heating was very welcome indeed.

Dinner is normally at 6 o'clock. Mrs Moore says people seem to prefer this, as it allows them to enjoy York's hopping night life. I can see the point, especially during the Festival or if there's something decent on at the Theatre Royal, but otherwise you could be stuck for a long evening in front of the telly or walking in the rain, as I was. Mind you, I'm not complaining: seeing the Minster at night was worth getting wet for, and wandering around inside without hordes of schoolchildren and tourists was a treat. But getting back to dinner, I had warned Mrs Moore – apologetic as always – of my limited diet, expecting no more than the basic vegan-type menu, minus any wheaty-frills, which usually means pretty simple stuff. But not here. Mrs Moore had really gone all out, though not in an elaborate or laborious way, to make a really interesting dinner, finding imaginative substitutes for both potatoes and wheat. And although I was the only diner that night, I was still given a choice of starter and dessert. The first course was avocado vinaigrette or celery soup. I had the soup, which was odd to look at (rather transparent) but very tasty, with rye bread. Next came a ratatouille with rice and haricot bean rissoles fried in sesame seeds. The rissoles were delicious though very filling (I ate too many and was sorry). Next a very fresh salad, I suspect straight out of the garden. For dessert, a mixed fruit crumble made with barley flour (which I have never thought of using), with peaches, blackberries, pears, bananas and apple, and topped with a soya cream, which she made by whipping soya milk with oil and adding vanilla, and which I cannot, alas, reproduce. Chamomile tea in the lounge followed. A really wonderful meal. Mrs Moore certainly gets full marks for thoughtfulness and invention in the service of the special diet; in any case, she is a wonderful cook and I'm quite sure will do you proud even if you're a plain old vegetarian or vegan. (It evidently runs in the family. Her daughter is Janet Whittington of the splendid Lancrigg Vegetarian Guest House in Grasmere.) The only criticism I can possibly make is that she seemed a bit nervous serving and rushed the courses as if she wanted to get things over with in a hurry; but this may have been because she had her daughter and grandchildren staying with her. Perhaps I took too long over my food, savouring it with my Anita Brookner novel (appropriate reading for a solitary lady guest).

After my walk, I came back and watched television, their very friendly black cat on my lap for company. After that, a hot bath (plenty of hot water; there's also a shower) in the luxurious new bathroom, then to bed. My bedroom was the small single, but was quite comfortable. The double room is much larger with en suite bathroom. There are basins in all the rooms and kettles, and chamomile tea bags very welcome too. The decor, again, was not wildly exciting – pinky-brown, flowery wallpaper, net curtains, sobersides wardrobe – but there was a pretty duvet with cotton sheets, including a top one under the duvet. Only two criticisms: the small bedside lamp was not very good for reading, and the newish bed was not great.

Breakfast was up to the same high standard as dinner, though there wasn't a wheat-free cereal substitute except for cornflakes. But there was a terrific fruit salad, with melon and green and purple grapes in addition to the usual fruits, plus orange juice, soya milk, rye toast and herb tea; eggs, mushrooms and tomatoes on toast were also on offer.

Mrs Moore runs a (in the best sense of that word) gracious establishment – warm, comfortable, friendly and generous (she wouldn't take payment for a telephone call), though she doesn't waste a lot of time standing around chatting; perhaps she would when she was less busy with family. It seemed a happy home, what with the sounds of Mr Moore's violin and their grandchildren's laughter. Of course it could take on a quite different character when other guests are staying and the family are fewer. I noticed there are ashtrays in the lounge and bedrooms (though not in the dining room), and my guess is that Mrs Moore – like her daughter and son-in-law at Lancrigg – does not stop people from smoking if they wish. I would have found it problematic had there been a smoker.

I enjoyed my short stay and would certainly recommend it to anyone visiting York. Unlike the Dairy Guest House (which is

B & B only and has a two-night minimum stay), it is strictly vegetarian and will cope handsomely for vegans and other special diets. You can choose to have an evening meal (highly recommended) or vary things by going out to one of the vegetarian restaurants in York.

CATERING Exclusively vegetarian; vegan and other diets catered for.

SMOKING Smoking restrictions.

PRICE CATEGORY Medium.

FURTHER INFORMATION Mrs Muriel Moore,
       21 Park Grove,
       York YO3 7LG
       Phone (0904) 644790

Other Places to Stay

NORTH YORKSHIRE

Harrogate: Amadeus Vegetarian Hotel, 115 Franklin Rd.
Phone (0423) 505151
XV, NS, B & B + EM, 'elegant modernised Victorian house, home baking, real coffee, etc.'

Kildale, nr Whitby: The Low House, Baysdale.
Phone (0642) 722880
XV guesthouse. Remote area, views, eighteenth-century small guesthouse; simple, no c.h., short season. Sounds wonderful – I tried to go repeatedly but it was always fully booked.

Pately Bridge:
Phone (0423) 711123.
XV, B & B + EM, 'restored eighteenth-century farmhouse, quiet location'.

Ravenscar: The Gypsy Vegetarian Guest House, 'Ranworth', Church Road, Ravenscar.

Phone (0723) 870366
XV, beautiful setting overlooking Robin Hood's Bay. I tried to go but failed.

Ripon: Riga, 22 Primrose Drive
Phone (0765) 2611
V-T, B & B + EM. Newish-, smallish-looking bungalow on private housing estate.

Scarborough: Lea-Grae, Crossgates, Scarborough.
Phone (0723) 862465
XV, B & B + EM only one day a week, otherwise you eat at Sarah Brown's. House on main A64 outside Scarborough.

Scarborough: The Red House, 46 Westbourne Park.
Phone (0723) 378836
XV guesthouse, 'peace, comfort, books and meditation, massage'.

SOUTH YORKSHIRE

Holmfirth:
Phone (0484) 683158
XV, B & B + EM on request for vegans – 'one bedroom (4 foot bed!), super view'.

WEST YORKSHIRE

Leeds (outskirts):
Phone (0532) 579639
XV, B & B only.

Places to Eat

NORTH YORKSHIRE

Scarborough: Sarah Brown's (XV), 13 Victoria Rd. Phone (0723) 360054.

Settle: The Kitchen Table, Market Pl. Phone (07292) 3638.

Skipton: Herbs (XV), 10 High St. Phone (0756) 60619.

Whitby: Shepherd's Purse (XV), 95 Church St. Phone (0947) 604725.

York: Gillygate Wholefood Café (XV), Millers Yard, Gillygate. Phone (0904) 24045.

York: Tullivers (XV), 55 Goodramgate. Phone (0904) 51525.

York: York Wholefood Restaurant (XV), 98 Micklegate. Phone (0904) 56804.

SOUTH YORKSHIRE

Barnsley: Down to Earth (XV), 36 Shambles St. Phone (0226) 282862.

WEST YORKSHIRE

Huddersfield: Blue Rooms (XV), 9 Byram Arcade. Phone (0484) 512373.

Leeds: Wharf St Vegetarian Café (XV), 17–19 Wharf St. Phone (0532) 449588.

Leeds: The Wholefood Shop (XV Takeaway), 182 Woodhouse Lane. Phone (0532) 435018.

V

THE NORTH-WEST AND LAKE DISTRICT

Cheshire, Cumbria, Isle of Man, Lancashire, Merseyside, Greater Manchester

Places Reviewed

42. Brocklebank Ground Country Guest House, Torver, Coniston, Cumbria
43. Brook House, Boot, Eskdale, Cumbria
44. Charrosa Guest House, Blackpool, Lancs
45. Fair Place Wholefood Guesthouse, Watermillock, Penrith, Cumbria
46. Greystones Guest House, Arnside, Cumbria
47. Lancrigg Vegetarian Country House Hotel, Grasmere, Cumbria (XV)
48. The Old Vicarage, Witherslack, Cumbria
49. Orchard House, Keswick, Cumbria (XV)
50. SKADI – Women's Walking Holidays Among Northern Hills, Sedbergh, Cumbria (XV)

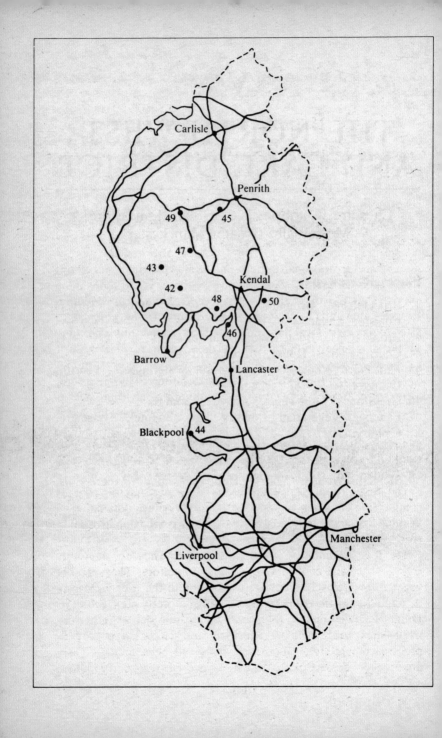

42. Brocklebank Ground Country Guest House

Brocklebank Ground is a late eighteenth-century farmhouse set in beautiful woodland above Coniston Water, in the shadow of the Old Man. You can tell it's a relaxed, friendly place by the number of dogs draped over the garden furniture. You get a loud but benign greeting. Lilian and Roy Cooksey, Brocklebank's proprietors, are professional potters. You can visit their workshop, which is on the premises and, if you stay there, you will be eating off their work. Roy is also a team leader of the local Mountain Rescue Team and (so it says in their brochure) is always happy to give advice and local information. They sound like charming people, but since we met neither of them when we were there, I cannot really say.

The interior of the house is a bit disappointing. In our bedroom, for example, somebody had made an attempt at 'style' by sprinkling it liberally with Laura Ashley (1970s vintage) mix 'n' match curtains, wallpaper and duvets, but the effect, ironically, was to increase rather than lessen the gloom. A lick of fresh clean paint would do wonders. It was also overcrowded with beds, twins and unmade-up bunks. Our mattresses were pretty soggy.

The dining room is small but pretty. The guests' sitting room is comfortable but when we were there was very much dominated by Wimbledon on the telly, so we had to hole up in the dining room to read our books.

The food: hmmnn . . . well . . . hmmnn. They are obviously trying very hard and deserve a big E for effort. They are not vegetarians themselves but are responding to the ever-increasing demand for veggie/vegan food, and doing a pretty good job of it. Dinner included melon, followed by a gigantic slab of rather dry wholewheat aduki bean pie (which my stomach took a few days to process completely); cauliflower, peas and new potatoes (very good). For dessert there was a choice of strawberry gâteau (homemade) or Walls ice cream with aerosol whipped cream topping – both very sweet – followed by cheese and biscuits. (The latter were a brand made with animal fat.) It was the sort of dinner you might welcome after a strenuous climb up the Old Man in winter. For my taste, it was too heavy and filling, also too sweet and starchy.

Breakfast arrived before we'd even been asked if we wanted it – egg, mushrooms, and fried bread – which I sent away. My companion ate his and looked a bit green around the gills. But the bread was marvellous: a whole, home-baked crusty wholewheat loaf for each table. It would be a good idea if they asked people what they wanted rather than just plonking down a standard cooked breakfast. I know such things take more thought and effort, but, to me – and I'm sure to others – it makes all the difference betwen an impersonal and a personal service.

Smoking could also be a problem, although no one actually smoked when I was there. When I telephoned before booking, I asked 'Is smoking allowed?' to which the answer was an unequivocal 'Yes'. When he (Roy Cooksey, I believe) realised that was the wrong answer (he must have thought I was a smoker), he quickly changed his tune and said that actually people didn't usually smoke in the dining room; anyway, if somebody objected it was up to the guests to work it out amongst themselves. 'But,' he added, still trying to soothe, 'very few seem to smoke here.' Well that may be, but the odd truculent puffer can still make things pretty miserable. In any case, I'm not too keen on 'working things out', which usually means me having to ask the wretched smoker if he/she would please put it out. Much better (especially when you're on holiday) not to have to worry about such things.

Still, there are some good things about Brocklebank, and it's the only place in the Coniston area, so far, that does cater fairly seriously for vegetarians. And they *are* trying, though they should read the small print on biscuit packages. Further encouragement and gentle criticism ought to bring improvement.

CATERING Traditional and vegetarian; vegans also catered for. Licensed.

SMOKING Allowed.

PRICE CATEGORY Low.

FURTHER INFORMATION Lilian and Roy Cooksey,
Brocklebank Ground Country Guest
House,
Torver, Coniston,
Cumbria LA21 8BS
Phone (0966) 41449

43. Brook House

Brook House is definitely not a farm or a cottage. It's a solid
Lakeland house facing squarely onto the road and as we
approached on a rainy Saturday afternoon it seemed severe in
aspect, all sombre pebbledash and creepers. It's situated in the
Eskdale Valley just at the cul-de-sac turning into Boot Village.
This is the remote western edge of the Lake District, no coach
loads of tourists, but lots of good walking and fine views. There's a
four mile steep hike up to Wasdale Head overlooking stunning,
sheersided Wastwater for the enthusiastic walker.

Less strenuous attractions within a few hundred yards include
the Ravenglass–Eskdale steam railway, an historic cornmill and a
fine riverside walk with (in March when we were there) impressive
waterfalls, white water and deep pools.

Boot is an attractive village to stroll through with a welcoming
pub, the Brinnmoor Inn, tastefully modernised with log fire.
Brook House is, as its brochure says, an excellent centre for
walking, and the 'Lakeland Experience' based at Brook House
will organise your day for you – canoeing, rock scrambling, caving,
abseiling or whatever you fancy.

Inside, Brook House is less severe than its exterior suggests.
The halls and landings are attractively done out. At this time of
year, the place felt stiff and empty, as indeed it was: apart from us

there were one other couple and a single man enjoying the Lakeland Experience out of season.

The separate lounge was over-stuffed with settees, heavy furniture and back issues of magazines you never wanted to read; as well as P.G. Wodehouse, *The Art of Coarse Golf*, British flora, herbal lore and an electric bar fire and piano. Green candles and china spaniels on the mantelpiece. Cheerful and warm in spite of all this.

The dining room – big, functional, and tidy – could not deter visitors from whispering over their meals at separate oak tables and chairs. Two dogs and a cat appeared only at breakfast.

The bar was small and potentially friendly if full of people (but who would prefer it over the pub except those lacking babysitters or wellington boots?).

Our bedroom, a bit on the small side for a family room, had standard brown B & B furniture, but the beds were comfortable, there was good lighting for bedtime reading, and a black and white TV. We felt snug and warm and safe from the stormy night outside. There was central heating throughout, continental quilts on the beds, and a fan heater provided for extra warmth. The bathroom, too, was pleasantly warm, clean, carpeted, with lots of hot water and nice colours. This was my favourite room in the house. I even liked the curtains.

Two more pluses. Brook House is very quiet at night and you wake up to lovely views from the bedroom windows.

The owners of Brook House are a young couple, and pleasant if a bit distant – there were no enquiries about where we'd come from or where we were going. They cater for a variety of guests from climbers and walkers to car-bound strollers. They were not geared to children but they're not unfriendly either, accepting our three-year-old. The owners are vegetarian and serve mainly vegetarian food, though discreet carnivores can be catered for. The vegetarian food was 'traditional' – a vegetarian dish and two veg and potatoes, but not particularly 'health' or 'wholefood' conscious. Breakfast, for example, was absolutely standard B & B with commercial cereals, followed by eggs and toast (shop bought wholemeal sliced) and marmalade.

Our evening meal was good, home-cooked, thoughtful and

filling, with delicious sweets. We had pea soup or fruit juice, vegetable croustade; red cabbage/peas and potato caraway bake. Dessert was cheesecake or homemade apple and blackcurrant pie with ice cream or cream. Coffee followed.

In summary, Brook House is a comfortable and convenient base for an active holiday in a beautiful setting. But, for us, it didn't have the special spark to make us note it down as somewhere to return to. In any case, the vegetarian food seemed rather incidental to its main attractions. If we wanted a holiday in Eskdale, we'd probably stay there again, but we wouldn't suggest going out of your way for the Brook House experience. M.H. and D.B.

CATERING Vegetarian and traditional. Licensed.

SMOKING No restrictions.

PRICE CATEGORY Medium.

FURTHER INFORMATION   Mr R.L. and Mrs J.E. Davis,
Brook House,
Boot,
Eskdale, Cumbria CA19 1TG
Phone (094 03) 288

44. Charrosa Guest House

We found ourselves in Blackpool on the night the Illuminations were turned on so we got the full works: crowds, lights, fruits, soldiers, even a trolley-cum-rocket bombing its way up and down the Front. We were filled with nostalgia – Moira for her childhood day trips to Blackpool from Manchester, and I for my Coney Island equivalents. Moira had her fortune told by Gypsy Boswell (while I gawped), we ogled people on the streets and in the boarding house windows, and we bought old jazz records from a market stall. We did not have Blackpool rock or fish 'n' chips. Hugging our records to our bosoms (good wind shields), we left

Staying Vegetarian

the Front and made our way back to Clifford Road, and to our shared attic eyrie at the Charrosa Guest House.

The Charrosa looks much like all the other backstreet, terraced boarding houses in Blackpool. It's on a nice street within a few minutes' walk of the Front. It boasts the usual swirly lurid carpets, knick-knacks, fake wood panelling, chandeliers and flocked wallpaper. Loud music played in the dining room. There was one small, thin towel for the two of us, and the hot water never made it up to our attic. On the plus side, we had a view of Blackpool Tower and the full moon out of our tiny skylight window, while the first-floor bedrooms – though probably better provided with the basic amenities and closer to the toilet and shower – overlooked bleak back alleyways. In general though, the Charrosa is clean, the hall and bedroom (at least ours) are painted a cheerful white, there are lots of plants, and one nice photograph of two elephants. I have seen worse.

Charrosa 'welcomes' vegetarians. Mike Elliott served us with lentil soup (which might have been homemade), wholewheat pancakes and mushrooms in a rather plodgy white sauce, garlicky green beans (very nice), jacket potatoes, and Peach Melba (a lump of vanilla ice cream sitting on a couple of tinned peach slices and drizzled with sticky pink syrup). Except for the dessert, quite a good effort, and certainly plentiful. Ditto breakfast. An impressive choice here, including cooked cinnamon porridge or baked apple muesli, followed by a full cooked vegetarian breakfast. We had the muesli porridge – interestingly fruity and peanutty, though sticky – and toast, and stopped at that. What with the music blaring and the sight and smell of the surrounding bacon, sausage, kippers, haddock and egg breakfasts, we bolted, never to discover what the full veggie breakfast was.

A word of warning to vegans: Mike does *not* welcome you. He is not much in sympathy with the idea or the products and simply finds it too time-consuming and bothersome to cater for three different diets at a time. So although he has had the odd (I mean that numerically) vegan – and he did find me a box of Flora instead of butter – he makes his feelings clear.

I will probably not return to Blackpool, but the memory of the Charrosa, inextricably linked with Gypsy Boswell the Palmist and

150

the Illuminated Strawberry with the Terrible Eyes, will remain. If you find yourself in Blackpool – for whatever reason – the Charrosa is probably your best bet.

CATERING Traditional and vegetarian; vegans not welcome (sic).

SMOKING Allowed.

PRICE CATEGORY Very Low.

FURTHER INFORMATION Sue and Mike Elliott,
Charrosa Guest House,
17 Clifford Road,
Blackpool FY1 2PU
Phone (0253) 28143

45. Fair Place Wholefood Guesthouse

Fair Place is a small (three bedrooms) family guesthouse catering for special diets and music lovers in one of the most spectacular areas of the Lake District, about 1 mile above Ullswater. Sadly, there is no view of the lake from the house ('a fine view from the roof', say the proprietors), but from just outside the front gates you get the whole panorama of Ullswater and the North Eastern fells.

The Bewleys serve primarily vegetarian food, but will accommodate vegans and carnivores too. They are very conscientious about using 'natural' foods, which to them means no chemical additives, growth promoters, antibiotics, etc. Dinner is a six-course set meal. Ours included a mushroom, onion and nut roast, mountainous potatoes, a heaped and chock-full-of-goodies grated salad, and a gingery apple muesli crumble. Choice of coffee or tea (plain Indian). Bring your own wine.

Everything about Fair Place is homey and unpretentious, from the Flora in tubs to the bright ceiling fixtures. No candlelight and roses, matching Cranks-type earthy pottery or Laura Ashley tableware. Had there been, my verdict would likely have been 'a gourmet feast'. As it was, the words 'hearty vegetarian fare' spring more readily to mind. But then I did not climb Helvellyn that day. And I am a sucker for atmospheric/decorative twaddle. Either way, the food was excellent.

The Bewleys offer music in a big way: two pairs of stacked Quad speakers look over the dining/sitting room like a couple of monoliths. But they are friendly enough monsters who woof and tweet only the best classical music, many from new compact discs.

The sitting area at Fair Place is very small and most of it is taken up by the Quads and the extremely efficient wood-burning stove. This dictates neighbourly interaction with the other guests, so you probably shouldn't go if you want solitude or if you don't like classical music.

Fair Place is not the ultimate in luxury, a good thing on the whole. There's no central heating but there are electric fires in all the bedrooms and, as I mentioned, the wood-burning stove in the lounge. No en suitery but three showers, two WCs and a shared bathroom; basin and kettle, etc. in bedrooms.

Ian and Dorothy Bewley are extremely nice people, especially after dinner when they are more relaxed and inclined to stand and chat. They are musicians themselves – they used to be the bass half of a string quartet – which explains their passion for music. They've made Fair Place a friendly, harmonious place to stay, in a naturally magnificent setting. But take note: they have a number of regulars who come back year after year, so book early.

CATERING Primarily vegetarian; vegan and other diets catered for, including non-vegetarian (naturally reared animal foods supplied by local farmers).

SMOKING No smoking.

PRICE CATEGORY High.

FURTHER INFORMATION Ian and Dorothy Bewley,
Fair Place Wholefood Guesthouse,
Watermillock-on-Ullswater,
Penrith, Cumbria
Phone (085 36) 235

46. Greystones Guest House

Greystones is just a snicket up from the Front in the village of
Arnside: a small, peaceful, very beautiful place on the Kent
estuary off Morecambe Bay, about halfway between Lancaster
and Kendal. The streets rise steeply from the curving Front, in
almost Greek fashion; there is a rocky beach to walk along and
watch the birds, a wonderful pub called the Albion where you can
sit out on fine days and watch the silver or golden sands,
whooshing tides, not to mention the Lakes in the distance on a
clear day and the Hornby Dublo trains chugging across the
estuary. It's also good cycling country and there are walks galore –
up Arnside Knott (where an even better view is to be had) or on
around the coast to Silverdale. A very special spot indeed.

If you are vegetarian, I suppose you must stay at Greystones
because there's no other choice. A pity, because Arnside deserves
better. Don't get me wrong. Greystones isn't dreadful, it's just a
bit blah, if you know what I mean; run pretty much along
traditional seaside boarding house lines. It's actually a splendid
semi-detached house. There's a large guests' lounge (shared by the
Bridgeman family) with maps and guidebooks, a small, freshly
painted white dining room overlooking a back walled garden with
sweetpeas growing up the window ledge; our bedroom was
enormous, with a partial view of the estuary. It's centrally heated,
there's plenty of hot water, towels, and so on; it's clean and quite
nicely decorated. So what's the problem?

Well, to be blunt, the food. It isn't exclusively veggie, though
they advertise in the *Vegetarian* and have a notice on their
doorstep saying they cater especially for vegetarians, and I think at

least one of the family is vegetarian. But the food is traditionally plain and rather dull. There was lentil soup and store-bought wholewheat rolls; quiche and two lettuce leaves, tinned or frozen peas and corn and potatoes; and for dessert, chocolate cake with chocolate pudding sauce; then a lump of cheddar cheese with biscuits. This was followed by coffee (decaf) or nothing (there was no choice of tea). Breakfast, I'm afraid, was equally drab: muesli or other dry cereals followed by eggs on toast; tea to sink the *Titanic* all over again. Again, no choice, which I really didn't like. I didn't want the eggs. I understand this too is typical boarding house style – you eat what you're given. I didn't.

It was all a bit grim, food appearing and disappearing with machine-like regularity through the hatchway. It seemed to be cooked by the younger of the two women (Pam Bridgeman, I suspect) and served by the older, a polite lady of few words who keeps her boarding house distance. She will also bring you tea for 45p and biscuits for 3p each (!) at other times. Pam is quite different, friendly and cheerful and very 'with it' (she even brought me a carton of soya milk for breakfast), but she stays mostly in the background. I realise what a big difference it makes when people are available to chat and be friendly; this was too impersonal for my taste, though you, of course, may prefer it. It felt too much like being at school where you are supposed to eat what you're given and not ask questions. We did not linger at the table.

Another problem is smoke. Mr Bridgeman smokes and shares the lounge and bathroom with guests, so the house is pretty smokey.

Not an enormously exciting place, to be honest, but if you want to go to Arnside, it's probably your best bet. Meanwhile I'm trying to interest someone in starting up an exclusively vegetarian country house hotel there (with panoramic views of the estuary, of course). Any takers?

CATERING Traditional and vegetarian.

SMOKING No restrictions.

PRICE CATEGORY Very Low.

FURTHER INFORMATION Pam Bridgeman,
                    Greystones Guest House,
                    Ashleigh Road,
                    Arnside, Cumbria LA5 0HE
                    Phone (0524) 761619

47. Lancrigg Vegetarian Country House Hotel

Lancrigg is an exclusively vegetarian hotel set in its own 27 acres in the Lake District, 5 minutes' walk from the centre of Grasmere. To reach it, you take the little road leading from Grasmere up Easedale. Just where the Easedale Tarn footpath sets off across the beck, you turn into a tall tree-lined drive and follow it winding uphill till you emerge on Lancrigg's terraces.

The house itself is, I presume, early Victorian, since almost everyone who was anyone in the Lakes lived, staying or visited there, from William and Dorothy on, though there seem to be both later and earlier bits. It's more like a rambling country house than a carefully coordinated hotel. When we were there shortly after they had opened, the lounge still had comfy old ex-nursing home furniture; the dining room was high Edwardian, the halls were tastefully modern with oatmeal carpets, stripped pine washstands and gorgeous Liberty drapes; some bedrooms and bathrooms were left plain and handsomely Victorian while some had been en suited and tarted up. We had the best double bedroom (with the best view), which had a traditional four-poster and spanking new bathroom with a corner bath for two with rather lurid pinky-bronze reflecting tiles.

The various styles don't necessarily all mesh, but the result is still tasteful and comfortable, with hardly a hint (except perhaps for the lounge) of its recent geriatric past. I think they've gone slightly over the top with their en suitery (there's one with a jacuzzi) and I find the naming of rooms rather silly (ours was 'The

Silver Howe Suite'), but I can understand them doing it; certainly many will be attracted by such things. For the more puritanical of us, there are still the plainer bedrooms with bathrooms down the hall fitted with lovely Victorian baths and taps; rather more to my style, and cheaper with it.

Guests are invited to lounge around at any time of day, as well as before and after dinner, ogling either the view or the log fire, which burns all day in winter. I don't need to sell you the joys of the Lake District, but a long wet walk, followed by tea and cake, then drinks, in front of the fire at Lancrigg is perfection.

The food is as good, if slightly more upmarket, as it always was at the Rowan Tree, the very successful tiny vegetarian restaurant Robert and Janet ran in Grasmere before they moved up in the world (literally) to Lancrigg. We had a three-course dinner, though I understand it's now four courses with more choices of desserts. The wine list covers a good range of prices, and is varied enough to include a number of organic wines, not all from the grape.

For starters there were fresh tomato and basil soup (delicious) or garlic mushrooms. The main course was lasagna made from a variety of fresh vegetables and – I can't swear, but I think – homemade pasta. The salad was a bit perfunctory, but friends who went more recently were given quite a number of interesting salady accompaniments. Pudding was either fresh gooseberry crumble with cream or peach gâteau with cream – very light and luscious. Yoghurt wasn't offered then but it may be by now. There was real coffee or tea (or herb tea), to be drunk in the lounge if preferred. Altogether a wonderful meal. And they are more than happy to cater for vegans, though they appreciate some advance notice.

Breakfast was equally plentiful and delicious though the buckwheat pancakes mentioned in their brochure were not available (they may be now). There was muesli and a variety of other grain cereals, as well as cooked porridge, fruit juice, fruit salad, stewed fruits, not to mention eggs, mushrooms, tomatoes, and toast. There was soya milk and margarine (vegetarian, of course) also available. Where would one put the buckwheat pancakes anyway? Unlimited fresh coffee rounded off a perfect breakfast and set us up for a really good trudge up the back of the Langdale Pikes.

My only real problem at Lancrigg was the smoke. Although ashtrays were conspicuously absent, there was a large party of people who smoked in the lounge and this drove us out into the cold. When we asked Robert about it, he explained that, though he doesn't smoke himself, he doesn't like rules. But he did ask them not to smoke in the dining room. I suspect we were simply unlucky. Friends have been there on several occasions and have not encountered any smokers.

I shall certainly go back, especially when the planned vegetable garden is flourishing and the 25 acres of woodland walks and pools are restored. They have a family suite now and there may well be a sauna one day on the landing or perhaps in the outlying barn. They also have plans for special interest holidays. It's not just Lancrigg but the Whittingtons I enjoy visiting: Janet's cheerful friendliness and Robert's care and forebearance are what round out that sense of a real country house weekend. I am very grateful to them for opening Lancrigg so near to me, and I am not in the least surprised that they are flourishing in the midst of the Lake District doldrums. L.A. and D. and A.G.

CATERING Exclusively vegetarian; vegan and other diets catered for.

SMOKING Smoking restrictions.

PRICE CATEGORY Medium to Very High.

FURTHER INFORMATION Robert and Janet Whittington,
Lancrigg Vegetarian Country
House Hotel,
Easedale, Grasmere,
Cumbria LA22 9QN
Phone (066 65) 317

48. The Old Vicarage

The Old Vicarage is one of those very special country house hotels. The service is efficient and unobtrusive, the bed linen snowy fresh, the hot water hot and plentiful, the interior decoration tasteful, the host full of goodwill, and the food sublime. It's also very expensive.

The ex-vicarage is a largish Georgian house set in 5 acres in the Winster Valley, in the pastoral fringe of the Lake District. It's 6 miles or so to Kendal, Grange-over-Sands and the foot of Windermere. It's tucked under Yewbarrow Ridge with views of woodland, gardens or Witherslack's village green and church out of its windows; if you climb the Ridge itself you see the whole of the South Lakeland fells. There are plenty of good walks on your doorstep, with a choice of Cartmel Fell and Whitbarrow Scar to climb, or the valley lanes to potter in; and you're close enough to the M6–Barrow road to give you access to the Lakes, but safely away from the worst of the Ambleside–Grasmere tourist crush.

The Old Vicarage, alas, is *not* a vegetarian guesthouse, but it is much more than the usual perfunctory 'we cater for vegetarians' type of place. At least one of the four owners (Roger Brown) is himself vegetarian and he oversees the preparation and cooking of the vegetarian meals. In fact (and I hope this isn't divulging a trade secret), Roger assured me all their soups and starters (and desserts for that matter; though not the cheese) are vegetarian, so you can be confident your soup isn't made with chicken stock, your salad won't be garnished with anchovies, and your pie crust won't be made with lard.

The dinner we had was stupendous: imaginative, fresh and interesting, beautiful to look at, and plentiful. For starters there was a terrine of carrot and hazelnut with Cumberland cheese, served with a rosemary hollandaise sauce. Then a leek and fennel soup with garlic croutons, which I would have sworn was made with double cream but Roger says not. The main course was a huge red pepper stuffed with two layered purees of parsnip and spinach and accompanied by no less than five fresh veges: baked new potatoes, green beans, cauliflowers, courgettes with pine kernels and mange-tout peas. Dessert was apricot and almond flan *and* – yes really – choice of chocolate or armagnac marquise or homemade damson ice cream (heavenly). Then biscuits and cheeses, including a couple of fine blue and white Stiltons. Portions generous. Wide choice of teas or coffee served with chocolate Kendal mints, just in case one still felt a bit peckish. The house wines were quietly superior: Sauvignon de Touraine or Côtes du Rhone, both AC and reasonably priced. The full wine list looks impressive. Final verdict is: worth every penny of the £15.95. And they are undeterred by other dietary restrictions or preferences (vegan, gluten-free, sugar-free, etc).

On to breakfast. We didn't stay overnight (couldn't afford to), but I will pass on the news from a friend who did. Apparently there are all sorts of goodies on offer for vegetarians, including nutalene (whatever that may be), fresh orange juice, free-range eggs, muesli, yoghurt, homemade wholewheat bread and rolls, and porridge with or without whisky, if you please, 'for the adventurous in spirit'. Yes, well, they do seem to go in for serious breakfasting. As they say in their brochure, 'We consider breakfast to be a very important part of our guests' stay.' What that means, however, is that in addition to the usual ham and bacon, they also offer more aggressively bloody delicacies such as Waberthwaite sausage and local black pudding. While I am quite sure no curl of bacon ever shares a pan with a free-range egg, the mere proximity (not to mention odour) of all that meat could be enough to put one off one's tipsy porridge.

The bedrooms as described sound lovely: plain duck-egg blue paint, fresh duvets, cotton sheets, pretty Victorianish wallpaper, Victorian chest and cane chairs. All spotlessly clean, perhaps too much so. By the time my friends returned from their breakfast (about 10 o'clock), their room had been tidied up and made ready for the next guests, which of course made them feel a bit unwanted.

Perfection is hard to come by at any price, but for a relatively high one I'd say the Old Vicarage comes pretty close. If you want a really special treat and fabulous food (and don't insist on an exclusively vegetarian place), then I would definitely recommend it. As they say in their brochure, 'Our aim is to offer first-class accommodation to a small number of guests with the accent on a relaxed and friendly atmosphere.' And that they do.

CATERING Traditional and vegetarian; vegan and other diets catered for. Licensed bar.

SMOKING Smoking restrictions.

PRICE CATEGORY Very High.

FURTHER INFORMATION The Old Vicarage,
Witherslack,
Grange-over-Sands,
Cumbria LA11 6RS
Phone (044 852) 381

49. Orchard House

Orchard House is somewhat unprepossessing from the outside, a typical back street guesthouse sandwiched between two car parks. But it is in Keswick, which means it has to be special. From all rooms at the back of the house (including the bathroom) and the garden, there are spectacular views looking out to Derwentwater and Causey Pike.

Orchard House was owned and run for many years by the legendary (to me) Monty Alge and Keong Wee. A hard act to follow for Australians Paul and Wendy Steele, who have only been there a short time, but they're working on it.

The interior of the house is nice: the hall painted with bright yellow trim, a capricious collection of artwork on the walls (paintings, drawings, plates, an oriental rug). A special luxury is having two separate guestrooms, one for watching TV, the other for reading and looking at the view. There is an interesting library, too, mostly books about the Lakes, nature and health. The dining room is in the basement, small but with a good view out of the back. Apparently there are plans to enlarge it in order to accommodate extra guests for evening meals. A good idea: how about a glassed-in patio area? Our bedroom (with a view) was well worth the £1 extra, especially as we chose a night with a tomato-coloured sunset. It was clean, the bed fairly firm and it had an electric blanket – though watch out, it was live!

Orchard House is exclusively vegetarian. To start, there was a carrot and orange soup followed by a mushroom quiche – both delicious. Then there was an onion loaf, which was not – soggy, plodgy bread stuffing with onion sauce. But then why have two main courses anyway? It seemed unnecessary, especially as the quiche was so good. Perhaps they like providing a vegan alternative; a good idea, but if so it would have been improved by the addition of some more interesting/healthy ingredients, like nuts. The beansprout salad was refreshing and complementary. The dessert – pink jelly trifle – was too sweet and fussy, though the sherry at the bottom was nice. One of our dinner mates (meals are semi-communal, three tables are shared), looking suspiciously at her quivering pud, asked Paul if it was made with gelatin. He drew himself up smartly and replied, 'Certainly not, it's agar-agar. It is my trade, you know.' Quite right too.

After dinner, we walked part of the way round the moonlit lake and then back for a quiet browse in their library, a hot bath (bathroom on the floor below our bedroom, but toilet and shower on our floor) and then up to our attic nest, where we stood for some time gazing at the shimmering water and lowering Causey Pike.

Breakfast was hearty and good: cooked fruits (apples, prunes and pears), yoghurt, muesli, Granola, wholewheat toast plus an assortment of jam and honey. The best possible breakfast short of homemade bread and yoghurt.

All in all, a satisfying stay. Paul and Wendy may not have Monty and Keong's colour (not many would) and the food may not be perfect, but their friendliness and a good line in teasing wit (that's Paul) go a long way towards putting people at their ease. They are also firmly smoke-free. 'Yes,' said Paul, 'we have a special smoking room. It's called the great outdoors.' All that and the location should ensure their ongoing success.

CATERING Exclusively vegetarian and vegan; other diets catered for.

SMOKING No smoking.

PRICE CATEGORY High

FURTHER INFORMATION Paul and Wendy Steele,
Orchard House,
Borrowdale Road,
Keswick, Cumbria CA12 5DE
Phone (0596) 72830

50. SKADI – Women's Walking Holidays Among Northern Hills

It was with some apprehension, most admitted later, that eight women met in a small village in Wharfedale to begin a week's walking holiday in the Yorkshire Dales. However, blessed with the hottest week of the summer, we had a highly entertaining holiday enjoyed immensely by all including our excellent organiser, Paula Day.

With the exception of two northerners most women were from London and had not stayed before in the Dales. However, by the end of the week we had walked a large part of Upper Wharfedale and the area on the map had become very familiar. As our week was graded as 'gentle walking', the emphasis was on rambles in the valleys or along moorland tracks which gave fine views over the surrounding area. We walked through lush meadows golden with buttercups and full of enough wild flowers and birdlife to excite the curiosity of the botanists and ornithologists in the party. We walked approximately 10 miles each day, though at a fairly leisurely pace with stops for dips, accompanied by much laughter, in the rivers and pools along the paths. Most days we did circular walks whilst at other times, by the judicious use of cars, we walked from one area to another providing a range of contrast in scenery and vegetation. Sometimes women chose to walk alone, meeting up with the main party at lunchtime and at the end of the walk. The walks were all led by Paula, who knew the area intimately, and we had much fun each evening choosing the following day's walk from among the many options she offered.

We stayed in an isolated seventeenth-century farmhouse which had beautiful views over typical Dales country. The house had cool, flagged floors and, though the accommodation was simple, it was comfortably furnished. There were three shared bedrooms with comfortable beds; blankets were provided but we had to take our own sheets or sleeping bag. There was one main living room with a comprehensive supply of books to cater for everyone's taste. Our evenings were spent round a blazing log fire with people reading, participating in animated discussions or, for those feeling the effect of the day's exertion, simply dozing in the warmth.

We had ample breakfasts of muesli, cereals, toast and fruit and were given a simple packed lunch to take on each day's walk. Most lunch stops, however, managed to coincide with a pub and we often squeezed in the odd afternoon cream tea to reward ourselves at the end of the walk! The evening meals were excellent, prepared solely by Paula whilst the rest of the party took baths, cups of tea or lay outside catching the last of the day's sunshine. We had a wide variety of vegetarian meals always accompanied by plentiful fresh salads and with a lovely dessert to follow. We took it in turns to wash up and clear away afterwards which seemed a small chore after the excellent meal.

Every aspect of the holiday ran smoothly due, in no small part, to Paula's efficient, calm approach. We had lively discussions and much laughter which was a lovely tonic in these somewhat serious times. To walk each day in the unhurried countryside with a group of friendly and interesting women and to be looked after in every way all contributed to an extremely enjoyable holiday.

Paula also organises more strenuous holidays, walking tours

(coast-to-coast, Dalesway, etc) staying at guesthouses en route, and runs weekend groups on the use of map and compass.

From spring 1987 most holidays will be based at Paula's new home, a purpose-designed barn conversion overlooking the beautiful Howgill Fells, within easy reach of both the Lake District and the Yorkshire Dales. M.J.

CATERING Exclusively vegetarian.

SMOKING Smoking restrictions.

PRICE CATEGORY Not applicable.

FURTHER INFORMATION Paula Day,
High Grassrigg Barn
Killington
Sedbergh, Cumbria LA10 5EN

Other Places to Stay

CHESHIRE

Chester:
Phone (0244) 383935
XV, B & B only.

Frodsham: Beechmill House, Bradley
Phone (0928) 33590
XV[?] small guesthouse; also Wholehealth Cookery and Nutrition School. See Chapter X.

CUMBRIA

Ambleside: Vegetarian Corner House, 14 Loughrigg Meadow
Phone (0966) 33142
XV, NS, B & B only. Price category VL.

Crooklands nr Milnthorpe: Loop Cottage
Phone (04487) 335

XV, NS, B & B + EM by arrangement. Hopes to do courses on painting, writing and dance. Price category VL.

Dent:
Phone (058 75) 439
XV, B & B only, own free-range eggs. Price category VL.

Nr Keswick: Sue Irving, 1 Crown Cottages, Braithwaite
Phone (0596) 82519
V-T, B & B only. Price category VL.

Keswick: Nutmegs, 48 St John St
Phone (0596) 74491
XV, B & B only. Price category L.

Nr Sawrey: 'Beechmount', Nr Sawrey, Ambleside
Phone (096 66) 356
XV/Vgn, B & B only.

Nr Penrith: Nunnery House, Staffield
Phone (076883) 537
T-V (prop recently won prize for vegetarian dinner menu). Eighteenth-century country house, Eden Valley.

ISLE OF MAN

Laxey: Glen Hotel
Phone (0624) 781230
T-V. Say they are 'the only vegetarian hotel/restaurant on the island', but are not XV.

Port Erin: Regent House
Phone (0624) 833454
T-V. 'Small friendly guesthouse overlooking bay.'

GREATER MANCHESTER

Chorlton-cum-Hardy: The Chalet, 58 High Lane
Phone 061–881 1788
XV/Vgn B & B + EM by arr or self-catering (self-contained chalet). Price category VL.

Manchester:
Phone 061–224 2551
XV, B & B + EM opt, home near university.

Places to Eat

CHESHIRE

Altrincham: Nutcracker (XV), 43 Oxford Rd. Phone 061–928 4399.

Chester: Abbey Green Restaurant (XV), 2 Abbey Green. Phone (0244) 319413.

CUMBRIA

Ambleside: Harvest Vegetarian Restaurant (XV), Compston Rd. Phone (0966) 33151.

Ambleside: Zeffirelli's, Compston Rd (XV). Phone (0966) 33845.

Bowness-on-Windermere: Hedgerow Vegetarian Restaurant (XV), Lake Rd. Phone (096 62) 5002.

Cockermouth: Quince and Medlar Fine Food Vegetarian Restaurant (XV), Castle Gate. Phone (0900) 823579.

Nr Grange-over-Sands: The Old Vicarage (*T-V, but prop V*), Church Rd, Witherslack. Phone (044852) 381. *See review.*

Grasmere: Lancrigg Vegetarian Country House Hotel (XV), Easedale. Phone (09665) 317 *See review.*

Kendal: Waterside Wholefoods (XV), Kent View. Phone (0539) 29743.

Keswick: Maysons Wholefood Restaurant (V-T), 33 Lake Rd. Phone (0596) 74104.

Keswick: Orchard House (XV), Borrowdale Rd. Phone (0596) 72830. *See review.*

Melmerby, nr Penrith: The Village Bakery (T-V). Phone (0768) 68515.

LANCASHIRE

Blackburn: Lovin' Spoonful (XV), 76 King William St. Phone (0254) 675505.

Blackpool: Nibbles Vegetarian Restaurant (XV), 14a Milbourne St. Phone (0253) 25337.

Lancaster: Libra (XV), 19 Brock St. Phone (0524) 61551.

Oldham: The Alternative (prop V), 103 Union St. Phone 061–624 0850.

Preston: Cornucopia Restaurant (XV), 33 Cannon St. No phone.

GREATER MANCHESTER

Ashton-under-Lyne: The Sunflower (XV), 153 Old St. Phone 061–339 3332.

Manchester: Greenhouse Licensed Vegetarian Café (XV), 331 Gt Western St, Rusholme. Phone 061–224 0730.

Manchester: On the 8th Day (XV), 111 Oxford Rd, All Saints. Phone 061–273 4878.

Stockport: Coconut Willy's (XV), 37 St Petersgate. Phone 061–480 7013.

MERSEYSIDE:

Liverpool: Carrageen (XV), Myrtle Parade. No phone.

VI
SOUTH WALES AND BORDERS

Dyfed, Gwent, Glamorgan, Gloucestershire (*Forest of Dean*)

The fact that at its southern end the national boundary runs down the middle of the River Wye is perfectly intelligible to historians with an eye to military strategy. Travelling vegetarians, however, may not care quite so much whether their feet are on English or Welsh soil, and for their convenience, not to mention international amity, we have included the Forest of Dean in this section. As far as places to stay are concerned, there are two marked clusters, one centred on the Wye Valley and the other in Pembrokeshire. Outside these two areas, the university towns of Cardiff, Swansea and Aberystwyth provide virtually the only opportunities for a vegetarian meal.

Places Reviewed

51. Castle View Hotel, Chepstow, Gwent
52. Duneside Guest House, Penally, Nr Tenby, Dyfed
53. The Nurtons, Tintern, Nr Chepstow, Gwent (XV)
54. The Old Brewery House, Redbrook, Forest of Dean, Glos (XV)
55. Old Dolphin, Angle, Dyfed (XV)
56. River View, Llanbadoc, Usk, Gwent (XVgn)
57. Springstone Studios, Llandyfaelog, Nr Cidwelli, Dyfed (XV)
58. Tregynon Farmhouse, Pontfaen, Nr Fishguard, Dyfed

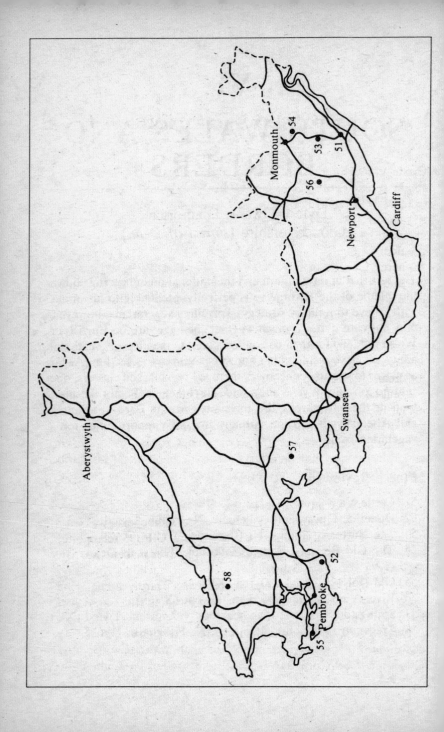

51. Castle View Hotel

Castle View Hotel (AA**RAC, Egon Ronay, Les Routiers, etc) claims to cater for vegetarians. So do many hotels these days. I exaggerate, of course. They do have a completely separate vegetarian menu, but separate, as any American will tell you, does not mean equal. Their non-veggie menu, by the way, starts off with shoulder of boar.

There's a surprisingly good choice of vegetarian dishes, including aubergine and nut crumble, mung bean curry, stuffed vine leaves, Gloucester and chive lasagna. The crumble was quite good though, like everything else on the menu, probably came out of the deep freeze. The desserts (I didn't partake) were uniformly rich, sweet and unwholesome looking: trifle with cream, gâteau with cream, ice cream with cream, apple pie with cream. Anyone for cream with cream?

Breakfast was more of a comedown. They had no idea what it meant to be vegan, since I was given cow's milk and butter pats and offered eggs, which I refused. Cornflakes and Weetabix followed by burnt white toast was about it; no fruit, vegan margarine or soya milk on offer. I asked for wholewheat toast and was told, 'We usually serve brown bread for breakfast, madam, but I'm afraid we've run out.'

Castle Park is an 'executive' hotel. This means it has many 'facilities'. My bedroom, for example – a dark shoebox – was over equipped with wall-mounted hairdryer and G.P.O. telephone, shower and toilet cubicles, fluorescent light over makeup mirror, and huge TV. Two ashtrays. Tea-making 'facilities' included eighteen packets of sugar and no tea bags. Hardly a charming room, to say the least, even if the lace curtains and carpet had been less dingy.

Castle View makes grandiose claims to eighteenth-century charm, history, personal attention, and so on, which in my opinion it does not live up to. It may be interesting to think its stones might

171

have come from Chepstow Castle, but that doesn't alter the fact that it is dark, airless and smokey; that it's next to the noisiest pub in town; that it plays non-stop wallpaper music, that it's deathly expensive, and that even to call it Castle View is stretching a point; Castle *Car Park* View Hotel would be more accurate, perhaps.

It's the kind of place where your host calls you 'sir' or 'madam' with Jeevesian irony. It also struck me as the kind of place which does not trust women on their own not to get drunk and make a spectacle of themselves. I was seated in the darkest, furthest corner of the back dining room. I was not offered the wine list, though our host bowed and scraped at the next table ('Any luck, *sir*?'). When I accidentally locked my key in my room, I was treated as if I'd committed a sin. I offered to unlock it myself, to which my host replied in his oiliest and most supercilious tones, 'We cannot allow you to take the master key, *madam*, for obvious reasons.'

And so it is for obvious reasons that I cannot recommend the Castle View Hotel to vegetarians, and certainly not to vegans. But do by all means visit Chepstow. It's a lovely town and the castle is splendid.

CATERING Traditional and vegetarian. Licensed bar.

SMOKING Allowed.

PRICE CATEGORY Very Very High.

FURTHER INFORMATION Mervyn and Lucia Gillett,
Castle View Hotel,
Bridge Street,
Chepstow, Gwent, Wales NP6 5EZ
Phone (02912) 70349

52. Duneside Guest House

This is a difficult entry to write, for reasons that will become clear. First of all, South Pembrokeshire is a lovely place, though not as lovely as when I visited it as a child, which may partly explain my discontent, and it would be a lot lovelier and more accessible without the caravans and the Army. And although Tenby in the summer is an appalling mess of seaside-tripper junk, it's still a spectacular town with its medieval walls and gates, still-functioning fishing harbour and decaying Georgian and Victorian houses perched on the cliffs above its huge sandy beach. You might well be tempted by the village of Penally, a mile away across the golf course – and Wales' largest caravan site – with its handsome villas in big gardens and an air of respectable solidity and peace. Closer inspection reveals, alas, first that the charming-looking pub has a concrete garden; secondly, that someone has built a giant shed at the edge of the village which looks like a hypermarket but is actually a nightclub; and thirdly, that Duneside is not one of the said villas but an example of interwar bypass architecture.

This wouldn't be so bad in itself. The road is quiet and Duneside is out of earshot of the nightclub; the back rooms look out over a little garden to open fields and the dunes of the golf course; and the sounds of the Army machine guns from the rifle range by the coast are, I suppose, no more horrible than anywhere else within 5 miles. The inside is, however, another story. How to make it clear without cruelty? Well . . . The house was not clean: no one had run a vacuum cleaner over our bedroom floor, even a sponge over the basin, for a good while past, let alone done more radical cleaning. The sheets *were* clean, but the fact that it occurred to me to wonder seriously tells you a lot. There were no towels. The dining room, on the other hand, is a pleasant, airy room looking out over the flowery front garden; and there's a small guest's sitting room with lots of local maps, guides and leaflets.

The food was something else again. I suppose that vegetarian places, even the bad ones, had unconsciously spoiled me more than I'd been aware. Not everyone in this book is a good cook, and there have been a lot of complaints; but I don't think any others provided a meal that came almost exclusively from packets and tins. Packet soup and white bread, cauliflower and packet cheese sauce, tinned potatoes, tinned peas, and for pudding a sugary pink concoction whose contents owed everything to technology and nothing to nature. This is, I now realise, the place that demonstrates by its absence that the stick-on label 'wholefood' actually means something. As for breakfast, I can't say because we left before that, but Roger Pattinson, Duneside's proprietor, pressed a vast bag of rehydrated dried fruit into our hands, which was very nice of him, and made up for quite a lot.

Now this is the difficult bit. First of all, Roger was much preoccupied by a friend's illness, which was taking up both his time and his energy, and he told us apologetically that he normally did more for evening meals. Perhaps that's so, but the whole experience was, to put it mildly, not confidence-inspiring. In any case, Roger is a teacher; this was the summer holidays, but during term time he must be equally distracted from his B & B, which is a lot of work for one person. I really can't imagine, even with a lot more time, Roger radically transforming Duneside into a place that I'd ever want to visit again. It isn't, you understand, that I felt angry or ripped off, unlike some places in this book: just plain miserable and sad for Roger. It all seems a bit much for him, though his heart is obviously in the right place. By the way, Roger is himself vegetarian, but Duneside is not exclusive. And there were some complimentary remarks in the visitors' book. But I'm afraid my advice would be to stay at the Dolphin House in Angle, and visit Tenby for the day. O.F.

CATERING Traditional and vegetarian.

SMOKING Smoking restrictions.

PRICE CATEGORY Very Low.

FURTHER INFORMATION Roger Pattinson,
Duneside Guest House,
Penally,
Tenby, Pembrokeshire,
Dyfed, Wales SA70 7PE
Phone (0834) 3365/2249

53. The Nurtons

It seems faintly irreverent to sit down and comment on The Nurtons. I'm not sure if it is (they are?) really more of an institution than other veggie guesthouses, or if I just happened to hear of it from veggie friends long before I became one myself. But it's certainly been going for a very long time and has that unmistakable feeling of make-yourself-at-home and take-it-or-leave-it self-confidence. Quite right too. In anyone's book it deserves a gold star.

The Nurtons is in the Wye Valley, halfway up the hill opposite Tintern railway station (now a museum – don't try to get a train there); so within 15–20 minutes' walk of Tintern village if you hurry, and with a lovely view from its hillside down the wooded curves of the valley. After I arrived I climbed up through the huge apple orchard and sat in a field watching the rabbits (for whom the Nurtons' jungley edges are a perfect refuge and I daresay the Nurtons' organic lettuces are a dietary staple) fooling around on the grass, and admired a perfect view of the abbey framed between the trees below. Walks abound: Offa's Dyke for the serious, the Wye Valley walk for the businesslike, and tons of footpaths for the rest of us. Or of course canoeing, pony trekking, cycling, castle-hunting, craftspeople visiting, or anything you fancy in the Forest of Dean or Gwent. And you're within 40 minutes' drive of Bristol, Gloucester, Newport or Cardiff.

But I think I'd just put my feet up, with an occasional stroll around the policies or down to the village, except that some exercise is essential to make room for all that lovely food. The

Nurtons is an organic smallholding, with five or six people working on it. When I was there in June it was a real pleasure to potter around in the huge, rambling gardens, where the ornamental areas merge into a huge herb garden, a paddock (two elegant horses, one properly melancholy donkey) and acres of fruit and vegetable garden, all separated by innumerable rows of comfrey (there's enough to keep the whole of the British Isles in tea and poultices) and leaping out of a wild green jungle of friendly weeds. It looks – and tastes – unbelievably rich and fertile, more like a French smallholding than an English one. Some very green thumbs work here.

The Nurtons is a three-generation enterprise. It was founded about 25 years ago by Harold Wood, now eighty but still a tennis champion I'm told. I found him digging in a corner of the garden, stripped to his underpants, like an elderly Pan. His son and daughter, Adrian and Elsa, also live in the house and do much of the gardening for sale, though Adrian also works for the Gwent Conservation Trust. Then there are David and Jo, no relations, who manage the guesthouse part as well as working outside. David welcomes you, waits on tables and does the upfront part: Jo is the disembodied voice and talent in the kitchen. There are also other inhabitants – a number of cats and one or two anonymous children.

The food really was magical. Dinner started with corn on the cob (their own, last year's from the freezer), a little tough but very good. The main course was deep-fried cheese and walnut balls with a pureed tomato–onion–tamari sauce 'in case they were dry', mashed potatoes (not a lump: an elegant little pottery dish) and then – the real *pièce de resistance* for me – broad beans fresh from the garden, cooked with a little spring cabbage, and tossed in butter and chopped fennel fronds. Superb. It all arrived, beautifully presented, on a separate serving dish, and I made a complete pig of myself, washing it down with delicious water from the spring behind the house. Then two salads: one with carrot chunks, tomato, apple, raisin and hard-boiled egg; the other of lettuce, cucumber and wild garlic flowers. Again, both looked and tasted superb. And to finish, the first strawberries of the year, picked 10 minutes earlier. Absolutely divine, though served with rather sweet ice cream. To round it off, lemon balm tea, made with a sprig out of the garden. I refused cheese.

The house is strange. Outside it's a kind of semi-battlemented Victorian two-bay house, with an absurd porch and a large circular-stone trough in the middle of a tiny circle outside under a huge copper beech. There are a series of grass terraces, one doubling as a croquet lawn; with benches to sit on and gaze at the view or smile and sniff at the sometimes quite exotic flowers, and little woody paths leading to other bits of the garden or orchard. Off at the back and to the sides are a series of rather tumbledown sheds, which seem to be slowly turning into living or studio spaces; and there's a splendidly rich and decaying conservatory with begonias and a huge vine. Inside, the house is a bit of a mixture: a huge bare, tiled hall ornamented with a giant Ordnance Survey map, a long drawing room ending in a bay with the view, and with a nice Victorian fireplace, but spoiled by a horrid carpet and rows of ugly chairs and a bare lightbulb. There's a big collection of mostly spiritualist books, but also some on wildlife; and a special bookshelf with copies (for sale) of the collected works of Alice A. Bailey, she of the Esoteric Knowledge. The dining room is sparser, but pleasantly so: if you sit in the window you can gaze out down the valley past the copper beech and across to a spectacular bluebell field a mile away above the Abbey. There is a back room, rather dark but friendly, with a huge fireplace with woodburning stove, black and white TV, books, maps, guides, etc, a piano and a fridge and kettle – help yourself anytime to drinks (instant coffee, barleycup, decaf, tea, herb tea, etc); also snacks for sale. Dark but probably cosy in the winter. The family wander in and out; the night I was there Jo was ironing (!) what looked like fifty sheets. My bedroom, a skinny room above the hall, had two comfortable beds (good mattress, cotton sheets, down pillows) but weird decor: red bed ruffles, green carpet, red and blue eiderdowns and curtains, mauve wash basin. The doors, nice Victorian on one side, have been fitted with fire-regulation panelling. There are lots of bathrooms and toilets, generally in 1950s primrose. The electric shower is at dwarf's height and swings away to point into the corner unless you hold it in place. Never mind; I didn't feel any of it mattered. As Elsa Wood said when a couple turned up on spec, saying the Wye Valley Hotel wasn't good enough for them (they fled at the mere mention of a vegetarian breakfast), 'People who want every mod. con. shouldn't come and stay here.' And if the decor seems weird, it's not active bad taste; it's just that other things – like the outdoors – seem more important, and someone with taste certainly makes up for it with lovely flowers in every room.

Talking of vegetarian breakfasts, it too was special: homemade apple juice and a grapefruit, a sideboard full of bowls containing stewed apricots (I was asked the night before what was my favourite stewed fruit), oat flakes, toasted wheat flakes, Granola, freshly toasted coconut and sunflower seeds, cashews and homemade yoghurt, toast from homemade bread, with Nurtons' own honey, and so on. Tea, coffee, barleycup, etc.

In sum, a place to dream, to work (I did, a little, very agreeably), to stroll, to grow fat, and to relax. In other years, they've done local interest courses – botany, wildlife, archaeology, gardening – but the wet summer of 1985 put a stop to such enterprise, so they're now sticking to their staple of yoga courses (though if you can find enough people, they'll still arrange a course on almost anything for you). But you don't need a course as an excuse. Go and enjoy. O.F.

CATERING Exclusively vegetarian; vegans catered for.

SMOKING Smoking restrictions.

PRICE CATEGORY Low.

FURTHER INFORMATION The Nurtons,
Tintern,
Gwent, Wales
Phone (029 18) 253

54. The Old Brewery House

The Old Brewery House is one of the places I want to re-visit. It's on the edge of the village of Redbrook which is about 7 miles from Tintern in the Wye Valley, just at the border of Gwent and Gloucestershire. It's set slightly up from the main road, overlooking the Wye to the front and the steep Forest of Dean hills to the rear. The house was originally an old brewery which has been completely and lovingly renovated, painted white and simply but prettily decorated with nice fabrics, pine furniture, wood-burning stove, plants, and so on. It's lovely to look at both inside and out, is set in a scenic area with lots to do, serves gorgeous food and is reasonably priced, and – what makes it all so special – is run by Ms Avril Lord, a super, loving, caring person and talented cook.

I arrived at the Old Brewery at 5 p.m. one day in early June feeling tired and strained from travelling; I quickly recovered on seeing the house and meeting Avril. After a restoring bath (I couldn't make the electric shower work) I sat with a book on the grass in the upper back garden under a full flowering quince tree, while mouth-watering cooking smells wafted up from the kitchen.

Dinner was very special, a real culinary delight, though I fear my limited 'stoneage' diet cramped Avril's style. Not that I could tell; she is one of those really talented cooks who make food look, taste and feel good. First a choice of fried tofu with cress and orange slices, or lentil and lemon soup. I had the tofu and orange, which was a wonderful combination. There were wholewheat rolls or homemade cheese scones for those who could indulge; at other times there might be corn tamales from a recipe she got from a Californian who lives in the Napa Valley. Then there was a main dish of black-eyed beans with red peppers, served with bulghur wheat and yoghurt. Avril made me a special dish of hummus, which was the creamiest and best tasting I have ever had, plus new potatoes with homemade mayonnaise and parsley (she was afraid I didn't have enough to eat!). Then a salad of lettuce and spinach with fresh thyme and chervil. Dessert was a choice of hunza apricot and tofu whip, rhubarb and pear crumble with cream, or fruit and cheese. I had the latter: the fruit was lovingly cut up and presented and the cheese included a spectacularly fine Cheddar. On each table were individual bottles of Perrier water. Coffee I saw from my neighbours' table was real and served in a gold-topped cafetiere. I had a choice of herb teas.

After dinner I walked up the steep hill and onto the Offa's Dyke trail. It was one of those rare, warm, early summer nights. After a mile or so I came to the top of a rise and a lookout point where I could watch the sunset over the Black Mountains; a huge, red tomato plopping down such as I have not seen since California. I returned to my room feeling tired but very relaxed and well pleased with the world. My bedroom was a dream: very small, twin-bedded, at the back of the house and tucked under the eaves, painted white and with a lovely triangular skylight window looking straight up the hill. I sat on my bed, reading, enjoying the fresh, pale-blue cotton duvet and pillows, the rosy summer light and the sound of the millrace. I have never slept better.

Morning brought rain, a log fire in the wood-burning stove, and breakfast: juice, a choice of muesli or other healthy-type cereals, rhubarb and stewed apple (their own), followed by a cooked breakfast of tofu, mushrooms and potatoes, plus thick slices of wholewheat bread, toasted or not, from an organic bakery in Bristol, or Avril's cheese scones or, sometimes, corn muffins or other baked goodies. Yoghurt and real coffee. Because of my diet I had a special treat of last night's dessert: hunza apricot, tofu and honey whip, which was out of this world, and soya milk.

After breakfast I spent some time chatting with Avril, while she cradled her weak nineteen-year-old cat in her arms. (She had been treating him homeopathically for a face tumour, with some success.) We talked about diets and the feasibility of running an all-veggie guesthouse. At first they weren't sure a single soul would come through the door – so to be on the safe side they described themselves as 'Traditional and Vegetarian' – but it's now clear that they can go exclusive. They're planning new brochures (for 1986–7) to say so – hurrah! They're also experimenting with a variety of women-only weekends. Write for more information.

Go – for a gourmet vegetarian treat and a cosy, friendly stay any time of the year. They rent canoes and cycles. And don't forget winter is a special time in the Forest of Dean. Last year they had a solid month of perfect cross-country skiing, with blue skies and sunshine galore. And they rent skiis too. I shall certainly go myself.

CATERING Exclusively vegetarian; vegan and other diets catered for.

SMOKING No smoking.

PRICE CATEGORY Low.

FURTHER INFORMATION Ms Avril Lord,
Old Brewery House,
Redbrook, Forest of Dean
Phone (0600) 2569

55. Old Dolphin

The Old Dolphin is a double cottage, recently renovated and redecorated, on the main street of a tiny village on the far west coast of Wales in Dyfed. The back of the house and garden look out onto Angle Bay – very peaceful and picturesque but for the refineries and power station which lower and dominate the scene – though fortunately you don't see them from the house. It's a composite of two former dwellings – seventeenth and eighteenth century cottages; more recently one of them was a pub. It must have taken a great deal of vision to effect the transformation: rather unprepossessing on the outside, the inside is very nice indeed, especially the Shaws' half. The guests' half consists, downstairs, of a small living/sitting room with its own kitchenette, from which Mrs Shaw served (though did not cook) our meals, and a bathroom; and upstairs, the bedrooms.

Our bedroom, which looked out onto the bay, was gracious and comfortable, white-painted, with a high oak bed made up with fine cotton sheets and a warm but light duvet; just as I imagine the old feather beds must have felt like. The downstairs bathroom though perhaps inconveniently far away for some was spick and span, with thick towels and cork-tiled walls. The sitting/dining room was less charming than the bedroom; rather minimal and dominated by a large telly. A peek through to the Shaws' half revealed colour, music, wood-burning stove, books, stone hearth, and character galore. Silly, I suppose, to expect as much for guests, but the contrast was rather painful. But overall, I think, a fair amount of comfort and privacy.

Having had a drink in a fisherman's pub on the bay, we scurried back to our evening meal. There was delicious homemade bread, broccoli and potato soup, a sort of Mediterranean brown rice dish (cold) with roasted peeled peppers, black olives, walnuts and grapes. (I recall that the grapes were peeled but my companion says not.) In any case, it was one of those great taste treats – simple but magically delicious. The salad was an everlasting lettuce straight out of the garden, nicely oiled and garlicked. Dessert was a gooseberry fool. Here I confess to having broken my vegan diet; I just couldn't resist it.

After dinner we strolled the length of the village to the sea and watched the sun setting behind the absurd, crenellated Thorn Hill Hotel, on its own island just off the coast. Then home along the Coastal Path to a luxurious hot bath and finally to sink into the feather-like bed. Almost too good to be true; the end, as they say, of a perfect day which began with Skomer Island in the warm sunshine among puffins and daisies. Then this peaceful haven and the Old Dolphin, with its charming proprietor and magnificent food. I slept well indeed.

Breakfast was equally good: grapefruit, super-muesli with banana chips, peanut butter, homemade toast, apple juice for the muesli, marmalade and tea. Along with breakfast came advice for a herbal hay fever remedy.

Pat Shaw is a very engaging character; the old saying 'bright as a button' really fits her. She not only treated us to one of the best dinners I have ever had but to lively and interesting conversation on subjects ranging from homeopathic medicine to music. She even produced a long-wave radio so I could listen to a World Service programme, though I fell asleep before it came on, lulled as I was by the wonderful bed.

Altogether a very special place; I wish I could have stayed longer.

CATERING Vegetarian and vegan; also traditional if requested.

SMOKING Smoking restrictions.

PRICE CATEGORY Very Low.

FURTHER INFORMATION Mrs Pat Shaw,
Old Dolphin,
66, Angle SA71 5AP
Wales
Phone (064 684) 295

56. River View

River View is one of the few-and-far-between vegan guesthouses. It's located just outside the town of Usk (No. 1 in this year's Wales in Bloom contest), about 10 miles from Newport, in the middle of Gwent. Although I've called it a guesthouse, it would be more accurate to call it a private home open to vegan visitors. The distinction can be easily blurred but in this case it is not: dining room, lounge and bathroom are all shared with the Bryans.

Joan Bryan and husband are extremely nice people; she a retired schoolteacher and he a gliding enthusiast. Joan devotes much of her time to gardening, but also teaches vegan cookery through adult education courses and local groups. The rest of the time she devotes to her family, practising the piano and catering for the odd visitor who comes to stay. She is, or was, an active member of the Vegetarian Society and it was they who encouraged her to offer meals and accommodation. Certainly a good idea; vegan guesthouses are not thick on the ground in that part of Wales.

Although River View itself was once a handsome stone house, it has been transformed into a nondescript two-storey dwelling, completely clad in pink pebbledash. And while there is a view of the Usk from the upstairs back bedrooms, there's none from the dining room or lounge, thanks to the Welsh Water Authority, who have built a huge concrete dyke, admittedly to keep the Usk from overflowing its banks and flooding the ground floor, which it used to do regularly.

The Bryans' taste is not mine: there are opaque glass sliding doors with hand-painted donkeys and photographic Alpine murals grace the upstairs yellow-painted hallway. It is a neat and tidy house but full of unnatural fabrics, polyester-mix sheets (perfumed), built-in wardrobes, mirrors in curlicue frames, and even (despite their passion for real plants) pink plastic flowers trailing above the bath. Their pride and joy – an exotic orchid kept alive by two mauve ultra-violet strip lights in the front hall – I'm afraid I found rather lurid and sinister. The shower cubicle was not welcoming, very cramped and dark. Though the house was warm (we were there on a muggy day in June), I suspect it could be quite cold and damp in winter among the river mists, especially since there's no central heating.

Dinner had been promised as 'a simple salad' but turned out to be a four-course spread. (We ate alone, Joan deciding to wait for her husband to return from gliding.) There was a thick lentil and onion soup to start – very filling and delicious – with wholemeal rolls. The main dish was a kidney bean and hazelnut roast, (specially bound with vegetarian gelatin instead of flour or breadcrumbs for wheat-intolerant me), accompanied by celery sticks and two salads: one sprouted chick peas and mung beans, the other lettuce, tomato, avocado, cauliflower and melon. Commercial salad cream, unfortunately, but that was unusual; Joan usually makes her own. Dessert was fresh fruit salad topped with vegetarian jelly. Café Hag or herb tea to drink.

After dinner we walked along the river footpath into Usk, a handsome, small, rural river town, distinguished by an ancient church and some very beautiful houses. Usk is apparently of considerable archaeological interest: the Bryans have a friend who has identified an early medieval street plan, and before that it was an important Roman settlement.

It was not a restorative night, to be honest. The bed was not comfortable and the room, even with one window open, was airless. After breakfast (muesli, soya milk, nuts, coconut, fresh fruit, homemade bread/toast and various nut butters and honey) we went for a short walk along the Usk Valley Trail. You can go as far as Abergavenny and beyond to the Black Mountains. The weather was rather grey and cheerless, but I think River View would be a pleasant place to stay in warm, sunny weather. It would be lovely to sit out on the back terrace overlooking the river, taking intermittent strolls along the River Trail, or long day hikes through friendly wooded countryside. All in all – if you don't find the set-up claustrophobic – a pleasant, simple place to stay, with very kind, friendly people as your hosts. And compassionately vegan, which is worth a lot.

CATERING Exclusively vegan; special diets catered for.

SMOKING Smoking not in evidence.

PRICE CATEGORY Very Low.

FURTHER INFORMATION Mrs Joan Bryan,
'River View',
Llanbadoc, Usk,
Wales
Phone (029 13) 2429

57. Springstone Studios

The ex-farmhouse perches (or, if you like, *nestles*, as they say in their brochure) high up a hillside of the Gwendraeth Valley, south of Carmarthen in West Wales, remote and bleak among the marching power pylons. It is not easy to find. After about an hour of wandering up hill and down dale (looking for a non-existent sign from Ann Dobson's directions), I asked a farmer who pointed out the way: a rutted, muddy, deeply dung-covered track which grew terrifyingly more narrow and overgrown by the second. But take heart, determined guest. As Ann said, 'Oh, we've had all kinds of cars up here; we're a lot more accessible than most of our friends.' In that case, I hope her friends do not hope to attract too many paying guests.

The house has enormous, rather unlovely rooms, little effort having been made to decorate or furnish them. The guests' lounge is big, square and minimally furnished in second-hand style, with a library consisting almost entirely of Michael Moorcock and other mystical tomes, though there were a number of tourist brochures of the area. It was not a cosy room even in summer. I don't think there was an open fireplace and certainly no central heating, so beware in cold or damp weather. My bedroom was equally large and uncluttered, but the bed was tortuous, with its nylon sheets over a wool blanket and dingy bedspread. There was no reading light. No towel was provided (fortunately I'd brought my own), though I daresay that was an oversight. There's no shower, but there was plenty of hot water for a bath.

But on to the good news about Springstone – its food. Ann Dobson, its rock musician/organic gardener proprietress, is an extremely nice, sincere, earnest and enthusiastic person, who caters magnificently for her guests, food-wise. She has only been gardening for two years but has already wrought miracles: the sweet corn, for example, which she grew last year and froze, was as good as Pennsylvania white corn, and that's saying something. She makes her own bread, goat's milk cheese, yoghurt, sweets and so on. The food was really wonderful, and she will cope with almost any diet around (including, recently, a raw food freak from California). When I arrived, I was given tea and a delicious chewy vegan cake. For dinner there was egg mayonnaise made with very free-range eggs and homemade mayo (which didn't quite liaise, but never mind), a brown rice main course, chock full of garden peas and sweet corn, mushrooms and peppers (very simple and utterly delicious), a salad with more garden vegetables and the best lettuce I have ever tasted. Dessert was a bowl of strawberries from the garden – again, beautiful and simple. Then tea. Breakfast was equally wonderful, original and aesthetically pleasing: dense and delicious homemade bread, little ceramic pots of homemade jam, honey and peanut butter; muesli and homemade yoghurt. Ann was eager to make a cooked breakfast of eggs and tomatoes and mushrooms, or a vegan cooked soya burger. If anything, there was too much food; but so good that you don't feel stuffed.

By the time I left I was feeling much more friendly towards Springstone; that is, towards Ann and her wonderful, healthy, pure food. Even the house took on a kind of romantic, isolated magic, and its lack of creature comforts seemed less damning; indeed, unnecessary. It will certainly not be to everyone's taste. But I do recommend it for those who like remoteness, even wildness, rough tracks, simplicity, perfectly luscious organic food in quantity and the distant sound of rock music in the evening.

P.S. A word of warning: watch where you park your car. Put it inside the gates if you can find room behind their Land-Rovers. I parked mine outside the gate and found in the morning that the aerial had been snapped off by an over-excited cow. The repair bill greatly increased an otherwise very inexpensive stay.

Also, make sure to get a map and up-to-date instructions on how to find them.

CATERING Exclusively vegetarian; vegan and other diets catered for.

SMOKING No known rules.

PRICE CATEGORY Very Low.

FURTHER INFORMATION Ann Dobson,
Springstone Studios (Ffynnon Eiddon),
Llandyfaelog,
Kidwelly, Dyfed,
Wales
Phone (0269) 861256

58. Tregynon Farmhouse

Tregynon Farmhouse hardly needs my two pence worth of praise – it has received the Welsh Farm Holiday Guide Award, the Wales Tourist Board Farmhouse Award, and the Vegetarian 3 Star Award (self-awarded) – but I will give it anyway.

I did not actually stay at Tregynon; that is, I was not able to, since they were booked solid for six months. I did manage a meal there, however, including a leisurely drink beforehand and a chat with the proprietor afterwards, so I can risk comment. As far as the food was concerned, it was one of the best meals I have ever had. I had learned earlier in the day that the vegetarian main dish would be stuffed pancakes and my heart sank at the thought of the usual thick, congealing mess. It was nothing like that, but a lacy-thin eggy crêpe stuffed with ricotta cheese, walnuts, onions, celery, and mushrooms in a quiet tomato puree. A *liaison parfaite*, as François Couperin once said: it really did melt in the mouth. Vegetables were equally heavenly: tiny baby sugar peas, broccoli from the garden, out-of-the-ordinary mashed potatoes (with garlic and spices). Dessert was a cinnamon and yoghurt cake with a lemon yoghurt sauce – beautiful. My father-in-law, who is practically Dracula-like around garlic and dreads yoghurt equally, had second helpings of both.

Breakfast must be an equally satisfying occasion for the vegetarian or vegan, or for that matter the fruitarian, nutarian, macrobiotic . . . whatever. Peter Heard told us about a guest who was allergic to piped water, gluten, and all dairy and animal products, yet they coped. Sheila's bread was specially baked, all water and juices were made with their own spring water. After her, I should think vegans are a snip.

Peter Heard (Sheila is the magician in the kitchen) is a very competent manager, perhaps even a perfectionist; in any case, he obviously likes to see things work out. He did his best to accommodate us at a neighbour's house down the road and made room for our party of six in the dining room. It's no surprise that

Tregynon (praise runneth all over their visitors' book) is thriving when other places are just scraping by.

On the basis of the downstairs and the general care and taste with which things are done there, I suppose the bedrooms are comfortable and pretty. The house is not large and that could be a problem, especially during cold, rainy weeks when everyone wants to sit around the fire. The lounge is a lovely room but the ceilings are very low. If all the guests decided to stay in at one time, it could become a bit claustrophobic. Happily, smoking is discouraged.

As its luscious advertisements tell us, Tregynon is set idyllically in the foothills of the Preseli Mountains. As mountains – even Welsh mountains – go, the Preselis are not large but they are very beautiful. Tregynon performed a classic piece of magic for us: we drove up into clouds from Haverfordwest higher and wetter through ever-narrower lanes; then suddenly, as we arrived on the doorstep where we were greeted by ducks and goats, the mist parted, revealing a glorious panorama of hills, woods and crazily-sloping fields. You can walk on the hills, through the valleys, or down to the sea (4 miles for crows, a bit further for people) and then along the coast path. Lots of west and central Wales towns and other attractions within an easy drive.

Of course there is the sad fact that Tregynon is not exclusively vegetarian. Although Peter claims likeminded people tend by some mystical process to book simultaneously, there must always be the chance of having to co-exist and dine with omnivores. It would be perfection, of course, if it were exclusive, but alas it isn't; and I don't think they have any such ambitions. They simply like taking good care of everybody. Still and all (and I rarely feel this about a place which isn't exclusive), I felt very relaxed and satisfied there; it is certainly a gourmet vegetarian's dream. I plan to go for a weekend as soon as I can get a booking. Be advised: they are usually booked up six months in advance, except for one week in August. Unless you want to try to divine which week, I suggest you book now.

CATERING Traditional and vegetarian; vegan and other diets catered for. Licensed.

SMOKING Smoking restrictions.

PRICE CATEGORY Low to Medium.

FURTHER INFORMATION Sheila and Peter Heard,
Tregynon Farmhouse,
Pontfaen, Nr Fishguard,
Pembs SA65 9TU
Wales
Phone (0239) 802531

Other Places to Stay

Dyfed: Abergwenlais Mill, Cilycwm, Llandovery
Phone (0550) 20188
XV, B & B + EM opt. Newly renovated – 'warm welcome at our small family guesthouse, upper Towy Valley, near RSPB reserves'.

Dyfed: Pembs Nat Park
Phone (0437) 710744
XV, B & B only, NS. Watermill.

Gloucestershire: The Lawn, Ruardean
Phone (0594) 543259
V-T, V prop, NS guesthouse. Licensed. Activity holidays. Price category M.

Gwent: Croton House, Tintern
Phone (029 18) 215
XV(?) visited in 1985 under ownership of Geoff and Mary Joyce. Interesting house, beautiful garden with waterfall and grotto. New owners will be V, say the Joyces.

West Glamorgan: Gower
Phone (0792) 391041
XV(?) wholefood, B & B + EM optional.

Places to Eat

GLAMORGAN

Cardiff: Crumbs (XV), David Morgan's Arcade. Phone (0222) 395007.

Swansea: Ear to the Ground (XV), 68a Bryn-y-mor Road. Phone (0792) 46350.

VII

NORTH WALES, MID-WALES AND BORDERS

Clwyd, Gwynedd, Powys, Shropshire (*west of Shrewsbury*), Hereford & Worcester (*Hereford half*)

Considering the number of places to stay in some of the other scenic parts of Britain, like the West Country and the Lake District, North Wales is very disappointing: we felt compelled to include both mid-Wales and the English side of the border just to keep the numbers up. And eating out is pretty grim too. I have a suspicion that the availability of vegetarian food in the Celtic fringes (Scotland as well as Wales) has a lot to do with their penetration by Anglo-Saxons; and for better or worse there seem to be fewer of those in North Wales than in Pembrokeshire, say, or the Scottish Highlands. Even health food stores are few and far between, partly because there aren't many sizeable towns away from the north coast.

Places Reviewed

59. Buck Farm, Hanmer, Nr Wrexham, Clwyd
60. Gwalia, Cemmaes, Nr Machynlleth, Powys
61. Llwyn-y-Brig, Trefor, Nr Caernarfon, Gwynedd (XV)
62. Pen-y-Bont Fawr (Wild Wales Walks), Cynwyd, Nr Corwen, Clwyd
63. Plas Dolguog Hotel, Nr Machynlleth, Powys
64. Spring Cottage, Cefn Einion, Nr Bishop's Castle, Shropshire
65. Sundial Cottage, Lugwardine, Nr Hereford, Hereford & Worcester (XV)
66. Earthwalk (camping/walking holidays), Nr Newtown, Powys

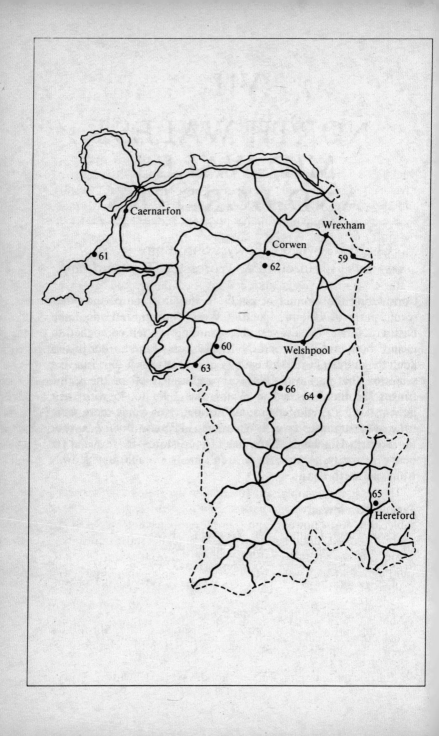

59. Buck Farm

Buck Farm is technically in North Wales, in an odd little bulge of Clwyd inserted, by some accident of history, between Cheshire and Shropshire. The house is 2 miles outside Hanmer on the main road between Whitchurch and Wrexham (7 miles from each). In the dark, it looked very like an ordinary Welsh roadhouse pub, with a big B & B/Teas sign hanging out front. But take heart, it is nothing like ordinary; quite the opposite.

Buck Farm is a sixteenth-century half-timbered farmhouse, warm, comfortable and beautifully restored. But its specialness results from the melange of styles reflecting the cosmopolitan background and experience of its proprietors. Cedric is English, Frances Trinidadian Chinese, but both spent most of their early adult lives in Ottawa. They have also lived in France (Frances has a diploma from a French charcutier in lower Normandy) and the West Coast of America (she has family there). It all adds up to a rich and eclectic combination of colours, tastes, fabrics, spices, artwork and music; not to mention the delightfully divergent personalities of Cedric and Frances. Ten years ago they decided to give up their Canadian civil service jobs and open Buck Farm – Canada's loss and our gain.

The house is simply and originally decorated: white walls, Japanese lanterns, woven baskets and jugs, dried grasses, Greek tablecloth, fresh flowers, and – in December when we were last there – a potted rhododendron in the front hall. Goose quills, from a friend, were for sale (5p) in a jug on the front table. Upstairs, our bedroom which was warm and cosy, had matching flower-print wallpaper and curtains, real goose down duvets, cotton sheets, a handsome Victorian washstand and chairs with embroidered cushions. Very pretty indeed. The bathrooms are downstairs, which posed no real problem for us but might for some. The dining room is a beautiful room with tiled floors and lath and white sugar icing plaster between ancient oak beams; modern prints done by

Frances' artist sister. On the tables were white cloths, jugs of winter heather and egg-shaped glass dishes containing salt and pepper. A tape, including 'Men of Harlech' arranged for Welsh harp, was playing discreetly in the background.

The food is the real star of the show. Frances and Cedric are not vegetarians but are seriously sympathetic to the vegetarian/vegan diet and lifestyle. We felt totally relaxed, reassured that all ingredients would be purely vegetarian. The first course arrived in a handsome blue and white ironstone tureen, containing a carrot soup made with fresh chili peppers, cream and herbs (no meat or chicken stock, Cedric thoughtfully assured us), accompanied by wholewheat pitta bread and butter. Next came a sweet corn souffle in wholemeal pastry, diced beetroot and apples, and a hot salad of leeks, walnuts and peppers; then another green salad of lamb's lettuce. All of the vegetables that the Welsh climate permits (i.e. possibly not the sweetcorn and peppers) came straight out of the garden; and Cedric's was the kind of loving and respectful cooking that brings out all the subtlety and freshness of the ingredients. Frances' cooking (they take turns) can be hotter and more exotic, with Portuguese, French, Spanish, Indian, African and even British influences. Dessert was Buck Farm Strawberry Coupe with whipped cream.

Excellent coffee followed, served to us in front of the fire (well, stove) in their dining room, along with special monster Canadian chocolates sent to them by friends. It was quite simply one of the best, most aesthetically pleasing and most relaxing dinners I have ever had. Added to the delicious food and atmosphere of the place, we enjoyed the pleasure of Cedric and Frances' company. Between courses Cedric told us some of the house's history as well as their own. After dinner, warmed by food and fire, we talked late into the night with Frances, with whom we found we had much in common.

Breakfast – this time cooked and served by Frances – was an elaborate and luxurious affair with a distinctive North American touch. First, apple juice followed by muesli, hotcakes, then a Buck Farm omelette made with cheese, peppers, leeks and tomatoes. There was also a big bowl of fresh fruit and wild plum jam which was sharp and magnificent. Toast was on offer, but we steeled ourselves and declined. An hour and a half later we waddled out of the dining room, stopped for a moment to chat to Cedric and Frances over their breakfast, gradually sank into chairs by the fire, were brought 11 o'clock coffee (fresh ground, of course) – and there we sat chatting with Frances for the next 3 hours while Cedric went about Farm business.

By rights, Buck Farm ought to be booked up months in advance. It is every bit as good as Tregynon Farmhouse (which is that booked up), though it is much much simpler and less 'done up', which I prefer. Its location may have something to do with it. It's true that at first glance it's in the middle of nowhere: Wrexham isn't on anyone's shortlist for favourite town in North Wales. But there are advantages to that: the country is friendly and unspoiled, and there are good lane- and field-tramping walks on the doorstep. I suppose it misses out on the tourist circuit since it's not exactly chapel, castle, mountain and *hwyl* country. (Though it is 5 miles from Erddig, one of the National Trust's most extraordinary stately homes.) But you can be in Llangollen in half an hour by car if you want, and Cedric can supply you with maps, guidebooks and personalised tours of half of Wales, as well as of fascinating towns and villages close by. He is an impressive, rather more than amateur historian. You can also borrow bicycles and it looks to be splendid cycling country; Cedric and Frances will even drive you around in their van for a modest fee.

I can't imagine a better place for a wonderful, quiet holiday. You will be exceptionally well looked after, and eating will be a memorable treat. I suppose if carnivores are staying at the same time (this has not been our experience so far), you may have to put up with meaty smells but, rest assured, Frances and Cedric will be fastidious about your vegetarian ingredients. The house is smoke-free. There is a telly, and an interesting, quirky collection of books for rainy days and evenings. And, most of all, you will enjoy if you choose – for they don't at all force it on you – the company of Frances and Cedric: I certainly felt I had made friends, and I plan to go back again often. But go soon, go often, and send your friends; at the moment Buck Farm isn't exactly coining money, and I would *hate* to lose them to southern France or San Francisco.

CATERING Traditional and vegetarian; vegan and other diets catered for.

SMOKING No smoking.

PRICE CATEGORY Medium.

FURTHER INFORMATION Frances Williams-Lee and Cedric
Sumner
Buck Farm,
Hanmer,
Clwyd, Wales
Phone (094 874) 339

60. Gwalia

The steep lanes in the narrow valleys of North Wales are punishing tests for the touring bicyclist, vegetarian or otherwise. Arriving at Gwalia, tucked into the rounded green hillside, its top floor windows at the level of the tiny road (2 miles up towards Commins Cock behind Cemmaes), you are likely to be hot and out of breath. You receive a calm welcome with an offer of draughts of water from the spring beside the door. And this is the sign of what Gwalia has to offer the traveller: quiet simplicity.

There are 'extra' features. In case you need further cooling and relaxing (this being summer) you are directed to the swimming pond. Down the garden past an immaculate and abundant vegetable plot and the goats' paddock, across the miniature stream by a single-plank bridge, there is the pond behind the hedge in a large excavation with a small island in the middle. It is brown but not uninviting. Perhaps those who like to see the bottom when they are swimming would not be tempted. But the compulsive swimmer in us plunged in unhesitatingly and pronounced it good. Bathing costumes are definitely not needed in this private place.

We had rather forced ourselves on the Chandlers, who live at Gwalia with their two small children. They had a houseful of their friends, but they agreed to put us up for the night. Over the telephone they had been unwilling to provide us with the (usually available) evening meal but, hearing that we were cycling, had said that we certainly would want to eat after tackling the hill; would soup and bread be all right? As it turned out, it was delicious and satisfying. The soup was thick and tasty, with vegetables and lentils; there was lots of homemade bread, perhaps a touch heavy and yeasty but a good basis for the meal; pickled beetroot from the garden; lentil curry spread; various homemade jams.

The house is almost self-sufficient in vegetables. There are goats for milk and free-range hens for eggs. The Chandlers do eat meat sometimes, their own cockerels and goats and sometimes one of their sheep, which they slaughter themselves. Gwalia is a small-holding run on a cheerfully pragmatic philosophy of a balanced use of resources rather than on a vegetarian or non-exploitation of animals principle as such. Meals for guests, however, are totally vegetarian and vegan food is also provided. They take this seriously and do it properly, with no animal products used, completely vegetarian margarine, etc. Our impression was that the cuisine was not gourmet but was simple and good. Pots of tea, etc, were available whenever anyone wanted it.

The dining/sitting room for guests is small with small cottage windows, but is quite comfortable; armchairs are slightly severe, the lighting poor. This is a pity because things to read are provided: back numbers of *Birds* (RSPB), *The Vegan*, *The Welsh Vegan*, *Soil Association* magazine, etc. Also leaflets on things to do and see in the area and a small collection of books – light/humorous, Wales, countryside, outdoors and so on.

The house is a converted farmhouse/cottage. Guests' rooms (two, sleeps four) are on the top floor of the wing at the back, looking over the garden to the hills on the other side of the valley. The style is plain and unpretentious: green painted wooden window frames, beautiful new wooden interior doors. Everything is relaxed and quiet. Like its owners, the house does not pretend to be other than it is or try either to preach or ingratiate. The aim seems to be tranquillity rather than luxury and this is achieved. The feeling is of a family house which accepts you calmly and does not make too many concessions to the B & B business. It is probably excellent if you visit with children of your own; less so, obviously, if your idea of peace excludes them. The Gwalia children do wake up early and are not shy of engaging strangers in conversation. The garden has children's things lying about and there is an adventure/climbing house structure in the intriguingly chaotic yard.

Everything is perfectly clean. There is a shower (no bath) with plenty of hot water. The beds are comfortable, with non-allergic duvets and cotton sheets and covers, important to us in high hay-fever season. We spent a peaceful night, the absolute quiet enhanced by the babbling of the spring outside and a gentle rainstorm after midnight. Breakfast was muesli, lots more fresh bread (an old-fashioned toaster on the table), boiled eggs, good coffee, homemade jam and marmalade. The Chandlers offered to make sandwiches (£1.50). We asked just for bread and were given the rest of our loaf as a gift. (We were charged only £1.25 for our evening meal.) We packed and paid and whizzed off euphorically down between the hedges towards Machynlleth, refreshed and soothed. We would be happy to think of going back.

Not everyone's cup of tea, perhaps. Too Bohemian for some; too plain for others; others, again, might not stomach the practical approach to animal husbandry. Certainly not a place for sophisticated haute veg. cuisine, nor for hotel luxury. But, for us, a good practical example of what people ought to mean by a family atmosphere, and of an exercise in how to accept guests and make them feel comfortable while remaining yourself. S.R. and D.F.

CATERING Exclusively vegetarian or vegan for guests. Evening meal on request (not always).

SMOKING Smoking restrictions.

PRICE CATEGORY Very Low.

FURTHER INFORMATION The Chandlers,
                                Gwalia, Cemmaes,
                                Machynlleth, Powys, Wales
                                Phone (06502) 377

61. Llwyn-y-Brig

Head west across North Wales, don't cross the Menai Bridge and follow the coastline south. Suddenly you will turn a corner and, behold, The Rivals (Yr Eifl), a spur of Snowdonia sweeping straight down into Caernarfon Bay. And tucked halfway up its/their slope – which you get to by one of two narrow, bumpy lanes (one of which may already be improved if Chris Lloyd has his way with the County Council) – you will find Llwyn-y-Brig – 'where the mountains sweep down to the sea'. It's a traditional, 200-year-old Welsh cottage, but unusual in that it's on three levels, following the contours of the mountain. It reminded me of split-level New Mexican adobe houses which also tuck themselves into the surrounding landscape, both for aesthetic reasons and for protection from the fierce weather. If the weather is different, it is not gentle in this part of Wales. The weekend we were there it was wild, fierce rain alternating with bright sunshine, and while the sea and sky were dramatic, it was no time to sit out. But I kept thinking how gloriously idyllic the garden must be on a hot summer day.

It's a really memorable spot. The cottage is high on a hillside, just at the level where steep fields, with thick hedges and wooded cataract-filled gullies, give way to rock and heather covered hillside. You look down on the rooftops of Trefor, a rather gloomy village which housed the quarrymen who left great scars on the seacliffs of Yr Eifl, and over to other heathery hills or across the sea to Anglesey. All around are ancient hillforts, settlements and burial chambers, and you're at the beginning of the Lleyn Peninsula, one of the holiest parts of Wales, with more saints per square yard than anywhere else in the world. The other side of Yr Eifl is a museum village preserved by the Welsh Language Society. The great mass of Snowdonia is still within easy reach if you want. Though you wouldn't have known it on our visit, I suspect the weather is quite a bit better than in the heart of the mountains.

The inside of the house has thick, whitewashed walls, exposed beams and stonework, shapely niches and irregular, lumpy protrusions. Here and there you have to sqeeze through a doorway where an ancient stone juts out, or duck down to avoid a low beam. It's been carefully renovated, but not at all destroyed. The decoration is beautiful: white walls throughout and plain carpets or rough coir matting, except for the dining room. This room (in spite of its swirly-whirly brown carpet) is especially lovely and cosy with an inglenook fireplace and wood-burning stove, pine tables, and a very unusual porch door with a stained-glass panel. Then there are the spotlighted fruit bowl on a black slate shelf, the old family photographs on the wall, the white porcelain pots and jugs sitting on lace cloths, all delights to the eye.

The house is kept fastidiously clean. When we visited there was a bath only, but there were plans for a shower room. All three bedrooms are lovely. Ours was white with a white duvet with delicate pink and green sprigs, eyelet-trimmed matching pillowcases, and white furniture. Even the built-in vanity unit managed to be inoffensive: a round porcelain sink built into a cork-tiled shelf, under a window looking out to the garden. Only problem: the bed, aside from its pretty, cottony freshness, was not, honestly, the most comfortable, and in such a damp part of the world an electric underblanket would have been a goodly thing.

The guests' sitting room was the other disappointment. It's very small, even by troglodyte standards, with not very comfortable wicker seating, a TV, a gas fire, and rather bald overhead lighting. With only one sitting room there is always the problem of the telly-watchers versus the readers, and here the situation is aggravated by lack of space. It is possible to retire to the dining room with your books and/or Scrabble (as we did), but Chris and Sharon's bedroom is just at the top of an open stairway, so it all feels a bit public.

The food, however, could not be improved upon. We had intended to stay for one night only but the food was so good and we liked Chris and Sharon and the wildness of the place so much that we decided to stay on. On the second night we had melon and grapes for starters followed by black-eyed bean stew with almonds, carrots and parsnips, and brown rice – an enormous helping, actually too much for the less greedy among us; a salad of lettuce, sprouts, celery, raisins, apples and walnuts; and for dessert, cheesecake with kiwi fruit. Coffee, alas, was instant decaf; but you could have barleycup or herb tea (a wide choice). Breakfast was a thing of real beauty: grape juice served in long-stemmed wine glasses, an arrangement of sliced fruits served in a porcelain dish – the first morning, nectarines, the second bananas – with nuts and grapes, homemade muesli or Granola and yoghurt, followed by wholewheat toast and homemade plum and blueberry jam in tiny white porcelain dishes. Real coffee would have been the *coup de grâce*.

Chris and Sharon Lloyd are young, cheerful and enthusiastic hosts. Everything is so perfect that one would suspect them of playing house but for the fact that they are mature and competent business people, as well as being warm and friendly. They'd only been open a few weeks when we visited, but any knots there may have been had already been worked out. Had they had enough money, they confided, the Lakes would have been their first choice for a vegetarian guesthouse. All I can say is, it's Cumbria's loss and Gwynedd's gain. It's well worth the journey. Do go: they deserve a big success. L.A. and O.F.

CATERING Exclusively vegetarian; vegan and other diets catered for.

SMOKING No smoking.

PRICE CATEGORY LOW.

FURTHER INFORMATION Chris and Sharon Lloyd,
Llwyn-y-Brig,
Trefor, Nr Caernarfon
Gwynedd LL54 5NB, Wales
Phone (0286 86) 693)

62. Pen-y-Bont Fawr

Pen-y-Bont Fawr is a handsome converted double barn in a beautiful setting in rural North Wales, about 2 miles from the town of Corwen. All rooms are white, light, airy and spotlessly clean, and have lovely views to hilly green fields. The five upstairs bedrooms have been fitted with large Velux windows and face south, so (when it shines) the sun pours in.

The food at Pen-y-Bont is wholefood, which can mean anything of course. But the proprietors are themselves vegetarians and are happy to do vegetarian and vegan cooking on request. Kay is a conscientious and knowledgeable cook. The food, which we ate *en famille* with the Culhanes, was good and plentiful, though not inspired. There was an unadorned carrot puree, a rather stodgy lasagna made with mashed swede and curiously bright green noodles, and a salad of militarily uniform portions. Dessert was fruit salad with commercial yoghurt. Drinks were apple juice (very sweet), tea and instant coffee.

After dinner we sat in the sombre lounge, with its bookshelves filled with serried ranks of maps, and huddled around the storage heater, which was not turned up very high (this was a bitter March weekend). Fortunately, the other guest there suggested turning on an electric bar heater. As it was, I retreated to bed to thaw my toes and escape from the conversation, which was exclusively centred around maps, routes and number of miles covered on walks and cycle trips.

Walks seem to range from the long and strenuous (6–10 miles) to the longer and more strenuous. A poem written in the visitors' book is revealing: 'There was a fine man called Tom/Whose walks were exceedingly long . . .' So be warned. Also, there are no baths for après bike or hike; only a trickle of a shower, alas.

Pen-y-Bont Fawr is very inexpensive, both as a guesthouse and activity centre (Wild Wales Walks). If you go for simple, basic accommodation and food without frills, if you value quiet, varied countryside and someone to lead you on stretching and improving walks or bicycle rides, then I recommend it.

CATERING Traditional and vegetarian.

SMOKING No known rules.

PRICE CATEGORY Very Low.

FURTHER INFORMATION Tom and Kay Culhane,
Wild Wales Walks,
Pen-y-Bont Fawr,
Cynwyd, Corwen, Clwyd, Wales
Phone (0490) 2226

63. Plas Dolguog Hotel

Plas Dolguog is a proper country house hotel, with all the fittings and atmosphere money and good taste can buy, from the splendid antiques (courtesy of Mr Brown's previous antique business) to André the French (well, sort of, see below) waiter. The house itself dates from 1632 and, although a bit 'improved' since then, has been lovingly restored and furnished. The downstairs rooms are warm, elegant and comfortable: two grand lounges, one with bar and open fire, where you can smoke; the other, with a Franklin stove, where you can relax (with or without a drink), read, and enjoy the view northwards over a wide lawn across the Dyfi Valley to the mountains south of Cader Idris, which rise abruptly out of the river's green and sheep-dotted floor plain. The upstairs echoes the elegance and comfort of the downstairs: our bedroom had an en suite bathroom which was panelled and painted, with generous old-fashioned fittings and lots of hot water for baths. (There may be rooms with showers, if you prefer; do check.) The bedroom wasn't enormous but had a lovely view, a very comfortable bed with fresh, good cotton sheets and blankets, a telly, kettle, and bottles of Perrier. The ultimate in unostentatious comfort.

As for the food, well, here is the problem. Plas Dulguog advertises itself in various vegetarian and health food magazines, yet it is by no stretch of the imagination a vegetarian hotel. It not only boasts salmon fishing, but proudly serves (and is redolent of) all forms of fish, fowl and animal flesh. Having said that, vegetarian cooking *is* a speciality. David is a long-time vegetarian and Eileen is very interested and skilled in vegetarian cooking. She would love to open an exclusively vegetarian hotel, run on the same lines as Plas Dolguog, but fears no business. As it is, she gets loads of enquiries from vegetarians but rarely any bookings. No surprise, when you catch a glimpse of the tariff.

Still, the vegetarian dinner we had was worth every penny: garlicky mushrooms, walnut roast, a splendid array of freshly cooked vegetables, blackcurrant tart, fine cheeseboard. The wine list was short but good and very reasonably priced. All in all, the food was very good, although on the traditional (rich and sweet) side, and it was not 'wholefood' by which I mean the pastry was white rather than wholewheat, and cream flowed rather than yoghurt. Along with dinner came André, a sort of Inspector Clouseau of waiters, down to the little blond moustache and towel flung over the stiffly cocked arm. For dessert, he offered us a chocolate cream 'leug' – meaning *log*. My private hunch is that he's from darkest Machynlleth . . .

I left from Plas Dolguog with very mixed feelings: on the one hand I felt happy, relaxed, thoroughly indulged and well nourished; on the other I felt highly critical of all the 'upmarket' razzmatazz (inch thick, gold-tooled leather menus; proliferation of Porsches and Mercedes, with matching owners parked inside, etc, etc); turned off by the pungent odours and general huntin' and fishin' ambience, and worried sick at having spent so much money. Still, still, I had a glorious time: ambivalence, ambivalence; oh dear. I'd say if you can arrange to leave your puritanical conscience at home (and wash your Dyane), I recommend Plas Dolguog enormously.

CATERING Traditional and vegetarian. Licensed bar.

SMOKING Smoking restrictions.

PRICE CATEGORY Very High.

FURTHER INFORMATION David and Eileen Brown,
Plas Dolguog Hotel
Machynlleth,
Powys SY20 5UJ
Wales
Phone (0654) 2244

64. Spring Cottage

Spring Cottage is set in deepest Shropshire, one of the few parts of England which Euro-agriculture still hasn't reached: steep little hills, deep, narrow lanes, slow, winding, muddy rivers and, in a rainy July, wildflowers everywhere. It felt more like a set of illustrations from an old-fashioned children's book than anywhere I've been, and the landscape, like the house itself, has a dreamlike quality of utter satisfaction and naturalness to it. Antiquities abound – ditches and mounds, hillforts, castle sites and earthworks, nothing too spectacular – but you feel a steady continuity of occupation. For the practical minded, Cefn Einion is a little crossroads a few miles south-west of Bishop's Castle. If you drive you should allow for the last five miles taking as long as the previous twenty. If you come by train, Pat Townsend will collect you from the Craven Arms station in her 2CV for a very small fare. But the best approach (which many visitors prefer) is from Offa's Dyke. A good day's walk from Knighton northwards, or Montgomery southwards, will leave you an easy half hour's stroll down from the Dyke to the Unk Valley, and then a few minutes up to Spring Cottage on the other side.

Pat Townsend, who owns and runs Spring Cottage single-handedly, is an interesting person: an ex-teacher and feminist who only recently took the plunge into self-sufficiency. She has no regrets; being out of the London rat-race is, she says, 'like being without a toothache'. She is busy trying to reclaim a garden from the hillside; if the weather has cooperated, by now there should be organic vegetables on the table.

Everything about Spring Cottage delights the senses. The house itself looks fairly undistinguished from the outside, but inside it's a photographer's dream: huge stone fireplace with wood-burning stove and vase of highlighted wildflowers; shadow of a jug on a white wall; black slate floor with rag rug and black dog (Puddles) lying on it; organic-shaped alcove with hanging plant and lamp; and so on, still life after still life.

And yet, for all its interior artistry, it is no showplace; on the contrary, it feels very lived in, a place to be perfectly comfortable. I could easily have spent a week there walking, eating, sitting by the wood-burning stove and working my way through the library, which contains a feast of novels, poetry, literary criticism, feminist writing, cookery, etc.

For those who like serious walking, there is the Offa's Dyke path and innumerable other footpaths and bridleways, over the tops or along the valleys. Within an easy drive you have the Long Mynd to the north-east and half the hills of Wales to your west. Restless visitors can even jump in their cars and drive to the seaside for the day. For gentler strolls there are country lanes and Forestry Commission roads.

The food was wonderful, lovingly planned, cooked and presented. Although there were only four of us, there was a handwritten menu with alternatives for each course. Starters were mushrooms in garlic butter with homemade French bread (delicious) or hummus with crudites and brown bread. Entrees were red beans in wine sauce with brown rice and salad (very good) or pasta with blue cheese sauce and tomato salad (unusual and delicious according to the non-vegans). Dessert was apple pie with cream or yoghurt, or fresh fruit salad. Altogether a simple, elegant, delicious dinner in an equally satisfying setting. It was certainly easy to be vegan and happy with it. The only disappointment was the coffee, which was weak. Breakfast was wholewheat toast (homemade like the French bread), yoghurt, blackcurrant preserves, free-range eggs, mushrooms and tomatoes if wanted. We were unable to stay for a second night but drooled over its menu: pears with blue cheese, pancakes stuffed with courgettes with cream and rosemary . . oh dear. At least I was spared from having to choose between damson pie and gooseberry fool.

Spring Cottage is not your typical guesthouse or B & B where you are shunted off into your own separate guests' quarters. Here you feel you are a guest in Pat's home: you sit among her books, pictures and art objects; you may spend time talking with her (as we did, very enjoyably); you listen to her choice of recorded music. It was varied and not too loud, though pretty constant.

The house was very clean. The bathroom was as aesthetically pleasing as any of the other rooms; even the colourful piles of clean clothes on open shelves were nice to look at. The shower was a puzzle, however; I just couldn't get it to work. Alas, there is no bath – almost a necessity after a long walk as far as I am concerned – but you may not mind. Our bedroom was harmonious and restful; even the iris pillowcases in browny colours against the Cotswold stone wall were a treat to the eye. The bed might not have been the world's most comfortable, and not to everyone's taste (a mattress on the floor in a frame), but it fitted with the decor and ambience of the room.

Altogether a beautiful, tranquil, almost perfect place. Pat has all kinds of plans in mind for possible group activity holidays – walking, writing, painting, reading. Write to her if you like the idea. Like so many others, Pat is in the position of wanting to run Spring Cottage along strictly veggie lines but is worried about not getting enough business. So it's up to you: *go* so that she can throw away her bacon and egg pans.

CATERING Vegetarian and traditional; vegan and other diets catered for.

SMOKING No smoking.

PRICE CATEGORY Very Low.

FURTHER INFORMATION Pat Townsend,
Spring Cottage,
Cefn Einion,
Bishops Castle, Shropshire
Phone (0588) 638632

65. Sundial Cottage

It's a hard life for the professional travelling, vegetarian woman. Think of it: impersonal hotels and guesthouses, suspicious and curious staff, paper-thin walls and big bills. The sort of place that takes pride in one thing and one thing only, the meat, grease and cholesterol-filled English breakfast! Not exactly enticing, I agree, but are there any alternatives? Well, to my relief I found one in Sundial Cottage, near Hereford. Paradise to the weary veggie traveller and, I'm sure, equally welcoming to those seeking a holiday base.

Almost nicer than the food (and the food really is very good) is the proprietor, Mrs Sherlock. She is a retired teacher, with energy and talent in abundance. The idea of a vegetarian bed, breakfast and evening meal business has been founded on her own keen interest and awareness of nutrition, fitness and general well-being. The meals reflect this: they're tasty, balanced, and wholeheartedly vegetarian. I was extremely well looked after; cups of tea and homemade shortbread or malt loaf after work, the evening meal at a time convenient to me and hot bedtime drink if I wanted. Breakfast isn't my favourite meal. Tea, a small bowl of Granola and a spoonful of yoghurt is all I can manage but Mrs Sherlock always makes absolutely sure she can't tempt you with something more – toast, homemade marmalade, scrambled eggs, etc. There's always plenty of fresh fruit available, too.

Mrs Sherlock pays great attention to detail. Salads are pretty (and filling), dressings, particularly her walnut one, are expertly prepared and soups are nourishing and full of flavour. The main courses I enjoyed included a delicious black-eyed bean and mushroom strogonoff, a satisfying vegetable and walnut lasagne and a spicy kidney bean savory with brown rice. She's definitely got the knack of making you feel at home too, always sensitive to your needs and willing to talk, but never overdemanding or intrusive.

The accommodation is pleasant. The Sherlocks have extended their black and white seventeenth-century cottage into the large rear garden to provide the kitchen, bathroom, small guest sitting room and the comfortable double bedroom that I slept in. The sitting room (with black and white TV) doubles up as the guest dining room and, although there was ample space for one or two, it would feel a bit cramped with more. The bathroom is modern with plenty of hot water and warm towels. As I was staying there during our arctic spring, I was particularly glad of the electric blanket on the bed.

As I was a working (ah!) and not a holidaying guest, I didn't have time to explore the countryside or visit local places of interest apart from Hereford itself. However, it's just one of those areas which ooze picturesque sites and things to do. Hereford itself is a lovely old market town, dominated by its huge cathedral and black and white buildings. The Wye Valley is green and lush with plenty of apple orchards which provide the local cider and dotted with quaint villages. The accompanying hills take you out through towns like Hay-on-Wye to the Black Mountains in Wales.

Sundial Cottage offers friendly service, lovely food, comfortable accommodation and very good value for money. It's a place I'd thoroughly recommend to my friends and, to cap it all – and this from someone suspicious of dogs of all shapes and sizes – I even made friends with the household dog! A.F.

CATERING Exclusively vegetarian.

SMOKING Not in evidence.

PRICE CATEGORY Low.

FURTHER INFORMATION Mrs P. Sherlock,
Sundial Cottage,
Lugwardine, Hereford.
Phone (0432) 850298

66. Earthwalk

Most readers of the holiday advertisements in veggie and 'healthy' magazines such as *The Great Outdoors*, and even the *Guardian*, must have paused over the testimonials in Earthwalk's small advertisements, which start with the strikingly implausible juxtaposition of 'An idyll . . .' (*Evening Standard*) and continue with a great raft of glowing quotations from journals with every conceivable readership. (Even *Vogue*, according to Phil Brachi, sent a green wellied couple, who lasted just one day and left in a hurry before they had to face an actual *tent*, darlings.) Now, unlike those quoted, your fearless correspondent went incognito – for a genuine holiday, stayed the full week, and paid for himself. Here, then, the utterly unvarnished and unsubsidised truth.

But, since my experience, though memorable and in many ways enjoyable, was a little less than totally *idyllic*, it's essential and only fair to start with a caveat or two. The most important point to make is that while most of the much quoted journalists went, I suspect, in glorious 1984, my walk was in September 1985 at the end of the wettest summer in anyone's memory. No one on my week actually demanded their money back (apparently others have: the management's answer, reasonably enough, is to suggest sending the bill to a higher authority), though one person never showed up, despite being fully paid up, and another fled after two days pleading an unspecified physical malaise, but there was a bit of resignation in the air. It's true we did *see* the sun every day, but there's no denying it rained every day as well. The tents were indeed waterproof as promised, but wet boots and wet clothes made them pretty steamy none the less. Earthwalk is, as it clearly says, a holiday in which, inescapably, you (a) walk all day, and (b) sleep in small tents. If this is your idea of an idyll in sun *or* rain, well and good. Personally, I still enjoy wet(ish) walks, but with advancing years a warm dry bed is creeping up on my priority list. I really do think a fine week could be close to idyllic, but there is a reason why the Montgomeryshire countryside is that lovely green colour, and it can't do all the raining on Friday nights, between Earthwalks.

The second thing is that I have always had deeply mixed feelings about group holidays with strangers, compounded of a mixture of hope of new and exciting friends and fear of the group bore/idiot/racist/lunatic/minstrel. As with most of my fantasies, reality turned out considerably less extreme: I found myself one of a slightly sad and buttoned-up little group, of whom the most colourful was a somewhat self-righteous vegan who couldn't resist the cream. Again, I think I was unlucky; certainly the campfire tales from Earthwalk staff suggested there had been more dynamic weeks. The solution, I suppose, is to bring your own friend(s).

Our first campsite was a field of long wet grass between two tree-lined streams, dotted with twelve little orange tents, nicely spaced, one big green one and three ominously upright green rectangles. Outside the 'mess tent' (inside when it rained) were twelve folding chairs and a table surfaced with large-scale maps. Inside the rectangles the two loos contained reasonably civilised flushing systems. (The signal was a small wooden block: red side up means engaged. Despite Phil's solemn warning, people failed to turn it back after use. My habit of yelling 'Anyone *really* there?' seemed more strategic.) The shower was effective but brief and not exactly copious. The special offer to Earthwalkers for a £1 bath at the Bear Hotel, Newtown, on the mid-week day off seemed a better bet. The sleeping tents were reasonably roomy and the mattresses adequate: one doesn't, after all, expect a Posturepedic on a camping trip. The said 'mess tent' was neatly arranged with cookers, library (three old suitcasesful), chairs and powerful lamp to read and eat by.

The food was excellent by camping standards, and some of it truly classy by any. Dinners usually began with a warm and reviving soup: bean and potato, broth with fresh veges, thick spicy vegetable, celery, spiced chickpea. Main course offerings included: bean stews (adzuki, black-eye and sweet corn, chickpea and apricot), nutloaf, curries. There were always lots of accompanying veges and different kinds of bread, including a delicious herb-spice bread. Desserts were substantial and good: German plum tart (plums, custard and almonds in a pastry base), gooseberry crumble, fruit salad, shortcake, brown bread pudding; most with cream. Cheese (including Stilton and lovely local goat's) and biscuits to round it all off. *Not* real camp coffee, I'm afraid, but help yourself out of a jar. There is a travelling cellar, containing basic but acceptable *vins de table*, which are extras.

In the morning there were hot kettles ready for tea, coffee and washing – fill your private plastic bowl and take it back to your tent unless you're prepared to brave the shower. Breakfast was good: muesli/Weetabix/cornflakes, etc, cow's and soya milk, boiled eggs; brown bread, butter and Granose, and homemade marmalade, tea, coffee, barleycup, Ovaltine, etc. On the last day there were wholewheat pancakes – a farewell tour de force – with lemon and sugar. The packed lunches bear special mention: home-made rolls with garlicky lentil-mushroom pâté; carroty loaf and fruit cake; nutloaf and flapjack; vegetable–cheese pasties, fruit, plus tons of gorgeous blackberries for the picking. Tea and Boots' wholewheat shortbread were very welcome on our return to camp.

Earthwalk is a funny compromise. You camp in the (slightly) wild (an enclosed pasture, to be precise), but the food comes over the hill fresh from someone's kitchen; you come for a week's walking, and it is, to be honest, four days; and you're encouraged to be free and relaxed in a pretty tightly planned regime. It makes a lot of sense, and it's spelled out very clearly in the brochure before you book; but if you don't, as I evidently didn't, read brochures very carefully, it jars slightly with the picture of the spontaneous idyll which my excessively fertile imagination had conjured up. And like all compromises there's a certain tension involved. Take, for instance, Phil Brachi, the leader and inspiration of the whole scheme. I have to say at once that I liked him immensely and found him much the most interesting person on the trip. His opening spiel, for example, encouraged us to take off our watches and 'let go of time' for the week. Fine: the trouble was that the next morning – probably, I grant you, not much after eleven by the despised chronometer and certainly only one-third of the way through the preordained mileage – I announced that my biological clock thought it was lunchtime. I certainly wasn't forbidden to eat my lunch, but I was left feeling pretty clearly that it was a self-indulgent and disruptive suggestion. More seriously, I had a strong feeling from him of frustration. Many of Earthwalk's customers are, inevitably, novice campers or walkers, and Phil has gradually worked out – and pretty accurately, I'd say – what the market demands, in the levels of freedom or protection that they want or can stand. You can sense, however (and Phil makes no real secret of it) that it's not quite the level on which he himself would prefer to operate. Certainly the walks are so carefully planned that it would be hard for him not to be slightly bored at times.

And here is the problem. Experienced walkers – and there are usually a few – can feel a bit frustrated, regimented, or even tied down to lower levels and tamer country than they'd like, while the inexperienced are still very stretched. I shared the formers' feelings at first; but I have to admit that though I love hilltops, open spaces and filling in the broad outlines, by the end of the week I came to have a real warmth of feeling for the detail of Montgomeryshire which I'd never have found for myself. In any event, Phil was talking (in 1985) of changing the balance a little my way, and moving some days further south and to higher ground. My final feeling is that I'm very grateful for a week quite out of the ordinary; I'd have enjoyed more and better talk and better weather, but there are a lot of good memories to keep as the others fade. In particular, sunset and sunrise from the second campsite, high on a gently sloping field with a spectacular view of the Severn Valley, was truly unforgettable.

Finally, read the brochure carefully; besides its sensible suggestions you might also take wellies; a private dripfeed for snacks to keep up your blood sugar level; books, especially if you're not too keen on alternative literature (I was glad of two novels); money for drinks; lots of dry socks; hot water bottle; anti-blister nostrums.

Earthwalking is not really for complete novices, unless they're strong. But as long as you can climb (short) steep hills and cope with 10 miles a day, don't worry, you'll survive. It'll certainly be a memorable week, and if the sun shines a bit and your feet hold out, it could be really wonderful. O.F.

CATERING Most weeks exclusively vegetarian; vegans routinely catered for.

SMOKING Not allowed in tents.

PRICE CATEGORY Does not apply. Send for details.

FURTHER INFORMATION Earthwalk,
Pen-y-wern,
Kerry, Newtown,
Powys, Wales
Phone (0686) 28282

Other Places to Stay

Gwynedd: Clynnog Fawr
Phone (028686) 627
XV. 'Large, isolated farmhouse . . . home made dairy products.'

Gwynedd: The Old Rectory Hotel & Licensed Restaurant, Maentwrog, Blaenau Ffestiniog
Phone (076685) 305
T-V (V props)

Gwynedd: Ty'n Lon, Llangybi, nr Pwllheli
Phone (076 688) 618
V-T farm guesthouse specialising in riding holidays. Some weeks XV. Price category L. Weekend rates in winter.

Powys: Stredders Vegetarian Guest House, Bryncelyn, Park Crescent, Llandrindod Wells
Phone (0597) 2186
XV, price category L.

Powys: Mary Lewis, 28 Park Street, Newtown
Phone (0686) 25169
XV, B & B + EM. Medium-sized (three letting rooms) terraced cottage in town. Price category L.

Places to Eat

CLWYD

Wrexham, Clwyd: Mwyaren (XV), 19 Bridge Street. Phone (0978) 362046.

GWYNEDD

Barmouth: Isis Cafe (XV), The Harbour. Phone (0341) 280802.

Nr Llanrwst: Trefriw Woollen Mills (XV), Trefriw. Phone (0492) 640462.

HEREFORD & WORCESTER

Hereford: Fodder (XV), 27 High Street. Phone (0432) 58171.

Kington: The Blue Frog (XV), Church Street. Phone (0544) 230355.

POWYS

Llanidloes: Great Oak Café (XV), 12 Great Oak Street. Phone (05512) 3211.

Nr Machynlleth: National Centre for Alternative Technology (XV), Llwyngwern Quarry. Phone (0654) 2400.

Machynlleth: The Quarry Shop (XV), Heol Maengwyn. Phone (0654) 2624.

VIII

SOUTHERN SCOTLAND AND BORDERS

Including Northumberland

Touring vegetarians need to plan their trips with care. There's a little cluster of places to stay in Dumfries and Galloway, but otherwise they are few and far between, though I mean no offence to the determined souls like the McDonalds of Barnhills who are doing their best to spread enlightenment in a rural wilderness. Edinburgh is a haven as far as eating out is concerned; pity we haven't found anywhere good to stay there. If you're looking for health food shops they're pretty thin on the ground outside Edinburgh and Glasgow, but the Bean Machine, based on Barnhills Farmhouse, tours the border towns on a weekly rota.

Places Reviewed

67. Barnhills Farmhouse, Nr Denholm, Borders (XVgn)
68. Old School House Kirkwhelpington, Northumberland (XV)
69. The Rossan, Auchencairn, Nr Castle Douglas, Dumfries and Galloway
70. Windywalls, Nr Gatehouse of Fleet, Dumfries and Galloway

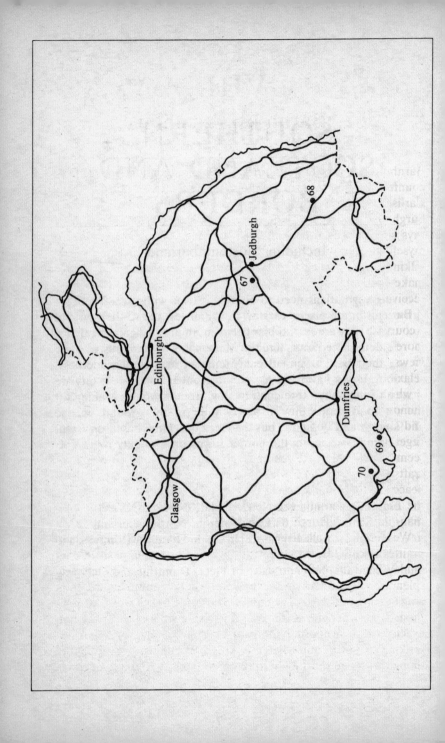

67. Barnhills Farmhouse

Barnhills is 'a private house offering accommodation' set in open country near the town of Denholm, about 50 miles north-east of Carlisle, in the Scottish Borders about midway between Edinburgh and the Lakes. Their letter (they have no fancy brochure) says simply: Vegan cooking. No smoking. No pets. I prepared myself for a spartan ordeal (no alcohol, no water, no music, no talking . . .?), anticipated the dreadful vegan faux pas I would make (pass the milk, please . . .), and the retribution I would receive (steely silence or the cane. . .?). But none of it.

Barnhills is a beautiful early nineteenth-century ex-farmhouse in a courtyard just across a cobbled yard from a working farm. It has more the air of a country rectory about it – huge rooms, lovely views, maybe just a wee bit of cold and dampness. There is a very relaxed feel to it – the overgrown garden, the weeds on the gravel – which comes not from neglect but from a deliberate, good-humoured live and let live attitude on the part of its owners, Kath and George McDonald. They also run a mobile wholefood and vegetarian catering shop called the Bean Machine, though it seems, sadly, they are feeding only their own kind, the artists, craftspeople, and so on who have come to live in the area for its peace and low rents, whereas the locals are still holding out against the Bean. Apparently the area suffers from an even worse diet than that in Edinburgh or Glasgow.

We went for a walk after arriving – up the farm track, across two prairie-sized fields, through waist-high nettles and up a steep and muddy semi-footpath through the wood to Fatlips (!) Castle, a splendid but fast-decaying seventeenth-century tower house on a crag looking out across Teviotdale. The castle is well worth seeing, though most people, Kath said, don't ever find it, since it's not exactly on a signposted footpath. It's not really very civilised walking country immediately around Barnhills, we thought, though with one short night to spare on the way to the Edinburgh

Festival, we didn't stay to explore further, and it wasn't the year for swimming in the Teviot, which is usually one of the other attractions. Still, it's not far to higher and less intensively exploited countryside.

We returned to our dinner: first, avocado, green pepper and spring onion (from the garden) soup – surprising (a) because it was cold, and (b) because it was so amazingly good (remember I was expecting vegan dullness) and homemade whole wheat rolls, also delicious. Then came an onion tart topped with sunflower seeds, both filling and pastry melted in the mouth. Next a salad of spring onions, sprouts, tomatoes, savoy cabbage and chinese leaves in a tangy vinegary dressing. Finally, dessert, hunza apricot and coconut cream whip. Then tea, which was nice and herbal. It was a wonderful and satisfying dinner, partly because it shattered all my preconceived notions of what vegan cooking is like but over and above that it was very, very good. I discovered flavours I had simply not tasted before. There is obviously glory as well as virtue in vegan food, especially if you are as talented as Kath McDonald.

Kath is also an intelligent and interesting person to talk to. She and her sweet, shy daughters served and bussed dinner and stayed to talk when we asked questions or just felt like chatting. I was interested in all things vegan, my companion in farming practices and malpractices round about. So we spent quite an entertained interval between our delicious courses. Yet at no time did Kath preach or lecture about veganism, in fact it turns out she is the only vegan in the family. But next morning there was a little pile of literature next to my muesli bowl. If I continue to be vegan (I have managed for two months so far), Kath McDonald will have been my light-handed inspiration.

After dinner we read and listened to music which drifted through from their sitting room. Fine Radio 3 classical music is obviously a feature of the place. I enjoyed most of it (good Telemann) but not all (long Bruckner) though it was always possible to close the door and not listen. It was certainly not intrusive, though if you absolutely hate classical music you might find it trying. On the subject of possible complaints, the only one I can think of is that the light in the lounge (and bedroom, too) was not very good for reading.

A hot bath in the huge old-fashioned tub (I nearly drowned!) and then to bed: not the newest of mattresses, to be honest, with a complicated arrangement of two single duvets for one double bed, but just very nice and homey and all part of the pure (in the best sense) and unaffected way of the place. Thank you, Kath McDonald. I recommend everyone to go, but not all at once since there's only one double and one single room. L.A. and O.F.

CATERING Exclusively vegan.

SMOKING No smoking.

PRICE CATEGORY Low.

FURTHER INFORMATION Kath McDonald,
                            Barnhills Farmhouse,
                            Nr Denholm,
                            Roxburghshire, Scotland
                            Phone (045 087) 577

68. Old School House

Only in 1986 did Frank and Rhona Young – themselves in their (vigorous) later years – start to take in guests at the Old School House. On the side of the adjoining building – the Parochial School House, erected 1858 – are carved religious maxims for a stern educational philosophy: 'Remember now thy Creator in the days of thy youth', 'Take my Yoke upon you and Learn of Me'.

Inside the Old School House on the evening of one of the few sunny days last year, the atmosphere was altogether more cosseting. The house is warm and comfortable and there are watercolours and sketches by Rhona Young on the walls. We were given a friendly welcome, with tea and homemade biscuits in the Youngs' sitting room before a log fire. The house is not large (a maximum of five guests, in one room with two single beds and one with double and single). Perhaps because the Youngs are new to the business – more probably because they are naturally inclined to treat people as guests rather than as mere customers – it is possible to feel even a little too much at home. It did not occur to us to wonder if we might be getting in the way; not that you are given a hint of this by your hosts, but it is obvious that while you are in their armchairs before the fire, they are sitting in the kitchen; and that they have to wait until you have finished in the dining room to pop in after you to watch the TV news. Our main problem, after huge meals, was how to get out of the armchairs before the fire once we had sat down. The Youngs are vegetarians and provide only vegetarian meals, and good and generous they are too. There was a menu, so we were able to set a pace to our indulgence in the celery and lovage soup, with delicious home-baked bread, then chestnut hotpot with cheese nuggets, with savoury rice, runner beans and a salad, knowing that there was still apple pie and cream to come. Vegetables are mostly from the garden. Afterwards, coffee, tea or herb teas.

We took a short digestive stroll around Kirkwhelpington in the dark under brilliant stars before bed. There were fresh flowers in the bedroom and a comfortable bed with cotton sheets. We were still feeling well fed by breakfast, which was splendid: three sorts of muesli, a fruit salad of figs, prunes and apricots, yoghurt, various kinds of egg with tomatoes and mushrooms, and toast and bread.

Daylight revealed Kirkwhelpington a pleasant village with some nice cottages and farmhouses which looks prosperous these days. There is a fine church tower and a churchyard with yews and leaning tombstones. The bathroom window at the back of the Old School House looks out over the church, a definite plus for those addicted to such lugubriously pleasant views.

All in all, you are well and kindly looked after here, and are also well placed to explore and enjoy Northumberland. The Old School House is almost equidistant from the coast and the National Park, on one of the Newcastle to Edinburgh routes, with the lovely upland spaces all around. We spent one hot and humid day on Hadrian's Wall, the next driving slowly over tiny roads up towards the Borders. S.R. and D.F.

CATERING Vegetarian (bacon stocked in freezer for odd carnivore passed on by her friend).

SMOKING Not in evidence.

PRICE CATEGORY Low.

FURTHER INFORMATION Frank and Rhona Young,
Old School House,
Kirkwhelpington,
Northumberland NE19 2RT
Phone (0830) 40226

69. The Rossan

The Rossan is a potentially beautiful Georgian house with a huge garden, just outside the tiny village of Auchencairn, Galloway, facing south-east across an inlet of the Solway to the Lakeland hills. Set in this quiet, unspoilt part of Scotland, full of archaeology, bird and plant life, it could be the perfect place to stay. Yet it isn't.

Guests get pretty short shrift when it comes to space in the Rossan. Their dining-cum-sitting room is pretty tiny to begin with, and is not made more spacious by being crammed with furniture: a huge round table with chairs in the middle (though with fresh flowers from the garden) and a giant sideboard against the wall, with telly and mouldering dried flowers. It was very claustrophobic with only the two of us. I hate to think what it would have been like with other guests . . . we'd have had to sit on each other's laps. After dinner we went for a walk and then spent the rest of the evening reading, sitting very close together beside the dining-room table. The Rossan has beautiful Georgian windows, but you don't get much view from this all-in-one guests' hidey hole at the back of the house. A pity in midsummer, when the light is so beautiful in Scotland.

The bedrooms are larger – ours was very large in fact – but had other drawbacks. The bed was distinctly uncomfortable with nylon sheets. The door was painted a shockingly bright glossy pink, a minor detail, perhaps, but a good, representative example of the Rossan's decorative style. Most of the doors were also pink. The bathroom, which you share with the Bardsleys, lacked a shower and the skirting boards and rugs were a bit dingy.

Mrs Bardsley smoked in the kitchen and, while she didn't actually smoke around us, I was aware of it most of the time. If you're allergic or sensitive to cigarette smoke, it's something to bear in mind.

The food was almost very good; just a bit hit and miss. For dinner we had a fresh garden vegetable soup which would have been wonderful (had it not been oversalted), accompanied by delicious homebaked, wholewheat bread. The stuffed aubergine was a rather unappetising grey, though the fresh tomato sauce was excellent. The accompanying vegetables were less distinguished – lumpy mashed potatoes and overcooked cauliflower. Dessert was oversweetened rhubarb, followed by mouldy Camembert and stale crackers. The herb tea was good, however. Breakfast was muesli followed by free-range eggs and more of Mrs Bardsley's lovely bread, with tea or coffee.

The Rossan is basically a traditional guesthouse serving traditional food, though Mrs Bardsley, who is herself vegetarian, goes out of her way to cull favour with the vegetarian tourist. She obviously has good intentions, serves reliably vegetarian food, often her own produce, and free-range eggs which, after all, is the most important thing for the travelling vegetarian. Too bad, then, about the cigarette smoke, cramped living/dining space, nylon sheets and lurid paint. Otherwise, you could do worse for a night.

CATERING Traditional and vegetarian.

SMOKING No known rules. Proprietor smokes.

PRICE CATEGORY Low. (Visitors are warned that they will have to pay for any damages.)

FURTHER INFORMATION Mrs Bardsley,
The Rossan,
Auchencairn, Castle Douglas,
Kirkcudbrightshire DG 7 1QR
Scotland
Phone (055 664) 269

70. Windywalls

Modest and unassuming, Windywalls is a real place to get away from it all: it's on top of the world above Gatehouse of Fleet with terrific views of the Solway and Isle of Man beyond; there are no other houses in sight. The house is really magical to behold, especially if like me you have a fondness for wooden houses. It was built by a Swede in the 1930s.

David and Hilary Hawker are caring, intelligent people. Both are ex-teachers. David, who works for the Nature Conservancy, is a very serious bird-watcher and also leads courses on birds. They and their pathologically shy great Great Dane, Bo, greeted us and made us feel instantly at home. Friendly and helpful but never intrusive, they've got the balance just right.

However: if you are expecting to be entertained in the grand manner, this is not the place for you. Windywalls is very homey: toys, books, well-worn sofas, no antiques and no Laura Ashley wallpaper. It is a very lived-in house. The guests' sitting room is large with a wood-burning stove and magnificent view. In the foreground, ducks and chickens range free; better than TV, especially in the mating season. Our bedroom was a bit out of the way (an eccentric house, remember) and could possibly be cold in winter. Not the best bed on the market in the past fifty years, but at Windywalls much is forgiven.

The food, I am reluctant to admit, was disappointing: the (homemade) wholewheat rolls too yeasty, the Waldorf salad too salad-creamy, the pineapple tartlets too fussy. Since the pineapple was fresh and perfectly ripe, I would have preferred plain fruit, perhaps with yoghurt or cream. The strength of a place like Windywalls is that it is simple and unselfconscious; that could easily apply to the food too, with a little *less* effort. The lasagna was delicious.

David and Hilary are splendid people and it's a treat to share their fine, remote house. They are not exclusively vegetarian themselves, but you can trust they will care for you meatlessly. Strongly recommended, especially for hearty types and nature-watchers, but not recommended for fuss-budgets or interior decorators. An excellent place for children – fairly childproof inside and plenty of space outside.

CATERING Traditional and vegetarian.

SMOKING Not in evidence.

PRICE CATEGORY Very Low.

FURTHER INFORMATION David and Hilary Hawker,
Windywalls,
Gatehouse of Fleet,
Kirkcudbrightshire, Scotland
Phone (055 74) 249

Other Places to Stay

Borders: Longformacus, Berwicks: Horn House Hotel
Phone (03617) 291
T-V specialist hotel for people who are allergic or environmentally sensitive, 'many of whom are vegetarian'. Price category M to VH.

Strathclyde: Glendrissaig, by Girvan, Ayrshire: (Mrs Kate McIntosh)
Phone (0465) 4631
V-T (wholefood), B & B + EM 'only at quieter times'. Owners vegetarian. Price category L.

Places to Eat

LOTHIAN

Edinburgh: The Breadwinner (XV); (a) 1 Raeburn Place. Phone 031–332 3864; (b) 47A South Clerk Street. Phone 031–667 9091.

Edinburgh: Helios Fountain (XV), 7 Grassmarket. Phone 031–229 7884.

Edinburgh: Henderson's Salad Table (XV), 94 Hanover Street. Phone 031–225 2131.

Edinburgh: Kalpna (XV), 2/3 St Patrick Square. Phone 031–667 9890.

Edinburgh: Seeds Cafe (XV), 53 West Nicholson Street. Phone 031–667 8673.

STRATHCLYDE

Glasgow: Asha Vegetarian Restaurant (XV), 415 Sauchiehall Street. Phone 041–332 4996.

Peebles: Sunflower Restaurant (XV), 6 Bridgegate. Phone (0721) 22420.

St Andrews, Fife: Brambles Wholefood Restaurant & Coffee House (V-T), 5 College Street. Phone (0721) 22420.

IX

SCOTLAND –
HIGHLANDS AND
ISLANDS

The north of Scotland is surprisingly well supplied with vegetarian places to stay, fairly evenly spread across the area apart from a cluster on Skye. And just as well, too; although fresh food is slowly spreading to rather more greengrocers than in the dreaded days when their only contents were potatoes, swedes, cabbage in summer and Brussels sprouts in winter, there are still plenty of cafés and restaurants where you'd never know it, and where a non-smoker, let alone a vegetarian, is still a freak. Health-food stores are few and far between: as well as major towns (Aberdeen, Inverness), look in the back of the delicatessen in Aviemore (near the station) and in the greengrocer/fishmonger in Portree.

Places Reviewed

71. Ben Tianavaig, Portree, Isle of Skye (XV)
72. Brook Linn Country House Hotel, Callander, Central (XV)
73. Ceilidh Place, Ullapool, Highland
74. Langdale Guest House, Nr Broadford, Isle of Skye
75. Letterbea, Boat of Garten, Highland (XV)
76. Minton House, Findhorn, Grampian (XV)
77. The Osprey Hotel, Kingussie, Highland
78. Rosebank House, Dornoch, Highland
79. Samadhan, Nr Ullapool, Highland
80. Strathlee, Nr Kilcreggan, Strathclyde
81. Tigh Cuileann, Nr Inveraray, Strathclyde (XV)
82. Vegancroft, Nr Dunvegan, Isle of Skye (XVgn)

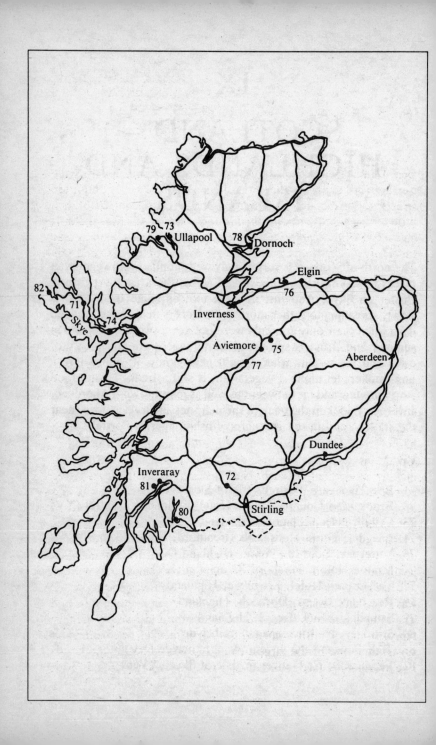

71. Ben Tianavaig

Ben Tianavaig, the guesthouse, on the grandly named Bosville Terrace (but don't get the wrong idea – there are only about ten streets in Portree and it's better known as the Staffin Road), is a little terraced house run for the last few years by Viv Mansfield. It has been strictly vegetarian for the last three. I didn't actually stay there: the only rooms available are double or bigger, and Viv understandably didn't want to give one away to me on my own at the height of the season. So she arranged for me to stay at a conventional B & B nearby (over which I prefer to draw a veil: if you don't fit in at Ben Tianavaig try to avoid the one I stayed in) but took me in for the evening meal and, as it turned out, an evening's conversation afterwards and a rendezvous with her and some friends at a curious Anglo-ceilidh two days later. She's that sort of person.

So I can't tell you first hand about the bedrooms, though I've no doubt they are at the very least adequately comfortable, and all of them will have superb views south-east over Portree's picturesque harbour to Ben Tianavaig, the eponymous mountain. They have, Viv Mansfield says, proper firm mattresses, and kettles/tea-making equipment in each. She is scathing about her Portree competition's 'mustn't spoil them' attitude and I'd trust her to do it properly. To judge by the powerful kitchen range there's plenty of hot water, too. I also have to rely on her description of breakfast, which sounds substantial and good – cereals, juice, fruit fresh and dried, yoghurt, toast, etc, plus eggs if you want. (She herself is a lacto- but non-ovo-vegetarian of some years' standing.)

I *can* tell you about supper. To begin with, it was enormous – I was glad I'd cycled 50 miles to earn it – but it's in keeping with Ben Tianavaig's generous style, and no doubt most visitors are hungry types. It started with a hot baked grapefruit half with cinnamon sugar; then one of the largest chunks ('slice' is hardly the word) I've ever got my face round of a rich and tasty nut-seed loaf, with baked potato and about half a sizeable cauliflower; next a salad full of good things, at the sight of which my less energetic neighbours folded up; and finally a date and apple slice made with oat pastry, with yoghurt. Almost dauntingly substantial, but not the sort of lumpy and indigestible excess that one or two places in this book think they ought to provide to outdoor enthusiasts. There was the usual wide assortment of coffee, teas, etc.

The dining room, which doubles as a lounge, is pretty small: one window looking out on the road; two or three new looking varnished white pine tables and matching chairs, a small sofa and a bookshelf with an interesting variety of books (it seems the kind of place where guests donate everything they've finished with to the house library), Monopoly, Scrabble and so on. I suspect visitors go out a lot, presumably to one of the many pubs in Portree. I intended to, or at least to stroll around and admire the lights twinkling on the water and the reflections of the pastel Georgian houses on the pier; but when I wandered into Viv's large and cosy kitchen to pay my bill and discuss a packed lunch in the morning, I was immediately drawn into the conversation going on there and it was hours before I dragged myself away for my walk. Viv was (sometimes still is, in the winter months) a community social worker in London, and is definitely not your average Portree landlandy. She has travelled to India, and studied down the road from me, in search of different kinds of enlightenment (the Indian kind evidently 'took' rather better), and is, she says, getting just a bit restless in her present career. So perhaps you should go before too long, though she promises that if she does sell up she will only sell to a committed vegetarian, and it won't be for a while yet. I found lots to talk about with her and her friends, both the night I ate there and a couple of days later when we met again at a 'folk night' (generously interpreted) at the Three Rowans, a half-vegetarian restaurant on the way to Dunvegan, which I'd also recommend.

A good place, then: not *grand luxe* and not exactly *cuisine minceur* either, but very good of its kind. Oh yes, the packed lunch was superb. Notably the sandwiches made with some wonderful sticky black rye bread which got me up some ferocious hills the next day. I'll be back. O.F.

CATERING Exclusively vegetarian/vegan.

SMOKING Smoking restrictions.

PRICE CATEGORY Low.

FURTHER INFORMATION Ms V. Mansfield,
Ben Tianavaig,
5 Bosville Terrace,
Portree, Isle of Skye
Phone (0478) 2152

72. Brook Linn Country House Hotel

The publicity for Brook Linn Country House Hotel is strong on television connections. 'The Country Diary of an Edwardian Lady' was filmed, in part, in the house and Callander was the setting for 'Dr Finlay's Casebook'. Brook Linn has been a vegetarian hotel/guesthouse for forty years, no less – though Fiona and Derek House have owned it for only one of them – and although only one of the visitors, at well over eighty, could be described as an Edwardian gentleman, several seemed to me as if they'd been coming for all of the forty years. The house itself is a large, rather lumpy Victorian villa, built around 1840 as a country retreat for a Scottish tycoon. It sits on a hillside away from the clutter of modern Callander (its back parts look as if Dr Finlay never left) whose main street is dominated by ice cream, curios and charabancs (you see, it's catching . . .). Behind it are the dense conifers of Lady Willoughby's Crag, in front are treetops, then the meadows where the River Leny joins the Teith, and above them Ben Ledi, looking down on the beginnings of the Trossachs. It faces west and if, as so often in perverse Highland style, a rainy day is followed by a magnificent sunset, you have the full view of it from the sitting room, the dining room, and the best of the bedrooms.

Inside, the house is not exactly my idea of Edwardian authenticity: no doubt the TV company brought some period enchancements and I daresay the last owners took a few away when they sold it. The dining room has some splendid wooden grotesques – a huge table, a lumbering sideboard (or do I mean a chiffonier?) and so on; and there's a very odd thing in the sitting room – a kind of blue, shiny, padded bench with a bookshelf attached to it above your head; also a nice grandfather clock in the hall. The hall has a tremendous flaming red Turkish carpet on the stairs, and a stained-glass stair window, which is also mainly red but with some other pretty strong panels. Unfortunately, the walls are acid green . . . But my bedroom (a small single without the full view) was simple and friendly, except for an extraordinary wall-mounted boiling water dispenser with elaborate instructions for making your own tea and coffee; the bathroom was huge, warm and splendidly unspoiled.

The food was less than inspired. There was tomato soup (tinned tomatoes, I think, but fresh herbs in it) or egg mayonnaise (suspiciously bottled looking mayo); then hazelnut roast which – perhaps after days of Scottish oversalting – I found a bit bland, with cranberry jelly, bread sauce, and 'stuffing' (little round balls of mostly sage); also whole boiled onions, roast potatoes, buttered cabbage and caraway flavoured carrots (all, including, I regret to say, the onion – a little too *al dente*) and a celery and apple (red and green) salad. Then sherry trifle (not much sherry) made with anonymous cake, tinned mandarin oranges, yellowish custard, cream(?) and coloured sprinkles on top. Ho hum. Then a Coffee Ceremony, a huge machine which gurgled ostentatiously with real coffee. We 'went through' to the drawing room to drink it with After Eights. I went out, to escape the conversation, rather elderly and fractured, several of the company being hard of hearing, and to walk it all off. I followed what was described as a Victorian ladies' saunter up a vertical path which pauses, breathlessly, at the top of a splendid beech-covered cliff overlooking the town, and ends on a mini-mountaintop with a 360° view.

In the morning, a lot of breakfast was laid out on the sideboard: cereals (mostly Kellogg's) in glass jars, stewed prunes, figs, hunza apricots, yoghurt; and the mighty coffee machine (alas, we all had tea). Then scrambled eggs and almost anything else you could ask for in a vegetarian cooked breakfast, including very thin potato scones, which were disappointingly chewy; and finally, good toast.

How does one sum it up? Callander is a good place to be – very strategic for the southern Highlands, both east and west, if you have a car – and there are quite a lot of activities on the doorstep. The town would make an excellent base for a youngish family on holiday. As to Brook Linn, I liked Derek and Fiona a lot but I think they're in a difficult position. They took over a going, in fact longstanding concern, and evidently also its clientele, and I rather think they're trying to live up (or down in my view) to the previous management's style in decor and food. It's not altogether successful and since, to judge by the sample of the clientele I met, it will certainly not last as long as Fiona and Derek, I think they should relax and adapt a bit, to try and appeal to a younger and rather different generation of vegetarians. Not altogether easy in that house but I think some changes in style would be possible. I certainly think there's great potential. By no means unqualified approval then, more in that peculiar class which the *Good Food Guide* describes as More Reports Please. O.F.

CATERING Exclusively vegetarian.

SMOKING No smoking.

PRICE CATEGORY Medium.

FURTHER INFORMATION Fiona and Derek House
Brook Linn Country House,
Callander, Perthshire FK17 8AU
Scotland
Phone (0877) 30103

73. Ceilidh Place

Ceilidh Place advertises itself as having vegetarian proprietors and 'catering for carnivores'. In practice it is a carnivorous hotel. You are not invited to share the proprietors' meals, after all, and the hotel menu for dinner when we were there showed the familiar score of one (uninspired) vegetarian main course out of five. This was a spinach roulade, rather dry and indigestible, served with potatoes, leeks and carrots. The à la carte menu advertised was not available. The other courses were all vegetarian-friendly: starters were minestrone, hors d'oeuvres (good but over-mayonnaisy) and stuffed mushrooms which were delicious. The sweets and puddings were the best course, with trifle, fresh fruit salad, a Viennese coffee cake, a carrot tart and a large selection of good-looking cheeses. Dinner was £9.50, plus wine; the house wine was acceptable. If your concept of vegetarianism embraces seafood this will buy you a good dinner; but not if, on the other hand, the sight and sound of a local langoustine being dismembered nearby puts you off. This was not our problem, but we were a little irritated by the whole page of the menu taken up by gushing and whimsical self-congratulation of the beauties of the experiences provided by the hotel and its surroundings. Once you're there you can presumably judge for yourself. And besides, the advertised virtues of quiet and space and good music were represented on this particular evening by a Dave Brubeck record playing rather too loud in the background. Good points about the ambience were the no-smoking rule in the dining room and the friendliness of the very young staff.

The hotel has been created by converting an old Ullapool town-house, and this has been beautifully done. The dining room is a wood and glass extension at the back, behind the huge comfortable bar which is furnished in wood and has Peace and Green movement magazines to read. Upstairs is the residents' lounge, a serene room with a low ceiling, beautiful decoration and furniture, and a view over the harbour up Loch Broom. People who have stayed in the rooms in the main part of the hotel say that they too are comfortable and have an individual style. We spent the night in the Clubhouse annexe. This is pleasant but basic, rooms with a combination of bunks and double beds, a sturdy table and chairs; basin in the room, shared toilets and a shower room on the ground floor. The clubhouse accommodation would be good for family groups, though expensive compared with bed and breakfast prices. It is practical and pays attention to fire precautions, but it is not at all soundproof; neighbouring children and, when we were there, a lavatory imitating the Stornoway ferry leaving port, were all too clearly audible. The bar and music room for live folk music and jazz are also in the same building; ceilidhs take place on Saturday nights.

Breakfast was excellent and lavish, self-service with a good range of cereals and fresh and preserved fruits and fruit juices, good coffee and toast freshly and generously provided. Cooked breakfasts on offer were carnivorous. The same background music as at dinner was even less welcome at this time of day.

We enjoyed the hotel's own small bookshop, which has a good stock of local interest books, but were distracted by explosions of bad language from behind the reception desk where our bill was being sorted out. From the harassed personal welcome from one of the proprietors to this muddled departure, Ceilidh Place gave us an impression of a system under strain. We felt that this was a place which needed to pay attention to the smooth and happy running of the basic things it offers before being distracted by the variety of good ideas built around the hotel. The concept and the style are attractive, and the Ceilidh Place experience could even fulfil the large claims made for it. Certainly a lot of vegetarians and part-time vegetarians will be attracted by what has been created; but at present they should be prepared to pay quite highly, and they should announce their dietary preferences in advance rather than expect to find them catered for. S.R. and D.F.

CATERING Traditional and vegetarian. Licensed.

SMOKING Smoking restrictions.

PRICE CATEGORY Hotel – Very High; clubhouse – High.

FURTHER INFORMATION Ceilidh Place,
West Argyle Street,
Ullapool,
Wester Ross, Scotland
Phone (0854) 2103

74. Langdale Guest House

When I first visited Broadford on Skye many years ago, it had a kind of native Highland squalor – sprawling, messy and rather depressed. Coming back in 1986 I found it no nicer but curiously changed: it now seems to be trying hard to imitate one of those Mediterranean coastal strip developments, with tacky amenities for the tasteless tourist covering several miles along the main road. Even the smell of drains was authentically Greek. My heart sank a bit, I will confess, and the first half mile along the road to the improbable sounding Waterloo didn't help a lot, being full of rather ugly bungalows among the occasional older house by the shore of Broadford Bay. But peace descended, the seaweed began to smell of sea instead of other things, the bungalows did at least have gardens, and the view got better all the time.

Waterloo (which is sadly named in honour of the appalling number of Skye men who lost their lives in a battle that can have made not the slightest difference to their island) is at the end of the road, where two bays meet at a little promontory sticking out into the Inner Sound. And the last house on the road is Langdale Guest House, purpose-built by Ted and Dorothy Green to accommodate eight visitors in considerable comfort. It's not, to be frank, a thing of great beauty, certainly not in Skye. It's a long single-storey house set in a rather suburban looking piece of landscaping, with two lawns with flowerbeds, a big expanse of gravel, and so on. But inside, despite rather a lot of frosted, patterned, coloured and even bubbly glass and a fair number of knick-knacks, it's a very friendly place: plain paint in innocent colours, several bookshelves with good reading and, best of all, huge (and double-glazed) picture windows from which to admire the truly cosmic view. The arrangement of the drawing room furniture makes the point very nicely. There is a fireplace, but nobody in their right mind would choose to stare at it given the alternative, so the chairs are set in a semi-circle around the east-facing window, with a pair of binoculars lying handy for seal-spotting on the skerries, submarine-hunting in Loch Carron, or just plain bird-watching. Even in the garden there is, say the Greens who are enthusiastic amateurs, quite an exotic selection, including short-eared owls who come and stare in at the visitors. And that's only one window: the other faces north to north-west, with the other half of the Sound in front and the Red Cuillin off to the left. The dining room and two of the bedrooms have the same outlook and I was much distracted from my excellent supper by the superb sunset.

Supper began with a big choice of starters: fruit juice, melon, mushroom soup or lentil pie. I chose the soup, and it was freshly made and delicious. Then came a rich nut roast or casserole – too moist to be neatly sliced, more the spooning kind – full of walnuts with olives, peppers and tomatoes and topped with cheese. It came with very fresh cabbage, broccoli, which seemed slightly over-cooked (perhaps frozen?) and an astonishing number of tiny bite-sized new potatoes straight from the garden, some of the best I've ever eaten. I scoffed the lot. Pudding was ice cream or fresh fruit salad with cream: after my potato orgy I settled for the fruit, which turned out to be strawberries, raspberries, nectarine and kiwi (merely!) though the cream, alas, was aerosol. I moved back to the other view for a big pot of good real coffee and After Eights, and was permitted to make friends by the shyest of the household's three cats.

My bedroom was extremely comfortable. The house has been designed to provide everything a visitor might want: central heating, good bed, wash basin, big cupboard, kettle and drinks, and of course the view. I slept very well. Breakfast, as you might predict by now, was pretty good, too: a huge array of things to help yourself from – muesli, Granola, commercial cereals, fruit of all kinds and so on. Cooked possibilities seemed pretty limitless also: I settled for scrambled eggs and tomatoes but there was lots more on offer.

Altogether, I felt thoroughly restored by the time I left, having approached tired and cross and suspecting this was no place for the discriminating traveller. Ted and Dorothy Green, who retired here from the south of England a few years ago, are extremely friendly in the kind of warm and chatty if slightly impersonal way that you expect from a good small hotel. A great deal of care and thought has gone into the design of the house and the way it's run. My own complaint, and I'm having to scratch around for one, was the Greens' TV: their kitchen/living space is right next to the main drawing room, and I found the 9 o'clock news and bits of canned laughter coming through the wall a bit disruptive to my mellow and contemplative mood. But I'd love to go back, perhaps for one of those blessed patches of fair weather in autumn or winter, and curl up with some good books and my binoculars; or perhaps in early summer and go out with the Greens on their 22' motor boat which is on offer for nature watching. O.F.

CATERING Traditional and vegetarian; coeliac by arrangement.

SMOKING Smoking restrictions.

PRICE CATEGORY Medium.

FURTHER INFORMATION Ted and Dorothy Green,
Langdale Guest House,
Waterloo,
Breakish,
Isle of Skye IV42 8QE
Phone (047 12) 376

75. Letterbea

Letterbea is a large late Victorian/early Edwardian Scottish villa in Boat of Garten, between Aviemore and Grantown on Spey in the Cairngorms. Much of it is still in the original state: beautiful natural wood (pitch pine and mahogany) window frames and panelling, open fires, a bath that's big enough for two with lots and lots of hot water and a warm and comfortable old wooden loo seat. There's a sitting room/dining room for guests, which is very homely and welcoming once the fire is going. When we were there, in −20°C weather, beautiful fresh irises and daffodils gave an impression of spring (thoroughly belied by the delicate hoar frost patterns on the windows in the morning). At that time there were two big guest bedrooms, one with a double bed and bunks, the other with two singles. (More rooms to come shortly, I believe.) Nice cotton sheets and duvets and, what was most important considering the climatic conditions, electric blankets. Bits of the house were obviously still being done up: doors inadvertently left open revealed ladders and paint pots, but all those parts given over to guests were finished and tastefully decorated.

Throughout the weekend we were extremely well fed despite a conspiracy of events which would have led many B & B owners to despair. Breakfast was porridge, barley one day, oats the next, muesli, stewed apricots and homemade (delicious stringy culture) yoghurt, wholemeal scones, toast and a series of spreads; tea or freshly made coffee, and one day, proper fresh orange juice out of an orange and not a square carton. We were offered eggs but had no space. However, as a fellow guest (non-vegetarian) remarked, there was plenty of roughage. Those who like a bland, smooth and unchewy breakfast had better go elsewhere.

Supper (we only had one night's, alas) was barley and seaweed soup, which was delicious, then a lentil bake with celery in lemon, haricot beans in garlic butter and bulghur wheat, all followed by fresh fruit salad, cream and yoghurt. It sounds deceptively simple: it was all perfectly cooked and beautifully arranged, a very special treat in any circumstances. But that this particular meal arrived at all, in any form, was amazing. Like us, Helen Geddes and her friend Moira had gone out cross-country skiing that day, but one of their party broke a ski and had to walk miles; then their road home was blocked by another car in a ditch. At that point Helen telephoned a neighbour to come round and put the oven on; she did so, and announced herself to us by blowing all the fuses in the process. Helen and Moira arriving in due course, set to cooking our supper with a vengeance and blew the fuses again. Finally, while we were peacefully if hungrily drinking our wine and listening to her records, Helen reappeared to ask with great calmness if we would very much mind moving our car to let the fire engine into the drive, as the central heating chimney just happened to be on fire . . . Even this, however, only delayed the production of a magnificent meal. Later still we learned that on top of all this, the dishwasher had frozen up. One of us, who ventured into the kitchen with some minor request, found a scene of total exhaustion. That they managed to cook supper at all, let alone such a truly elegant and considered meal, in the face of such adversity, is an astonishing tribute. I must go back soon and see what they do on a less eventful night.

There are endless opportunities for activity around Boat of Garten, in both winter and summer. We had gone for the cross-country skiing: skis can be hired quite easily in Aviemore, about 6 miles away. The main downhill skiing centre of Scotland is also nearby. At other times there are lots of walks to suit all energy levels, cycling, swimming (for the brave) in fact anything outdoor including a limitless supply of wonderful scenery for the more sedentary. Boat of Garten is famed as an osprey village, although some idiot has cut down the ospreys' official nesting tree; but there are evidently other ospreys and plenty of other birds around. Helen Geddes knows the area well, and can advise you on good, out of the way places for skiing or, I suspect, almost any other activity you want. She is planning a whole series of special interest/activity weeks, including wildflowers, geology and land use, cycling, hillwalking and skiing. S.R.

PS

I went back in the summer, by which time a lovely single room was available, looking out of the front of the house at the good view. I got my revenge for the late supper in March by arriving at 9 p.m., exhausted, soaked and with a borderline case of hypothermia. I was whisked upstairs and put straight into the palatial bath. By the time I'd staggered out of my wet clothes, and told not to move till I was alive again, a huge teapot was waiting for me. Nobody reproached me, miraculously, and supper was ready when I was. I stayed for two days and everything was as good as before or even better: magnificent breakfasts – one day banana pancakes, the next oatmeal scones with cheese and a kind of hummus without the garlic, each after porridges made of exotic grains. Packed lunches were imaginative and wonderful: peanut butter and sliced apple, cream cheese and sprouts sandwiches and so on. Dinner one night was soup and about seven salads, all interesting and all improved with something unusual from the garden such as herbs, endive or dandelion. The other night's dinner was a magnificent Indian feast, starting with pakoras, then two subtle curries (one with fresh peas and carrots) and fresh pineapple and lychees for pudding. Fellow-guests said there was a different nationality nearly every night: French, Mexican, Indonesian and so on. Even better than I'd remembered. I'm going to be a regular so don't all come at once. O.F.

CATERING Exclusively vegetarian.

SMOKING Restricted.

PRICE CATEGORY Low.

FURTHER INFORMATION Helen Geddes,
Letterbea,
Strathspey,
Boat of Garten,
Aviemore, Inverness-shire PH24 3BD
Phone (047 983) 209

76. Minton House

Minton House is on the doorstep (well, across the road) from the Findhorn Foundation Caravan Park. As the Meynells say in their beautifully written information sheets, which you find on your desk/dressing table, 'We are completely independent of the Foundation, but we gratefully acknowledge that we would not be here without it.' The house is primarily a house of peace, relaxation and healing, and a number of alternative health practitioners are available, either on the premises or nearby, offering Alexander technique, massage, reflexology, dietary therapy, etc. But until the healing side becomes full time, they are happy to have guests who may or may not be interested in a massage while they are there, in the use of the Sanctuary, a beautiful meditation room with big windows looking south and west, or in any of the other facilities. Much of the house's passing trade, if that's the expression, comes from visitors to the Foundation – people who, for instance, need a few days to prepare for re-entry to real life after their Experience Week. The night I stayed, there were four or five of these, of a number of different nationalities and in various emotional states. Judith and Peter-John Meynell, the owners, are perhaps surprisingly unfreaky – if I dare use the word – for such a place: they are friendly and hospitable, but perfectly businesslike. I suppose they may play down the more exotic side of their offerings for non-Findhornies like myself (possibly I looked a little nervous) but they certainly seemed reassuringly normal.

The house is quite bizarre. Built in 1957 by a couple who 'did a lot of entertaining', according to the Meynells, it is an enormous, ugly, rather nondescript lump of granite, painted pale pink and sitting in vast areas of lawn, with the shores of Findhorn Bay behind a wall on two sides. As the brochure says, it is a peaceful place, though the amount of traffic on the road to Findhorn village and beach was astonishing (it was an August Saturday) and as there was an easterly wind blowing, I was always aware of the traffic in the distance. But I sat on the wall facing the bay, watched ospreys doing their kamikaze diving, and soaked up the late afternoon sun feeling quite reasonably at ease, before going to find the bath, for which hot water was promised on the dot of 6.30.

Inside, the huge house turns out to be a small house with huge rooms, if you follow me. The main room is a gigantic drawing room, at least $30' \times 20'$, with, leading off it at one side, a slightly smaller study (housing a superb and apparently mint condition vegetarian cook book collection), and on another, an enormous ballroom, even bigger and entirely bare. The Meynells have accepted the inevitable and left it entirely unfurnished and decorated. Even the main drawing room swallows up quite a lot of furniture. The dining room is on a similar scale: it has a good sized table in the sunny, east-facing window which looks equally insignificant. But the Meynells are trying hard. They have a long way to go in decorating the inside of the house, which at present has a large variety of hideous wallpaper, but meanwhile there are wallhangings, pictures and photographs to cheer things up. The Sanctuary, at least, is beautiful, very simply decorated and with giant soft-coloured cushions on the floor; but as it was rather full of meditators I decided to go out and watch the sunset over the beach instead. My room, finally, was not attractive. It was a decent size for a bedroom, if a bit long and thin: it was built as a mere dressing room for a master bedroom next door. It was papered in striped yellow, with one or two sheets of the same pattern but different colourways (pink and cream) at one end. There was a large double bed, which turned out to be rather soggy and very lumpy, a dressing table/desk and that was it apart from two built-in cupboards, one containing a wash basin. But most other bedrooms are en suite so I had an enormous bathroom down the hall to myself.

Some things about Minton House may soon change. The house is in the process of redecoration, and Kathryn, who did the cooking – and dietary therapy, massage, reflexology, etc – is not committed to next season. In fact, she was away for my visit but had prepared the food before she left. For what it's worth, dinner was rather unrelenting: there was a black-eyed bean 'cordial', said the menu – stew to you – made with a few other vegetables and hiziki seaweed, with mixed grains and cauliflower. The latter two came unadorned on a huge plate with one inside the other. Then a mixed salad which, by contrast, did in fact taste and look beautiful, and fresh fruit salad with lots of different summer fruits. Kathryn's cooking is evidently firmly salt, sugar, dairy and wheat-free; but in her absence someone smuggled in a bottle of tamari sauce for the first course and a jug of yoghurt for the fruit salad. I found it wholesome and filling rather than inspiring but that, no doubt, was the intention. Breakfast was help-yourself-at-any-time: there is a kettle and a toaster and all the usual drinks, jars of cereal, fruit (Outspan oranges!), raw, dried fruit, brown bread, peanut butter, etc. You really could have it any time – an exhausted Experiencee was eating hers at midday as I left.

'As you walk in the peace hits you', the brochure says, in its one infelicitous phrase. I have to be honest and say that I'm not a good healee; I found the Findhorn Foundation, with its inherent internal contradictions and its incongruity with its surroundings, a bit oppressive; and I was, bluntly, glad to get away, peace or no. (And I didn't feel that at Grimstone Manor where some of the same things go on.) If healing and spirituality are your thing, you'll surely like it a lot: if they're not, maybe that's your problem and mine. O.F.

CATERING Strictly vegetarian; vegan in 1986.

SMOKING No smoking.

PRICE CATEGORY High.

FURTHER INFORMATION Minton House,
Findhorn, Forres,
Moray IV36 0YY
Scotland
Phone (0309) 30819

77. The Osprey Hotel

The Osprey is in many ways an unusual, indeed idiosyncratic place. It is small but unashamedly luxurious. It feels like a country house but it's in the rather dreary main street of a grey Highland town but with lovely places in easy walking distance as well as further afield. It certainly isn't exclusively vegetarian and the personality of one of the owners is a bit powerful. But a glance at *The Good Hotel Guide* for many years past will tell you, like Duncan Reeves (the host), it cannot be ignored, and it has made genuine efforts ever since its opening to cater well for vegetarians.

First, the place. Kingussie has been transformed in the last few years by the new A9 bypass, and has reverted to a rather sleepy little town, home of the Highland Folk Museum, the golf course with the best views in Scotland, and access to the whole west flank of the Cairngorms and the beauties of Speyside. The tasteful person's Aviemore, you might say. As you drive into town from the south, you will see a monster plate-glass and tartan-carpeted hotel – the Duke of Gordon – on your left with twenty tour buses parked outside. Just across the road, but facing the town gardens, is The Osprey, converted from a modest family villa or perhaps the manse for one of the many large churches.

Inside, all is comfort. The bedrooms are lovely with delicate, flowery decoration with fresh or dried flowers as well, according to season. Big baths, lots of hot water, comfortable and cosy beds with electric underblankets and plain, oatmeal carpets. Downstairs there are two sitting rooms, one with TV, one without, with well-lit and comfortable chairs. The rooms are a bit crowded but this is so as to leave space for the dining room, the biggest room in the house. It's done up in handsome Edwardian style – dark paint and velvet curtains, polished tables, silver, candles, etc.

The food is distinctly good. I've been there for two dinners but on quite separate occasions; both times the main dish was oatmeal roast, a rather splendid if distinctly rich concoction of oatmeal, onions, herbs and quite a lot of butter and cream; a kind of superior, meatless haggis, I suppose. I'm sure other confections are available if you stay more than one night at a time, though I note the brochure says that vegetarians are offered unusual dishes such as . . . oatmeal roast. With it come beautifully cooked vegetables, astonishingly fresh for the Highlands, where everyone has them in their gardens but the greengrocers are enough to send you screaming to California. There is a wide choice of starters, some of which are always vegetarian; puddings are mostly sweetish and there's lots of cream on offer but not everything is made with white flour and white sugar. There is also a splendid, indeed formidable, wine list, especially with a most polite kilt waiting while you make up your mind. A proper hotel dinner. The biggest problem about staying several days must be the sense of over-indulgence though, after long days skiing, walking or climbing, it can be very welcome.

As for breakfast, this is probably the real *tour de force* of The Osprey. What chiefly sticks in the mind, if not the stomach, is excellent, true Scottish porridge, with double cream. (I believe milk is available for the pathetically weedy.) There is, of course, anything else you might wish: muesli, prunes, yoghurt, eggs in any shape or form, and there's no problem about wholewheat toast. Others will be eating kippers, oak-smoked haddocks and for all I know devilled lamb's kidneys in silver chafing dishes, so be prepared. But at least they won't smoke in the dining room: the Osprey's management has no problems about making rules. There is also heather honey and ground coffee.

The Osprey is an exceptionally comfortable, indeed luxurious, small country house hotel which takes very seriously the business of meeting its guests' physical needs, be they vegetarian or anything else (though I don't somehow think it's a place for vegans). Food is important mainly because it *is* important, but also because most visitors will be out on the hills all day. Our breakfast certainly kept us going during a long, hard morning's skiing. Pauline Reeves (you won't see much of her) is an exceptionally warm and welcoming person, and trustworthy, too: you can be sure she won't confuse the vegetarian margarine or oil with the vast amounts of dripping that must come out of her kitchen.

Duncan Reeves, who does the serving and socialising, is one of those people you meet in the Highlands who has what sounds to my doubtless insensitive ears like a thoroughly English accent (perhaps it's Scottish public school?) and a somewhat dubious kilt. He is ex-Army S A S I suspect, or something else rather special. I add these gratuitous details because at the Osprey you feel a bit like a guest at a country house weekend with a host who expects you to do your bit to add to the general jollity, though I think you can be private if you choose. Either way, go for a luxurious, pampered stay. O.F.

CATERING Traditional and vegetarian. Licensed bar.

SMOKING Smoking restrictions.

PRICE CATEGORY Medium to Very High.

FURTHER INFORMATION Duncan and Pauline Reeves,
The Osprey Hotel,
Kingussie, Invernesshire PH21 1EN,
Scotland
Phone (05402) 510

78. Rosebank House

Cheryl Carter and her family came from Derbyshire to Sutherland a few years ago and have rescued Rosebank House from a state of neglect. It is a large and friendly looking nineteenth-century Scottish farmhouse, white with steep gables, and looks over fields towards the Dornoch Firth. Inside the house is less inspiring; clean but impersonal, standard B & B rather than the more individual style we had come to expect from vegetarian places. There is a large bathroom with a fine Victorian floral basin (now cracked and out of use), but here too some forbidding notices; there is also a shower downstairs. The bed was comfortable – cotton sheets and duvet – but no little friendly touches, of flowers, etc; on the mantelpiece was a gruesome horned skull which did not seem well judged to appeal to a vegetarian guest.

The food offered is either whole food or vegetarian; from the cooking smells, the family is certainly carnivorous. The separate dining room for guests is dominated by what seems to have been a large railway station clock, whose tick would have been better at the far end of platform 6 than overhead while drinking one's soup. We had booked our vegetarian meal several days in advance, and although admittedly one of us was pregnant and feeling choosy, we did not enjoy it. First course was lentil soup or orange juice; the soup was adequate though uninteresting. Next came a large pile of wholewheat lasagne with a few bits of carrot and courgette in it and some glutinous cheese sauce on top. It was extremely stodgy, with little flavouring. There was also a salad with fresh crispy lettuce, but no dressing or even oil and vinegar. Dessert was either apple crumble and ice cream or an orange, fig and date salad. These were edible but extremely sweet. The underlying idea seemed to be quantity rather than quality. There was a choice of tea or coffee afterwards; again, none of the special or herb teas offered by many vegetarian places, but extremely strong tea bags. By far the nicest aspect of the meal was being waited on engagingly by the eleven/twelve year-old Carter daughter. Her father's landscape paintings, of which there are a lot about the place, weren't quite our thing; a bit loud and unsteady, like the dining-room clock (though not at all like the artist, who seems just the opposite).

Breakfast was an improvement. A menu states the alternatives available; orange juice or fresh grapefruit or cornflakes, Weetabix or All Bran. (Some of us like orange juice *with* our cereals.) Then there were boiled eggs, scrambled eggs with mushrooms or tomatoes or baked beans on toast. The eggs were delicious, free-range from the garden; but the toasted sliced bread, Golden Shred marmalade and Gales honey detracted from this good impression.

Although there is no sitting room for guests, you are invited to sit with the Carters in their room where there is an open fire and a TV. We were offered tea and biscuits in the evening, which in fact turned out to be quite a spread of cakes, spice bread and biscuits, many of them homemade. One rule of the house which we much appreciated was the very strict no smoking. Mrs Carter's determination to have no smoke in her house seems to be a principal motive in her move towards the wholefood/veg market; she makes this clear when accepting bookings and says she has refused casual visitors in the past if they wish to smoke inside.

We walked down the small road past the house towards the Firth and enjoyed the quiet, the yellow gorse and blue sea, and the open skies of the east coast. Dornoch is about 3 miles away, and this could be a good base from which to explore this part of the world, or on the way to the far north and Sutherland. Our tranquillity in the morning was disturbed by the RAF from the nearby base practising their tree-trimming skills. And when the new Dornoch Firth road crossing is built it will cut through the meadows between Clashmore and the sea in front of Rosebank House.

We found this a pleasant enough place to be in but not especially appealing, and the food only ordinary, to say no worse. It felt like many bed and breakfasts, and from those that advertise themselves to vegetarians we have begun to expect something slightly special. Enthusiastic comments in the visitors' book (including some about the food) suggest that others have felt differently. S.R. and D.F.

CATERING Traditional and vegetarian.

SMOKING No smoking.

PRICE CATEGORY Very Low.

FURTHER INFORMATION Cheryl Carter,
Rosebank House,
Clashmore, Nr Dornoch,
Sutherland, Scotland
Phone (086288) 273

79. Samadhan

Samadhan is not the easiest place to get to, but that is half its virtue, and it's worth every step. On the Scoraig Peninsula between Loch Broom and Little Loch Broom it is a beautiful and calm retreat from the world. To get there you either park your car at Badrallach and walk 4 miles along the coast track which rises high above the sea at one point, with waterfalls and the chance of seals to encourage you; or, if you are staying for a few days, Tom Forsyth can pick you up by boat from Badluarach on the other side of Little Loch Broom. There are no cars on Scoraig, and the only electricity is provided by small windmills which whizz away constantly above the houses. The peninsula has a population of about thirty-five adults and thirty-five children, all of whom have arrived from outside in the last twenty years. Most of them live in houses built up from the ruins of the old crofts.

Samadhan itself is a large house and one of the earliest; Tom has been here for twenty-two years and Sundara for nine, and they have lived in the house itself for the past five. The garden shows the years of patient care and skill. You step in from the wild heather moorland and windswept rocky slopes, through the wind-break of trees into a magically sheltered garden, full of azaleas, rhododendrons, apple trees, flowers and scents and a vegetable garden. Inside the house you enter the huge kitchen/living room where you can eat, sit and just be. There are beams with pans and skillets hanging down and little vases of flowers everywhere; you look out of the low windows to the garden and glimpses of the loch. The bedrooms are small and comfortable; Laura Ashley and, again, lots of good wooden furniture and bunches of flowers. A shared bathroom is as relaxed as the rest of the house; even the messages about what the septic tank will or won't consume do not come across as orders to guests so much as useful information. The most pleasing room is upstairs: the meditation room (but which can be used for a variety of purposes). A large room with parquet floor, a few rugs and cushions, a cassette player, it is light and tranquil and as quiet as everywhere, with a huge window in the gable end looking out to the west and the sea. You realise why Sundara looks upon her house as a retreat rather than a guest-house. It is designed to be used in this way, for individuals or groups. Sometimes there are courses and activities: the ones mentioned in this year's brochure were a women's art workshop, a hiking retreat and a week of Alexander technique. We just came for a rest and a pause for reflection – two long, twilit June nights when the cuckoos never stopped calling, and a day of exploring Scoraig. We left refreshed.

Meals are *en famille* in the kitchen, where cups of tea and cakes and biscuits seem to be on offer whenever you want them. The food is good though not over-elaborate. For example, the first night we had avocado vinaigrette, salad, lasagne and huge slices of chocolate gâteau and cream. It's a 7 mile walk to the nearest pub, but those in need of alcohol need not despair; excellent homemade stout, beer and wine are provided in liberal quantities. The regime is basically vegetarian though apparently there is fish and seafood occasionally. We said we were vegetarian before arriving and it certainly created no problems. Breakfast was good, too. Muesli, juice, home-baked rolls fresh from the oven, scrambled, boiled or omeletted eggs, fresh from the hen, homemade marmalade, and honey, which in a good year (when the bees haven't all died as they did in 1985–6) is probably fresh from the garden too. The milk comes straight from the cow and the quark is homemade. As if that weren't enough, there are extremely generous packed lunches.

Even if you have no particular spiritual or artistic end in view, there is plenty to do provided you like the outdoor life and have good waterproof clothing. Of course, you could sit in the calm world of the house and garden at Samadhan all day and meditate, but the outside is too attractive. There is a respectable mountain at the back of the house, and the secrets of the coastline and the little inland lochs to explore. On the north side of the peninsula is a mysterious sixth-century Christian settlement and fine rock forma-tions. There are otters, but we saw seals and a porpoise and enjoyed the flowers on the cliffs. Tom has great knowledge of the area and will tell you where to go and what to look out for. The more energetic can always walk the 4 miles to the road, drive through the beech woods at Dundonnell, rush up the several thousand feet of An Teallach, down again and walk back in time for tea – but you need to be fit! Provided you are prepared to do the walking required at each end there are endless mountains to climb, brochs to explore and lochs to swim in.

It's difficult to write about a place which charmed and calmed us so much; we found no disappointments and would not like to set them up for others who will experience it differently. What we particularly liked about Samadhan was that we were made to feel as though we were friends visiting. This is partly to do with the eating and living arrangements; you get to know your fellow-guests and Tom and Sundara in a way which doesn't usually happen in a bed and breakfast or a hotel; and you may also end up helping with the washing-up, but that's part of feeling at home. But mainly it is because Tom and Sundara, having chosen the best and much the bravest way of opening their house to people, seem to have the patience and the inner resources to enjoy and welcome them all. Of course, a lot depends on who you coincide with, if you haven't arranged to go to Samadhan as a group. We met people we wouldn't normally meet, the one disadvantage as far as we were concerned being that one of the other guests smoked – a lot – and seemed rather insensitive to complaints. But this was gracefully managed and the man who did smoke was persuaded to go outside at breakfast time – there's plenty of wind out there to disperse the smoke. Smoking is banned in the bedrooms and the meditation room.

What else? There is a diminutive wind-powered TV, if you want that, and a piano upstairs – musicians and musical people are especially welcome, it seems. We didn't discover how the piano had got there, nor some other technical mysteries like the endless hot water. Scoraig is a retreat and an escape, but towards a saner way of life. To live there all the time, build a house and make a living is obviously hard work and neverending; as a visitor you can envy, but you enjoy the tranquillity others have created. We came with some apprehension and scepticism about the implications of 'alternative' living, and left impressed by Samadhan on both the practical and the spiritual planes. We gave it an embarrassing 10/10, but you can't recommend your friends to others. 1986 was only the second year of opening; it will undoubtedly be a success and will certainly evolve and change. Other people will have to make their own way there and their own discoveries. S.R. and D.F.

CATERING Vegetarian; occasional seafood. Homemade wine, stout and beer (included in price).

SMOKING Smoking restrictions.

PRICE CATEGORY Low.

FURTHER INFORMATION Samadhan,
Scoraig Peninsula,
Dundonnel, By Garve,
Wester Ross, IV23 2RE
Scotland
Phone (085 483) 260

80. Strathlee

Strathlee is a paradise with the devil close at hand. Coming by car I headed west out of Glasgow down the Clyde and up the Gareloch. The sun glittered on the water, the rhododendrons were flowering under the tall beeches in their first green leaves; I turned a corner as the loch curved, and there was Faslane Peace Camp, its caravans huddled across the road from the double chain link fences, TV monitors, police with dogs, and of course the invisible missiles themselves in the monstrously spreading Trident base. Resolutely jamming on my rose-tinted, tunnel-vision glasses I gritted my teeth and drove on, feeling thoroughly guilty at the prospect of a comfortable night, while the campers faced the physical discomfort of their caravans and the far worse one of looking our crazy future in the eye. Turn left at Garelochhead,

Margo Scott had said, then look for the sign to Coulport. Another military road sign; more anti-Trident slogans on the gravel boxes on the roadside; the worse one just says THINK. A whole mountain top of construction camp – miles of fences, cops and dogs. Down the hill, at last, turn away from the signs. Primroses, lambs, fishing boats, a fantastic view across Loch Long and right down to the mountains of Arran. Ignore the grey destroyer steaming up the Clyde; don't think; enjoy the sunset.

Strathlee helps a lot. It's idyllically placed: a little curve of a bay, with a strip of grass where people gallop on ponies, then the road, then the houses, all of them very stately. Glasgow merchants built them for their summer holidays, sailing down the Clyde to Kilcreggan to be met at the pier by their coachmen and driven the 2 miles to their sheltered south-west-facing bay. Strathlee, Margo Scott told me, though one of the less ostentatious houses (at least half of them are full-sized baronial castles) was the most expensive site of all, just at the best point of the curve. It's a wonderfully friendly house – 'cottage-gothic', not the absurd Greek Revival or Gothic Baronial of the others – with tall gables and tall slender windows letting in the light from floor to ceiling. The Scotts have painted it mostly white inside and filled it, mercifully sparely by authentic standards, with turn-of-the-century furniture and an elegantly mixed collection of other things: some rather vicious looking weapons (but of individual not of mass destruction, thank God), beautiful old china in a cabinet, old and newer family photographs on a table, school and factory long-service certificates in frames, a gorgeous modern ceramic vase filled with little magenta carnations; clearly a lot of thought and quiet taste has gone into it. It was, literally, Margo Scott's dream house. She had vivid dreams about it for fifteen years before setting eyes on it for the first time when house-hunting. She left her job in a building society two years ago to open up the guesthouse; and Hugh Scott gave up a full-time teaching job, though he still teaches art part-time between writing childrens' books.

The night I was there the food was plain and simple and none the worse for that: a rich lentil soup, followed by wholewheat macaroni in a tomato and onion sauce – rather too visibly oniony for my taste, but opinion will vary no doubt – with sauteed mushrooms on it and a green salad. And delicious homemade bread to go with it. My only complaint was that everything was a bit salty for my taste (same for the breakfast eggs) and the pudding a bit too sweet. I felt that this was typical of Scotland, where they do go in for salt and sugar more than we delicate southerners. The best of the meal was a rhubarb pie, picked fresh from the garden a few minutes earlier, in a lovely light wholewheat pastry, served with a homemade ginger syrup – again, slightly spoiled for me by brown sugar sprinkled on top. But the rhubarb made up for it. Then there was excellent coffee (real), which I took over to the fire where I toasted my feet and talked to Margo, who'd come in to chat after supper, as the summer light slowly faded over the loch. She is a vegetarian by conviction and for health; Hugh follows suit 'reluctantly' but goodnaturedly. Like others, they first opened as primarily but not exclusively vegetarian; she wants nothing to do with meat if possible, and would go exclusive if it weren't for some of their first guests, who are omnivores and will insist on coming back for more of the same. I certainly felt in safe dietary hands with her. She also knows about, and caters for, people with allergies, and both of her children and her first grandchild are vegetarian. Her daughter is a professional vegetarian chef.

What does one do at Cove? 'Walking, touring, sailing, fishing, ideal for artists', says the blurb, and that seems about right. Loch Long and its subsidiaries are spectacular, running from the open seaside at Cove, near its mouth on the Clyde, to the spectacular fjords up toward Arrochar (averting your eyes from the Trident depot, the US Poseidon depot at Holy Loch, the NATO Nuclear Weapons Store, and the torpedo range, to name just a few). Sailing must indeed be superb and it's not far to lovely mountains. Cove also claims to have a mild and dry micro-climate, which in the West Highlands is a distinct asset. I don't know if I could cope with the military for too long, hypocritically finding it easier to forget what's not under my nose. But I do very much recommend Strathlee none the less. There is something about both the Scotts, perhaps especially Margo, which makes you remember and agree with all those overworn phrases about 'Scottish hospitality'. Food is ample and good, the house is spotless and comfortable with good beds, well-equipped bedrooms, good electric shower and so on. I thought it a specially friendly place to be on my own, though I'm sure larger parties would enjoy it too. Margo will see that you're not lonely, and I could happily sit in the drawing room and stare all day. O.F.

CATERING Vegetarian and traditional; vegan and other diets catered for.

SMOKING Not in evidence.

PRICE CATEGORY Medium.

FURTHER INFORMATION Margo and Hugh Scott,
Strathlee, Shore Road,
Cove, Dumbartonshire G84,
Scotland
Phone (043 684) 2395

81. Tigh Cuileann

It was an appalling, classically wet Highland day in May when I went to Tigh Cuileann, Achnagoul. I had trudged all day through dripping birches and rhododendrons, peering at the primroses through my steamed-up glasses. As I drove through Inveraray, I thought it a smug, self-satisfied little town, sitting like a well-waxed moustache under the Duke of Argyll's extremely prosperous nose. But 2 miles further on there was a turning up a gravel road; through a field or two and there on a hillside were about six houses, two still being renovated. Achnagoul is a small hamlet now coming back from near-dereliction. And Tigh Cuileann, the highest and most lovingly renovated house, boasting the best view and the prettiest garden, belongs to Dianne and Peter Fairweather. Peter is the Duke of Argyll's factor.

It's a croft house, basically: two up and two down. But it's been enlarged, mainly by Peter's own hands, with a lovely dining room with French windows out to the garden at one end and an oversize kitchen and extra rooms above at the other. There's a bit of garden at the front, intensively worked with a variety of flowers and herbs, some nice bits of terrace and rockery at the side, and then a series of vegetable plots among the rocks and scrub on the hill behind the house. The inside, too, was full of beautifully arranged flowers – pheasant-eye narcissus and bleeding-hearts in a jug in my bedroom, for instance – and plants, especially in the light and airy dining room, where a huge and happy lemon tree flourished in a big pot by the window. The other rooms feel more like the croft they once were: the little living room has a tiny window facing the south-westerly view, and is basically inward-looking: warm and cosy in any weather. It's beautifully furnished with (mostly) antiques, including a long, low upholstered, bench for sitting staring into the fire, and cleverly chosen small pieces of furniture to make the most of the room. Lots of books and records, sanded wooden floors and rugs, pictures and ornaments. Dianne is a painter and some of the pictures are hers, including lovely flower drawings in my bedroom. She has a good eye for decoration and my room in particular was a dream. No real window (no room, low eaves each side), only a skylight: but the presumably tiny original had been replaced with a big Velux for star-gazing in bed – or listening to the rain . . . The bed (very comfortable) had flowered cotton sheets and a gorgeous patchwork quilt; I've already men-tioned the flowers on their little table: a bookshelf built into the old fireplace alcove; rush matting on the floor with simple rag rugs on it. It was a rural fantasy come true, and my hostile feelings instantly abated.

The house was beautifully warm: my bedroom was over the kitchen and there was a good fire in the living room. The dining room was also comfortable, and there I had an early supper, gazing out at the dripping garden and the misty hills. It began with excellent leek and potato soup (leeks straight from the garden, I suspect) with a rather special taste that I couldn't quite identify, but herbs also from the garden, I thought. With it came freshly baked wholewheat rolls with butter or vegan margarine, then aubergines in a rich cheese and tomato sauce, with brown rice and a plain green salad; and to follow a rhubarb crumble. All deceptively simple, as they say, and perfectly cooked and presented. The Fairweathers joined me for coffee and we talked of life in rural Argyll. Afterwards I took myself out for a walk, as the rain had finally stopped, and strolled up some oozing fields past sodden sheep to a huge Bronze Age 'kist', a chambered cairn of impressive size and with a superb view. (There are several others nearby.) The immediate surroundings are pasture, with nice woods down to a triangular glimpse of Loch Fyne, but very commercial-looking forestry elsewhere: new plantations just behind the fields round the house, and much of the view is of rather dour spruce plantations.

I returned, to be greeted by the dogs (Misha the retriever and Isla the spaniel) who'd been banished to the kitchen while I ate, and was promptly offered tea while I sat by the fire and read. It came in a lovely blue enamel pot and with two fresh scones beside it spread with homemade blackcurrant jam – irresistible, though I couldn't believe I had any room. Then I retired to my comfortable bed and slept happily while the soft rain pattered on the roof.

In the morning there was some of the best porridge I've ever had – a combination of fine and coarse oatmeal which made it both delicate and crunchy – and tasty as only Scottish oatmeal is; then scrambled eggs, mushrooms and tomatoes, last night's rolls reheated and wholewheat toast, homemade marmalade and the same glorious blackcurrant jam. Tea (without question) to drink, but I'm sure I could have had something else for the asking. A marmalade cat warmed itself by the heater while the dogs dreamed noisily next door.

In short, virtual perfection. It was also absurdly cheap. Dianne is not in it for a living, more for the pleasure of occasional and mostly sympathetic visitors. (She doesn't take passers-by as far as I know.) My only reservation is that you are very much in the Fairweathers' living space. They are consideration itself, making sure that you occupy it as if it's yours alone. But you do know better, and I felt it wouldn't have been a problem for me – though it might for them – if they'd acknowledged it by eating and sitting with me instead of discreetly retiring to the kitchen. It might not work – the rooms are small and they are both, I thought, quite shy though good company none the less – but I think I'd have felt less conscious of displacing them. In all other respects, however, I highly recommend it. There's plenty to do and see and it's an excellent base for all of the south-western Highlands. O.F.

CATERING Exclusively vegetarian.

SMOKING Not in evidence.

PRICE CATEGORY Very Low.

FURTHER INFORMATION Dianne Fairweather,
Tigh Cuileann,
Achnagoul,
Inveraray, Argyll PA32 8XT,
Scotland
Phone (0499) 2349

82. Vegancroft

The brochure for Vegancroft advertises a newly built guesthouse, but when I went it turned out to be still under construction. A bit cheeky I thought, but things will have improved, I trust, by the time you read this. Meanwhile, it's a pretty startling place. I cycled slowly from Dunvegan (as slowly as the evening midges would allow) up hill and down, looking for the landmarks that Nora Warby had mentioned in her letter: they came in a quite different order, however, and I was glad of my Ordnance Survey map. But at last I did see the large, gaunt, concrete-block frame of a new house, with no roof tiles, sitting on a ridge above the road. I pushed my bike up a very steep, rough track, dodged the abandoned cars, caravan chassis, cement mixer, lawnmower, and the piles of wood, scaffolding, etc, and found what looked like a front door. After making a lot of unproductive noise I was about to give up, but eventually Tony Warby appeared, guided me through the chaos inside to an almost-finished bedroom (walls painted if not windows and woodwork) and a very unfinished but functional bathroom, and left me to what was at least a mercifully hot bath.

Supper was in the temporary guests' sitting/dining room (the future kitchen). I ate off a new pine table with matching chairs, with a Belgian rug on the rather uneven concrete floor, and a large TV and four identical armchairs in a row for company, gazing at the concrete-block walls, loops of electrical wiring and so on. There was grapefruit juice for starter, then a plate with two rings of marrow stuffed with Sosmix, two of the biggest potatoes I've ever seen, and a pile of mixed frozen vegetables. There was also a gravy boat with some weird glutinous stuff which I didn't get on with very well: "I see you're not a gravy man,' said Tony reproachfully as he took it away. Then there was a slice of chocolate sponge pudding with chocolate sauce. There was a variety of drinks (help yourself any time) including instant coffee (decaf, too) and some herb teas. After a chat with the Warbys I refused the offered TV and settled myself in one of the rather uncomfortable chairs to thumb through a pretty comprehensive collection of local brochures before turning to my novel.

My bedroom was fine: a little dark – but the house is built in the vernacular style with fairly small windows – and painted in a nice soft yellow. There was also an oldish but comfortable bed, brand new built-in wardrobe and plain carpet. It rained hard during the night, but there was no sign of wet in the room, despite the temporary roof. The next morning I found more juice, stewed prunes and muesli or commercial cereals on the table. I'd been offered a cooked breakfast the night before, but since fried Sosmix was on offer and I'd had quite enough, I first refused firmly then, after further hospitable urging, asked for porridge. This was a disappointment: I didn't think you could go wrong in Scotland, but it was unmistakably rolled oats, and not very well cooked at that: my stomach protested for most of the morning. Packed lunch, however, was an improvement: sandwiches with vegetable pâté and marmite.

How does one sum it up? Let's start with the pluses: and that on the whole means the location. North-west Skye is pretty idyllic (utterly if you don't mind wet feet and midges in season), and Husabost, facing east over Loch Dunvegan, is almost lush by virtue of its shelter from the south-west. The views from the house, even in misty weather, were splendid: on a clear day you can evidently see north to Lewis in the Outer Isles, and to Macleod's Tables and the Cuillins in the south. If there's ever a garden it'll be too exposed to be as cottage as some nearby – you have to pay for the view – but I can certainly imagine peaceful days sitting contemplating the surroundings. Other activities, though, are a bit more problematic. Bird-watching and hill-walking are advertised, and the former sounds fine. But hill-walking would certainly require driving, at least according to the OS map: there aren't any footpaths within walking distance, though the roads are quiet, and Skye is *not* a place for off-path walking. The Glendale peninsula is incredibly well equipped with craftspeople, museums and so on, but again you'd need to get in your car for almost all of them. Bicycles may be hired, but even with a high-geared touring bike (which the rental ones aren't) I found the hills punishing.

On the other hand . . . it is possible that staying on a building site may have warped my usual level of tolerance. But it would seem prudent to read the brochure with some scepticism, and ask a question or two when you book. 'Newly-built' it wasn't; the 'guests' lounge and dining room' didn't exist; the only 'homegrown vegetables' at present are potatoes, and they're definitely not organic, by the way; and the 'good home cooking' was certainly not wholefood. But it seems a bit churlish to complain in the face of such efforts, like asking for flush toilets in a covered wagon. Things can only improve, and one thing's for sure: there's definitely nowhere like it in this book. O.F.

CATERING Vegan; dairy produce can be provided with advance notice.

SMOKING No smoking in the house.

PRICE CATEGORY Very Low.

FURTHER INFORMATION Nora and Tony Warby,
Vegancroft,
11 Husabost, By Dunvegan,
Isle of Skye IV55 8ZV,
Scotland.
Phone (047 081) 303

Other Places to Stay

GRAMPIAN

Dallas, Moray: Mansewood House (Miss Frances Edwards)
Phone (034 389) 287
*XV guesthouse/retreat. Availability of EMs unclear. Price category
VL.*

HIGHLAND

Aultbea, Wester-Ross: Mrs Cawthra, 'Cartmel'
Phone (044582) 375
V-T. 'Luxury guesthouse, sea 200 yards.'

Ledmore: 'Avalon' (formerly Shepherd's Cottage), Bridget Filose
Pursey
Phone (085 484) 243
*XV, guesthouse. Price category VL. Ms Pursey was away when our
veggie brigade was in the area, or we should certainly have visited.*

Newtonmore: Meall an Eireannaich, Kingussie Road (Caroline
Brown)
Phone (05403) 676
*XV B & B (+ EM sometimes): open during skiing season. Price
category VL.*

Talmine, Sutherland: Hillview, 148 Skinnet
No phone listed
*XV, B & B + EM by arr. Family home overlooking Kyle of
Tongue. 'No colour TV but six colourful cats.'*

STRATHCLYDE

Isle of Colonsay: Isle of Colonsay Hotel
Phone (095 12) 316
T-V hotel: vegan and vegetarian meals on request. Recently in The
Good Hotel Guide. *Price category H to VH.*

Isle of Iona: Argyll Hotel
Phone (068 17) 334

V-T Hotel: simple, friendly sounding: 'At least half our staff are vegetarian.' Price category M to VH.

WESTERN ISLES

Isle of Harris:
Phone (085 983) 311
XV, B & B + self-catering. Boat trips.

Places to Eat

GRAMPIAN

Aberdeen: Jaws Wholefood Café (XV), 5 West North Street. Phone (0224) 645676.

Findhorn, nr Forres: The Findhorn Foundation (2 cafés, health food shop) (XV). Phone (0309) 30154.

HIGHLAND

Edinbane, Isle of Skye: Three Rowans Café (V-T). Phone (047 082) 286.

Nr Kyle of Lochalsh: Loch Duich Hotel (prop V), Ardelve. Phone (059 85) 213.

Special Interest Holidays

There is a surfeit of special interest holidays being advertised these days, from decoy duck carving to fungus forays. Sports and other active activities, arts and crafts, nature watching and stalking, learning and health – the list is growing every year, and goes far beyond the scope of this book. If you choose the activity that interests you (look in the *Guardian*'s back pages, plus special interest magazine adverts) and negotiate yourself, you'll no doubt find that some (particularly the craft and outdoor-pursuits holidays) will cater for vegetarians (even cheerfully, though how well?); even university summer school caterers seem to have started branching out beyond those occupational hazards, the greasy omelette and the tepid quiche. According to *The Vegetarian Handbook*, The Holiday Fellowship (centres all over Britain) caters for vegetarians and vegans (write to Holiday Fellowship Ltd, 142–144 Great North Way, London NW4 1EG for further information). But it's still, I'm afraid, as with the ordinary hotels and guesthouses, a pretty hit and miss business.

However, rescue is at hand. There are now a small number of organisations (usually individuals) that have designed their activity/special interest holidays especially with vegetarians in mind. They include courses held at exclusively vegetarian guesthouses; walking, sailing and riding holidays especially for vegetarians; and some activity holidays which run special weeks for vegetarians; and – at least in the case of Earthwalk – the vegetarian weeks seem to be outnumbering the non-vegetarian. Health 'holidays' are a rather special case. They usually involve *de facto* vegetarian food, since dieting and health are part of their programmes. Again, we ask you to search these out yourself, but we've listed a few which seem to take catering for vegetarians particularly seriously.

Active Holidays

CYCLING

Bicycle Beano, 2 Pleasant View, Erwood, Builth Wells, Powys
Phone (09823) 676
XV. 'Designed for enjoyment rather than Olympian endurance.' All ages/abilities; bring your own musical instrument; luggage van.

Wild Wales Walks also do cycling holidays. See under 'Walking'.

RIDING

Forge Farm Riding Holidays, Garstang Rd, Bilsborrow, Preston, Lancs
Phone (0995) 40204
XV family. 'For "pony mad" girls.' Farmhouse accommodation living as one of the family.

Ty'n Lon Riding Centre, Llangybi, Pwllehli, Gwynedd, N.Wales
Phone (076 688) 618
Not XV but do 'vegetarian only' weeks.

SAILING

Squirrel–Holidays Afloat, Brian Burnett, 14 Allington Place, Chester CH4 7DX
Phone (0244) 675598
XV cruises in UK waters and abroad for people with little or no boating experience.

Slowboat, 7 Railway Cottages, Hardy Rd, Norwich NR1 1JW
Phone (0603) 663474
Canal holidays, some XV trips.

'Whisper' in the Hebrides, Vivian Finn, 88 Guildstead Road, Liverpool
Phone 051–226 4240
Some XV cruises to Western Is of Scotland. No experience, all ages.

SKIING

Letterbea, Boat of Garten, Strathspey, Inverness-shire, Scotland
Phone (047 983) 209
*XV Guesthouse. Cross-country and downhill skiing weeks/
weekends with instruction.* See Chapter IX.

Old Brewery House, Redbrook, Forest of Dean, Glos
Phone (0600) 2569
XV, NS guesthouse. Cross-country skiing weeks/weekends. See
Chapter VI.

'Ski Backcountry', Ian and Elizabeth Maples, Maelstrom, Insh by
Kingussie, Inverness-shire, Scotland
Phone (05402) 805
*XV, NS guesthouse. Nordic skiing with instruction at all levels.
Hand-built log house.*

WALKING

Bowland Treks, Lowgill, Lancaster, Lancs
Phone (0468) 61277.
*Guided exploration of Bowland Forest in N.Lancs. Week-long
holidays. Guides take your luggage in their minibus. They say
vegetarian food is always on the menu. This year only one week is
XV but they will include more if there's greater demand.*

C-N-Do Scotland Ltd, Howlands Cottage, Sauchieburn, Stirling,
Scotland
Phone (0786) 812355
*V props/guides. Walking holidays in Scotland, either centre-based
or cross-country treks.*

Earthwalk, Pen-y-wern, Kerry, Newtown, Powys, Wales
Phone (0686) 28282
*'Guided unladen walking and civilised all-done-for-you camping.'
Most weeks vegetarian.* See Chapter VII.

Head for the Hills, Laurence Golding, The Recreation Hall,
Garth, Builth, Powys, Wales
Phone (05912) 388

XV. Guided walking holidays; luggage van. Various areas through-out Britain; somewhat more rugged and self-reliant than Earthwalk.

Hillscape, Blaen-y-ddol, Llanafan, Aberystwyth, Dyfed
Phone (0597) 2186
Special XV weeks; thirty-five varied walks.

SKADI: Women's Walking Holidays Among Northern Hills:
Paula Day, Grassrigg Barn, Killington, Sedbergh, Cumbria.
XV all-women walking tours. 1986 included: The Dales Way, Coast to Coast Walk, A Lakeland Circuit. From 1987 will be based in newly converted barn overlooking the Howgill Fells, near the Lake District and the Yorkshire Dales. See Chapter V.

Walking for Weedies (sic), Castle Hill House, Lynton, Devon
Phone (0598) 52291
'Vegetarians especially welcome.' Guided walking on Exmoor.

Wayfinder Holidays, 83 Abbotsham Road, Bideford, Devon
Phone (02372) 78417
Walking on Exmoor, stay in hotel catered by V prop.

Wild Wales Walks, Pen-y-Bont Fawr, Cynwyd, Clwyd, Wales
Phone (0904) 2226
Strenuous walking and cycling holidays. Not exclusive, but prop-rietors, Tom and Kay Culhane, are vegetarian and do a lot of vegetarian catering. Also guesthouse. See Chapter VII.

Outdoor Activities

Boswednack Manor, Zennor, St Ives, Cornwall
Phone (0736) 794183
V-T (props V). Wide range of courses, e.g. Breeding and Migrant Birds, Bird-watching, Natural History of the Land's End Penin-sula, Autumn/Winter Birds, Natural History Photography, Mega-liths and Monuments – Prehistoric Cornwall, Landscape and Seascape Painting, Printmaking.

The Lawn, Ruardean, Glos.
Phone (0594) 543259

T-V 'fare' in NS house. 'Living Forest' weekend programme with Forest Ranger 'including badger watch, fungus foray, bird-watching and guided walks in ancient woodland'. Forest of Dean.

Letterbea Special Interest Weeks, Boat of Garten, Strathspey, Inverness-shire.
Phone (047983) 209
XV Guesthouse offers a wide variety of special interest weeks, including: Flower Hunting at Sites in the Scottish Highlands, Geology and Land-use, Cycling and Hill-walking; also Bird-watching weeks. See Chapter IX.

Health Holidays

Bournemouth Centre of Complementary Medicine, 26 Sea Road, Boscombe, Bournemouth, Dorset
Phone (0202) 36354
'Whole person therapies . . . meditation and diets. Vegetarian meals. Health restoration or restful holiday.'

Green Farm Nutrition Centre, Burwash Common, E.Sussex.
Phone (0435) 882180
Green Farm health foods (XV?). 'Give yourself a week of nutritional, physical and emotional healing. Exercise, swim, sauna.' Price category H.

Harmony House, Southerton, Ottery St Mary, Devon
Phone (0395) 68577
XV. 'Holistic Vegetarian Guesthouse for [self] Healing Holidays.' Day seminars and weekend courses.

Malvern Nature Cure Centre, 5 College Grove, Great Malvern
Phone (06845) 66818.
XV. Run by Miss Winifred E. Jones, S.R.N. Rest and relaxation, walking in Malvern Hills. 'Cordon bleu standard of vegetarian fare.' Price category L.

Mansewood Health Holidays, New Luce, Newton Stewart, Scotland
Phone (058 16) 281

T-V, Therapy, diet, massage, etc.

Middle Piccadilly Natural Healing Centre, Holwell, Sherborne, Dorset
Phone (096323) 468
XV/organic. Old Dorset thatched farmhouse. Weekend breaks or longer.

Roundelwood Health Improvement Centre, Drummond Terr, Crieff, Perthshire, Scotland
Phone (0764) 3806
XV. 'Slimming, health, fitness, stress control, stop smoking therapy', etc.

Shrubland Hall Health Clinic, Coddenham, Ipswich, Suffolk
Phone (0473) 830404
Eighteenth-century hall described in Country Life. *Not XV but diet consists mainly of elegant raw health foods. Colin Spencer went there. Price catory VH.*

Tyringham Naturopathic Clinic, Newport Pagnell, Bucks
Phone (0908) 610450
XV Residential Centre for Complementary Medicine. Georgian mansion in 30 acres; intensive therapies offered.

Other Activities

Beechmill House, Bradley, Frodsham, Cheshire
Phone (0928) 33590
XV Guesthouse and Wholehealth Cookery and Nutrition School. Cuisine verte, wholehealth, gluten-free cookery, tofu and soya, and more.

Buck Farm, Hanmer, Clwyd, Wales
Phone (094 874) 339
T-V guesthouse, international cooking. Yoga weekends with Mehr Fardoonji. See Chapter VII.

Centre for Alternative Technology, Llwyngwern Quarry, Machynlleth, Powys, Mid Wales
Phone (0654) 2400

Not quite XV (though their public café is). Short courses (weekends or weeks) on aspects of alternative technology, ecology, gardening, etc; also working weeks at the centre.

Claridge House, Dormansland, Lingfield, Surrey
Phone (0342) 832150
XV. 'Centre for renewal, rest and study.' Quaker Centre, host conferences, groups, etc, on religious, spiritual, healing, etc, subjects. See Chapter II.

Findhorn Foundation, Findhorn, Forres, Highland, Scotland
Phone (0309) 30154
XV. Numerous courses on elements of Findhorn life – horticulture, crafts, dance, self-development/actualisation, religious experience, etc. Most courses require you to join a Findhorn Experience Week (general introduction to life and beliefs of the Community) before you take them.

Grimstone Manor, Yelverton, Devon
Phone (0822) 854358
XV. Dance, drama, Gestalt, meditation, enlightenment intensives, yoga and more. See Chapter I.

Loop Cottage, Crookland, Milnthorpe, Cumbria
Phone (04487) 335
XV, NS, B & B + EM. Courses on painting, writing and dance.

Nash Hotel, Steyning, W.Sussex
Phone (0903) 814988
V-T. Sunday programmes on health and healing. See Chapter II.

Oak Cottage, Gretton, Cheltenham, Glos
Phone (0242) 602570
XV, B & B + EM in artist/potter's cottage, Nr Stratford. Pottery and art tuition; also vegetarian cookery.

The Nurtons, Tintern, Nr Chepstow, Gwent
Phone (029 18) 253
XV. Iyengar yoga. Other courses, e.g. 'The Purpose of Life', Vegetarian Cookery, Rambling in the Wye Valley, How to Start and Run a Small Farm, etc, have been offered in the past; could be

provided again if enough demand. See Chapter VI.

Runnings Park, Croft Bank, West Malvern, Worcs.
Phone (06845) 65253
V-T. 'Pegasus' residential weekend courses: Healing, The Way of the Warrior, The Growth of Sensitivity, Healthy Living. See Chapter III.

Spittal Farmhouse, Carnwath, Scotland
Phone (0555) 840991
XV, B & B + EM, traditional tapestry weaving in summer craft school.

Stredders Vegetarian Guest House, Park Cresc., Llandrindod Wells, Powys
Phone (0597) 2186
XV. Natural history holidays in central Wales; experts from the University of Wales.

Tekels Park Guest House, Camberley, Surrey
Phone (0276) 63723
XV. Conferences, group studies and social gatherings; theosophical peace, spiritual subjects, plus music and arts. See Chapter II.

Westbridge Open Centre for Arts, Highclere, Newbury, Berks
Phone (0635) 253322
T-V guesthouse and 'centre open to the arts and healing studies'. Also recitals and exhibitions. Holidays 'restful or roaming'.

Index of Places Reviewed

(Map reference numbers in parentheses)